SACRAMENTO PUBLIC LIBRARY

3 3029 05686 1636

SACRAMENTO PUBLIC LIBRARY
828 "I" STREET
SACRAMENTO, CA 95814

9/2005

D0016045

WITHDRAWN FROM COLLECTION
OF SACRAMENTO PUBLIC LIBRARY

SMART SEX

ALSO BY JENNIFER ROBACK MORSE
AND PUBLISHED BY SPENCE PUBLISHING

Love & Economics
Why the Laissez-Faire Family Doesn't Work

SMART
SEX

*Finding Life-Long Love
in a Hook-Up World*

JENNIFER ROBACK MORSE

SPENCE PUBLISHING COMPANY · DALLAS
2005

Copyright © 2005 by Jennifer Roback Morse

All rights reserved. No part of this publication may be reproduced or
transmitted in any form or by any means, electronic or mechanical, including
photocopy, recording, or any information storage and retrieval system now
known or to be invented, without permission in writing from the publisher,
except by a reviewer who wishes to quote brief passages in connection with a
review written for inclusion in a magazine, newspaper, or broadcast.

Published in the United States by
Spence Publishing Company
111 Cole Street
Dallas, Texas 75207

Library of Congress Control Number: 2005926622
ISBN 1-890626-51-1
978-1-890626-51-7

Printed in the United States of America

Contents

PART III
SELF-GIVING, RIGHTLY UNDERSTOOD

Foreword

Chuck Colson

T HIS BOOK is just what Christians and right-thinking citizens need to read now—extraordinary insights by a brilliant economist as to why the family is endangered and why it matters.

Calling the traditional family "endangered" or "in trouble" has achieved the status of a cliché in our culture. By "cliché," I mean the dictionary sense of the term—an idea that has lost its force through repetition.

The question is: why is it necessary to repeat this idea in the first place? Is it for lack of empirical evidence? Hardly. The numbers may not tell the whole story, but they do tell a compelling one. Fewer Americans are marrying and increasing number are opting for what Jennifer Roback Morse calls "marriage substitutes."

Those who do get married are marrying later and are having fewer children. And many of these aren't staying married. So much so that, by one estimate, 54 percent of American children can expect to spend at least part of their childhood in a single-parent home.

If the problem isn't the lack of evidence perhaps the need for repetition stems from the lack of any real consequences to family break-up. Maybe the warnings about demise of the traditional family are yet another example of cultural conservatives, especially religious ones, trying to impose their values on everyone else.

Wrong again. The weakening of the traditional family affects all of us. As Morse and others have pointed out, family breakup puts our children at greater risk for virtually every "adverse outcome," from drug abuse to mental illness, you can name. Even if I hadn't read a word Morse has written, I would know this from personal experience: more than thirty years of prison ministry has taught me the connection between what used to be called "broken families" and crime. I've seen it up close in the faces of thousands of the generation lost behind bars.

None of this is a secret. On the contrary, it's been more than a decade since the *Atlantic Monthly* declared on its cover that "Dan Quayle Was Right" (about the family). And, still, the uncritical embrace of—to employ another of Morse's expressions—the "laissez-faire" family continues unabated.

The most recent example of this destructive embrace is, of course, the crusade (is there a more apt description? yes) to legalize same-sex marriage. In nearly every respect, the case for this bit of social engineering disguised as civil rights depends on the discarding of the millennia-old rationale for marriage. It requires turning marriage from an institution whose purpose is rooted in the social good—the well-being of children—into a purely private matter, a gesture intended only to express the parties' shared affection.

None of this is new. It is the same rationale used to justify both the impermanence of heterosexual marriage and the "marriage substitutes" currently in vogue among many of our contemporaries. Any successful attempt at reversing the fortunes of the traditional family in American cultural must begin with a renewed appreciation for the historic rationale for marriage.

And that is what makes both this book and the larger effort undertaken by Jennifer Roback Morse so important. More than anyone I know, Morse makes the connection between the traditional understanding of marriage and freedom, prosperity, and other markers of cultural well-being.

Against the new libertines who insist that redefining marriage is essential step in furthering personal freedom, she makes it clear that if your goal really is to "do what [you] want to do, with a minimum of interference from other people," you have a stake in strengthening traditional marriage.

Likewise, in a world in which sex is simultaneously a "way to enlightenment and spirituality"* and a purely biological function with no moral consequences, Morse's insistence on the social consequences of sex is much-needed corrective. Just as we are not free to "reinvent" the family without suffering the social consequences, our attempt to treat sex as "morally neutral" has costs that all of us end up paying.

Just as important as demolishing the cultural myths regarding sex and marriage is being able to do so in a way that doesn't presuppose a particular religious commitment. While it may seem odd, or even disconcerting, to make the case for marriage in terms of both personal and societal self-interest (after all, isn't self-interest what got us into this mess?), it is the only language that stands a chance. I've learned through experience that, while the public square may unreceptive to the language of faith, it still retains its instinct for self-preservation and some sense of the common good.

All of which makes *Smart Sex* more than timely; it is vital. There's too much at stake for people of good will, religious or not, to sit idly by as our most important institution is redefined and deconstructed out of existence. That's why, for my part, when Jennifer Roback Morse calls out "every man to his post," I am happy to reply "Aye, aye, ma'am!" When you read Morse's compelling logic, you'll be ready to obey as well.

---

* Interview with Eve Ensler at Riovuelto.org, August 22, 2001.

SMART SEX

Love Makes the (Free) World Go Around

WARNING

This book contains no blueprints for utopia.
Please remove your political hat before reading.
This book will self-destruct in the hands
of politicians and policy wonks.

THIS BOOK IS ABOUT HOW AND WHY TO STAY MARRIED. This book is for married people who want to stay married. It is also for single people who hope to be married some day.

Maybe you've been married for a while, long enough for the honeymoon to be over. Perhaps you have a gut feeling that staying married is the right thing to do, but you need more motivation. If you are going to put forth the effort to make it work, you want to know that it really matters. Of course, you aspire to more than just staying married. You want more than just putting up with problems in the marriage, and soldiering on. You want to be happily married.

But like everyone else, you and your spouse have problems some of the time. You're bored; your spouse is bored. You're angry; your spouse is angry.

Maybe you feel aggrieved in your marriage. It isn't fair. You do all the work, earn all the money, provide all the excitement and entertainment, take the lead on creating and sustaining intimacy. Oddly enough, your spouse thinks that he or she makes the greater contribution.

Maybe you don't feel appreciated. You give and give and give, and your spouse is never satisfied. You want to be a generous and giving person, but you are starting to feel like a doormat. Oddly enough, your spouse feels the same way. She or he thinks you are the one doing all the taking and none of the giving. The two of you have argued about it endlessly, but you never seem to get anywhere.

You need more than a self-help book. Some books offer to help you "keep love alive," which usually means having a spicy sex life. Introducing sexual variety might help you stay more interested in each other. But if you are angry at your spouse, improving your sexual technique is not going to help. You can get so mad you can't even bring yourself to think about sex. Sex and sexual variety can become one more thing to fight or pout about.

Other self-help books offer to help you with communication skills. You've tried a lot of different ways of communicating. It helps some, that's for sure. But after all that communicating and relating and empathizing and expressing and role-playing and all that other touchy-feely stuff, sometimes you still have a problem. You know exactly what your spouse is thinking and feeling and you don't like it one little bit.

The books don't quite tell you what to do in this situation. The unspoken assumption behind the "improving life by improving communication" books is this: any two reasonable human beings can work out their differences, if only they communicate properly. And if your problems don't dissolve in the waters of talk, well, maybe you're married to the wrong person. An even less appealing alternative is this: if improved communication between you two wonderful people doesn't solve the problem, maybe you aren't so wonderful to begin with.

You don't want to believe that you are the non-wonderful one. That leaves your spouse. Your spouse must be the problem person. You think to yourself, "No one can reason with this moron. No one can live with him or her." The less you want to be the one in the wrong, the more you need for the other person to be the one in the wrong.

If improved communication isn't helping, either I am not a reasonable human being or my spouse isn't. Neither of these explanations is very appealing. So you let it slide, rather than look too closely. The self-help books don't usually come out and present these alternatives, of course.

You have let a lot of those things slide by. You sometimes ask yourself, "Are we sweeping too many disagreements under the rug? Are we just hiding from the unpleasant reality that we aren't really right for each other? Should we just bag the whole thing and forget it?"

There is another possibility: maybe the "improve life by improving communication" theory is false. Without disparaging improved communications, (sometimes it does help, after all) maybe there is something else that you need.

This book is also for people who are not yet married who hope to get married and stay married. Maybe you're in college, or just graduated. Maybe you've gotten the impression that marriage is a bad idea. You aren't sure exactly where you got this impression.

If you're a woman, it might have been the women's studies professor who told you the risks of domestic violence for women and children. Maybe it was a movie or television program depicting married women as frumps and losers, and single mothers as independent and hip. Maybe your political science professor told you how gifted you are and what a great career you could have.

Yet you want children someday, but you aren't sure exactly when. You spent a semester working at the university day care center. You've seen the forty-year-old women professors with gray hair dropping their kids off. You've heard the kids crying when their mothers leave them. You've heard the women talk about how they waited until they got tenure to start trying to have a family. You've seen that some of the kids were adopted from foreign countries. Reading between the lines, you figure out that some of these professors waited too long to have babies of their own. You're sure you don't want that for yourself, but you aren't sure what you do want.

If you're a man, maybe you're looking forward to some adventure after college: travel, skiing, windsurfing, rock climbing. You've been in school for a long time, and you're looking forward to some release. Or maybe you're looking forward to charging ahead into a career. But maybe something even scarier makes you reluctant to consider marriage as a serious option for yourself right now. You've heard about men who thought they had perfect marriages. Then their brides kicked them out and made them pay child support for years. They seem like good men. They appear to be guys who loved their wives and tried to keep their marriages alive. But their wives treated them as if they were no more than a combination wallet and sperm donor. They're broken men now.

Male or female, you've probably seen troubled marriages. Maybe a couple of them, actually. Your parents got divorced when you were in grade school. Your dad remarried right away and then divorced again. He has a new girlfriend. You like her better than his former wife. Your mom was in no hurry to get married again, but she had a couple of boyfriends. One of them even moved in for a while. You got attached to him. It seemed like he might be a new dad. But then they quarreled, and he moved out. She got married again last year. You're happy for her, and you hope it works out.

You've heard the sociology professors recount the statistics about the effects of divorce on children. It's hard for you to listen to them talk about the studies that show kids in single parent households are at risk for a variety of social pathologies. After all, you survived your parents' divorce. But you have to admit you know some kids who truly are struggling, maybe your own siblings, or step- or half-siblings.

You don't like listening to those statistics, but there's something else you dislike even more. The professor starts ranting about how the studies don't actually prove anything. The numbers really show that kids in all sorts of families can do just fine, if there are enough other resources. If the mother has enough money, if she spends enough time with the kids, they'll do just fine. If the parents continue to work together in a loving cooperative way, the children will be better off with divorce than in a family life of continual strife. If the stepdad is loving and attentive, remarriage is no problem for kids. If the children know that their parents love them, they will be secure and have minimal difficulties adjusting to the necessary changes in their parents' lives. You know from experience that those huge "ifs" hardly ever occur in real life.

The single moms you know don't have much money or time. You've seen plenty of divorces that don't end the conflict, but just transfer the strife to another arena. And you've seen divorces that produce legions of new issues to fight about.

Stepdads and boyfriends don't spend all that much time with kids. Sometimes the moms are so preoccuppied with their new men that the kids loose their mom's attention as well. As for knowing that your parents love you, well, you know it in an abstract way. During the times that they seem distracted or overwhelmed, you have to remind yourself that they love you. You find yourself parenting your parents, and maybe your younger siblings, as well. So when the prof says, "divorce is no problem to kids, if . . . ," you tune him out. You shrug and think to yourself, "this prof is clueless."

All in all, then, you think maybe you'll just wait a while before getting married. You can always pursue your career. Graduate school and a professional job will provide you with a ready-made path and a sense of purpose. The women among you might have a nagging feeling that you could wait too long and end up like one of those gray-haired mommies. The guys among you may feel sure you don't want to go through life alone, but still not feel much urgency about getting mar-

ried. But you can't figure out how you'd find a suitable partner, and if
you did, whether you would have any better luck keeping a marriage
together than your parents did.

Most of all, you know you want something better for your kids
than you had. You don't want to put them through the turmoil and
upheaval that you went through. You want to get married and stay
married, but you don't know how to go about it.

You know you need more than a self-help book. "How to find and
keep the man of your dreams!" is not going to be good enough. Nor
is "how to balance work and family" likely to allay the fears you have.
The shelves upon shelves of books on building a successful career
aren't going to do it either. "How to make a million bucks before you're
thirty" sounds nice. But you know yourself well enough to know that
you don't really want to give up all the things you'd have to give up to
acheive that kind of success. Besides, a million bucks isn't going to be
enough to take away the sting of a lifetime of loneliness if you can't
figure out this relationship stuff.

I agree with you. The self-help books aren't going to be enough,
because they deal with the superficial symptoms of much deeper problems. You'd like a new way to think about yourself in relationship to
other people. You need some help balancing, but not the usual mantra
of "work and family." You want help balancing your desire for independence and autonomy with your equally important longings for
interdependence and even at times, neediness. You need some way of
seeing your own value as an individual, as well as the value of others.
You'd like to find an alternative to the struggle for equality in relationships. You have an intuition that freedom is something more profound
than the right to do as you please. But you aren't quite sure what that
deeper meaning of freedom might be.

This book will give you two things: information and hope. The opening chapters will explain why your marriage matters, not only to you, but to the rest of the world as well. The decision to marry is a decision to engage in the noble enterprise of building up a community of life and love. This little community of the family is the foundation for larger, more complicated social structures. There is more at stake than your immediate feelings and your personal happiness. Keeping these larger issues in your mind will help you to see that your personal struggles are worth the effort. There is meaning and nobility in the struggle.

I maintain that we in modern America are working with a batch of concepts that are in our way. We can't build happy home lives around the ideas of equality or freedom, however attractive and appropriate those ideas might be in the political or economic realm. The family is a distinct social sphere that needs concepts and ideas of its own, not just concepts borrowed from politics and economics.

In a nutshell, here is my explanation for why your marriage matters to the rest of the world. A free society needs people with consciences who can control themselves and use their freedom without bothering other people too much. But no one develops a conscience and self-control in a social vacuum. We develop the groundwork for our conscience during the first eighteen months of our lives, in our relationships with our parents. Without that foundation, a child is much more likely to grow up without an ability to control himself. *Your marriage has the potential to create children who can strengthen a free society—or significantly weaken it.*

You might object that not every married couple has children. Maybe you yourself don't. There is a second reason your marriage matters to the rest of the world, a reason that is independent of children. *Human sexuality is the great engine of sociability.* Sexuality builds up the relationship between the couple, as well as building the family by creating children. You can treat your sex partner as a person to love, or as an object that brings you pleasure. If you treat your sex partner as more than an object for your use, you are building up a household of love, the beginnings of a society of love. If you treat your sex partner as exclusively something that gives you pleasure, you are reducing him or her to a consumer good. You are, in effect, bring the world of commerce into your bedroom. The way you treat your sex partner is your contribution to creating the social world.

In a nutshell, here is my explanation for the widespread disappointments in family life since the 1960s. In the last half of the twentieth century, we distilled from the Western tradition of freedom a peculiar elixir of sexual and personal freedom. We have come up with the idea that *freedom means being completely unencumbered by human relationships*. A woman is free only if she is not required to be in a relationship with a child or with a spouse. Reproductive freedom means having an unlimited right to sexual activity, as well as an unlimited right to abort or contracept. No woman can be truly free if she has a child that she does not want to have. Similarly, a person is not free if he is required to remain married. Unconditional marital or parental relationships constitute an unacceptable infringement on the modern person's freedom.

Finally, no self-respecting modern woman can consider herself free if she is financially dependent upon her husband, or any other man. This notion of freedom as monetary independence has created the almost hysterical demand that woman must work at any and all times during her life, regardless of her family situation. This in turn places a high priority on substitute childcare. If a woman's liberty depends on her financial independence, it follows that her liberty depends on the availability of alternative care for her children.

This social, sexual definition of freedom is in conflict with older notions of economic and political freedom. I define political freedom broadly to mean the right to participate in the governing process and economic freedom as the right to acquire and dispose of property. However desirable the new sexual and social freedoms might be, they are certainly not necessary for having political and economic freedoms. More important, this modern understanding of freedom is ultimately incompatible with these older, more modest definitions of freedom.

This is true for two reasons. One is a social, collective reason, while the other is a personal, individual reason. A society that defines freedom as the absence of unconditionally committed human relationships can not remain free. And individuals who define freedom in this way are abandoning the very thing that has the best chance of making them happy. In short, *I aim to show that the notion of freedom as complete personal independence is incoherent at the social level and inhuman at the personal level.*

The sexual revolution has been a disappointment, but people continue to acquiesce in its assumptions because no appealing alternative seems to be on the horizon. Many Americans think the only alternatives are some combination of *Leave it to Beaver* and the Taliban. They imagine that if it weren't for the sexual revolution, women would all be at home in dresses and high heals, in their spotless kitchens with cookies in the oven, waiting for the Beaver to come home from school. If it weren't for the sexual revolution, men and women alike would be in danger of ever-increasing surveilance by the state for deviant sexual acts. Without modern sexual mores, women would be but one step away from the burka and public stoning for adultery.

Many criticisms of the sexual revolution focus on the direct costs of indiscriminate or impulsive sexual activity: out-of-wedlock births, divorce, stepfamilies and the social problems associated with them. I focus on a different kind of cost: the opportunity costs. I want to show what we miss when we embrace the modern assumptions about sexuality and the family. This will provide an appealing and realistic alternative to the modern way. My alternative can be summarized simply: *Self-giving, rightly understood.*

For many people, the very thought of self-giving will set off alarm bells. People fear being manipulated by others who take advantage of their generousity. Those on the political Left might have images of women cooking and ironing for centuries out of an artificial and inappropriate sense of duty that someone else calls "love." Those on the political Right might have images of the massive totalitarian states of the twentieth century, demanding self-sacrifice from the citizens in the name of creating a utopian world in which everyone gets along nicely. These are reasonable things to fear. No one wants to be taken advantage of, either in the political or personal sphere.

On the other hand, everyone wants love in his life. Everyone wants to love and be loved; people want to feel secure enough to be generous and giving to others. In fact, this universal desire for connection and community goes a long way toward explaining the pathologies mentioned in the previous paragraph. Why would women spend their lives doing things for others, if not for some deep-seated need to give? Why did so many thousands of people give their lives to ideologies that turned out to be destructive and even murderous, if not for the belief that they were creating a world of connection and caring? The longing for human community is so deep, so universal, and so important to people that it can be used by the unscrupulous to manipulate others.

That is why the discussion of self-giving, rightly understood, is so necessary. People want to give of themselves. But few understand self-giving's proper place, how to bound it properly, and how to channel it appropriately.

The term "self-giving, rightly understood," is reminiscent of another expression that has a long intellectual pedigree in Western thought: "self-interest, rightly understood." Proponents of the liberal Enlightenment have discussed and dissected this term for two hundred years. The "rightly understood" part of the phrase is meant to explore the boundaries of self-interest. Where does my genuine self-interest lie? What obligations, if any, do I owe to others? What are legitimate limitations on my actions? This way of placing the individual at the center of analysis has been at the heart of western individualism for a long time, and has generated our understanding of universal human rights, the rule of law, and much else that is distinctive in the Western tradition.[1]

I think the discussion about "self-giving, rightly understood" will be a much more interesting discussion. For starters, we've about run out of things to say about self-interest. That set of ideas has pretty much been played out. Western civilization is ripe for a discussion about self-giving, rightly understood.

Like the traditional analysis of self-interest, the analysis of self-giving begins with the premise of the intrinsic worth of each individual. Thinking of oneself as a gift is a great act of self-valuing. If I am not worth anything, how could it make sense to give myself to anybody else and think I have done them any favor?

The self-giving perspective also helps to remind us of the worth of the other person as well. The other people in my life are gifts. (Admittedly, I sometimes have trouble seeing exactly how some of my more difficult relatives are gifts.) In this way, self-giving quite directly emphasizes reciprocity in human relations. Self-interest, rightly understood, has an element of reciprocity to it, but the reciprocity is something added after the fact. We are taught to say, "I am valuable. Oh, by the way, so is everybody else." With self-giving, there is no "by the way" about it. Giving presupposes a gift, a giver and a recipient. Community is the starting point of the discussion and at the center of one's life.

⁀

I think we not only need a new way of thinking about ourselves in relationship to others. We also need a new approach to the "nature versus nuture" debate. The question of what is "natural" behavior is actually quite crucial in having a reasonable understanding about sexuality and relationships.

Much of the current debate is rather sterile. The more scientific-minded members of the intellectual community are often the greatest champions of the idea of human nature. Believers in human nature also tend to believe that we are limited in our ability to change fundamental aspects of human motivation. Many of these scientists assume themselves to be in opposition to anyone with religious ideas. The presumed battle is between religion and science.

On the other hand, the greatest champions of "nurture" tend to be humanists who believe that the human condition can be continuously improved, if only we had the will to modify our social structures. The infinite maleability of the human condition is an article of faith for this kind of person. Many of the deconstructionists and post-modernists among humanities departments in major universities, as well as certain political parties, seem to think that anyone who opposes them does so solely out of mean-spiritedness. Post-modernists do not necessarily cast the intellectual conflict as one between humanism and science. Often, post-modernists are more offended by religious ideas than scientific ideas. Religions that claim that the human condition is inherently troubled are an affront to the idea of infinite perfectibility of human nature. Religions that propose limits on human behavior are an affront to the idea that we can construct and reconstruct our culture at will.

The scientist who believes in the permanence of human nature regards religion as his enemy. The post-modernist who believes in the infinite maleability of human nature regards religion as his enemy. Is n't there something odd about this so-called debate?

I propose a new set of battle-lines, at least for the set of questions under consideration in this book. The man of science has more in common with the man of certain kinds of faith than either of them has with post-modern man. Science and certain kinds of faith both agree that there is such a thing as human nature, which places limits on how much we can reconstruct the social world.

The man of science disapproves of religion because he finds its methodology disreputable: revelation does not and cannot take the place of scientific method. But religion and science need not be in conflict.[2] Theology can contribute something constructive to the human endeavor because religion asks a different set of questions than science. What should we do with our knowledge? How should we treat one another? What does it mean to be a good person?

My approach assumes that there is such a thing as human nature that is universal and enduring. My primary academic training is in economics, and most economists agree that human nature is something stable that we can observe and study. My approach is consonant with other theories of human nature, such as sociobiology and Christian revelation. Both of these seemingly disparate approaches assume that human nature is something specific that is not infinitely maleable. My approach contrasts with post-modern theories that assume everything interesting and important in human life is culturally or socially constructed and can therefore be reconstructed essentially at will.

I am confident that neither every devotee of evolutionary psychology nor every Christian will agree with everything I say. However, I am confident that they will understand what I am talking about. On the other hand, I expect that committed post-modernists will find much of my discussion not only offensive, but positively incomprehensible.

I promised this would be a practical book, with information that can help you in your own married life. And so it will. The first and ultimately most practical thing to say is why your marriage matters to people besides yourselves.

PART I

WHY YOUR MARRIAGE MATTERS
TO THE REST OF THE WORLD

1

The Gift of Marriage

AFREE SOCIETY REQUIRES PEOPLE WITH A CONSCIENCE. The vast majority of people must obey the rules voluntarily, not because they are afraid of what the police might do to them. The terrorist attacks on September 11, in which a handful of people turned our freedoms against us, showed how much our freedoms depend on people having a basic attachment to society. As a result of those attacks, everyone now accepts greater levels of government scrutiny and control than he otherwise would have.

In a police state, the government doesn't count on voluntary compliance or cooperation, but enforces rules with threats and punishments. A free society, by contrast, needs people to cooperate voluntarily. The culture of a free society must, therefore, nurture and cultivate people's willingness to collaborate peacefully with others. The continuation of a non-intrusive government depends on this cooperation. The operating assumption of a police state is that the primary human motivation is fear: if people are in a continual state of terror, they will do what the government wants them to do. Needless to say, this is a recipe for a society that is both fragile and joyless.

The very idea of a free society is one of the great contributions of the West. In a free society, most people, most of the time, do what they want to do, with a minimum of interference from others. Most people, most of the time, have the opportunity to define for themselves the shape of their own lives, unencumbered by law or tradition. But for this to work, people have to be willing to respect others and conform to basic laws of the society that apply to everyone. We can get along with a minimum of governmental control only if we are able to control ourselves.

We sometimes think about conscience and cooperation in terms of arguments and justifications for moral rules and prohibitions. Most abstract discussions about "rational self-interest" or "self-interest, rightly understood," concern the specific content of the conscience. But having a conscience at all depends on a whole host of prior conditions. A person has to have a desire to do the right thing, the willingness to learn about right and wrong, and the ability to follow through and do the right thing. All of this is logically prior to figuring out the specific content of the conscience.

The remarkable fact is that this moral groundwork is not rational at all, but relational. We do not develop trust, trust-worthiness, or self-restraint in a social vacuum. We develop these traits in the pre-cognitive, pre-verbal period of our lives. The groundwork for the conscience is laid in the first eighteen months of an infant's life through his relationship with his mother. This is why the family matters; specifically, this is why your marriage matters. *Your marriage has the potential to create children who can strengthen a free society—or significantly weaken it.*

Let me demonstrate by counterexample: the common patterns of life for a child without parents.

The Child without a Family

Children who are abandoned by their families often end up in orphanages. Their experience reveals some things about human development we might otherwise overlook. Children who are deprived of human contact during infancy sometimes fail to gain weight or to develop. This "failure to thrive" syndrome is well documented. Some scientists now believe that the presence of a nurturing figure stimulates the growth hormones.[1] All the bodily, material needs of the child are met in these orphanages. The child is kept warm and dry; the child is fed, perhaps by having a bottle propped up in the crib; the child contracts no identifiable illness. Yet the child fails to thrive and may even die. The widely accepted explanation is that the children die from lack of human contact.[2]

Their plight is reminiscent of monkeys that, in an experiment, were deprived of their mothers. Baby monkeys that received food but were kept from their mothers exhibited disturbing behavior: head-banging, rocking, and other forms of self-stimulation. Orphanage babies sometimes do these things, too.[3]

More important, these children often have difficulty forming attachments to others. Even children who are later adopted by loving and competent families sometimes never fully attach to them. Experts believe that children who do not develop attachments in the first eighteen months of life will have grave difficulty doing so later. And if the parents of such children do not intervene by the time the child reaches twelve years of age, the prospects for successful future intervention are thought to be diminished to the point of hopelessness.[4]

If loving adults do eventually appear in this child's life, he may not accept their care. He may resist being held or refuse to make eye contact. I once saw a photograph of a woman who took care of many babies in a ward in an Eastern European orphanage. She was holding one of the babies. She was an attractive, perfectly nice woman, so far as one could tell from the photo. But there was something wrong with the picture that I couldn't immediately identify. Finally, I realized what it was. The baby's face was not visible. The baby was arching its back, resisting being held. This baby, less than a year old, small enough to be held, was already at risk for attachment disorder.

The classic case of attachment disorder is a child who does not care what anyone thinks of him. The disapproval of others does not deter bad behavior, because there are no others significant enough to matter to the child. The child does whatever he thinks he can get away with, no matter the cost to others. Such children respond to physical punishments and to suspension of privileges, but not to disapproval. They lie if they think it is advantageous to lie; they steal if they can get away with it. They may go through the motions of offering affection, but those who live with them sense a kind of phoniness. Such childen show no regret at having hurt another person, or may offer only perfunctory apologies. They may enjoy torturing animals.

As they grow into adolescence, these children may become sophisticated manipulators. Some authors refer to them as "trust bandits," because they are superficially charming in their initial encounters with people, only to betray their trust by using them. Their parents, and anyone else who has long-term dealings with them, grow increasingly frustrated, frightened, and angry over their child's dangerous behavior, which may include lying, stealing, violence, and fire-setting.[5]

As the parents try to seek help for their child, they may find that he is able to "work the system." He can charm therapists, social workers, counselors, and later, perhaps, even judges and parole officers. This child is unwilling to consider others, or even to inconvenience himself for the sake of others.

Plainly, such a person is not fit for social life. This person cannot be turned loose with the ordinary freedoms of movement and choice that most of us take for granted. A society cannot manage very many people like this and still remain free.

The desperate condition of the attachment-disordered child shows us that modern Western society has, all along, been counting on something more than the mutual interests of autonomous individuals to hold it together. In spite of our proclamations in favor of individualism and personal choice, we have been counting on the very personal attachments of mothers to their children to produce consciences in those children.

The Child with a Family

How does love make the difference between the sociopath and the kind of person who can be trusted to pursue his own self-interest without causing too much trouble for other people? When an infant is hungry, he cries. His mother comes, picks him up, and feeds him. The baby gets food in his stomach. But the adult help gives the baby more than just satisfaction of his bodily needs.

When the mother picks up the baby, usually she will look at the baby. For a significant part of the nursing time, the mother and baby are locked in eye contact. The mother rocks the baby during nursing and burping; the rocking is comforting; the mother's milk is nutritious and sweet. The baby begins to make the lifelong association between sweetness and love. (Many of our pet names for people make this connection. When we are fond of someone, we call him sweetie, honey or sugar.) The baby's needs are met; he is satified and can relax.[6]

This cycle of need, adult help, satisfaction, and relaxation occurs many times each day of a baby's life. The baby becomes attached to the person who helps him. He learns to trust that his needs will be met, that his discomfort is not really as deadly as he may have at first feared. He comes to trust that the world is a safe place and that he belongs in it. He comes to see that human contact is the great good that assures his continued survival.

The contrast with abandoned children makes this connection even more stark. Suppose no adult appears to meet the child's needs. The baby cries. No one comes. The baby gets angry, as well as wet, hungry, and tired. Still, no one comes. He may give up crying: he has found it to be futile. Instead of developing trust in the world, or in adults, he become angry. Each episode of neediness increases his rage rather than his trust. Instead of building his connection to other human beings, every instance of the baby's neediness builds his sense of isolation from the rest of the world. Eventually, he stops looking for another person to help him. Instead, he may turn inward, on his own resources. He may conclude that the only way he will survive is by taking care of himself.

This may sound appealing to our independent-minded American way of thinking. We celebrate the individual pioneer, out blazing a trail for himself on the frontier. But the Lone Ranger is an adult. The people on the set of *Wagon Train* head out on the frontier together; they don't send babies or small children out on the trail alone. It is profoundly pathological to leave an infant to try to take care of himself.

If the adult world responds to the child's needs, the child learns that it is safe and beneficial to trust. Children of normal, loving parents learn that all the anxiety they experience is not really necessary. Mom and Dad are going to show up; they are going to do what is needed. Children eventually learn to relax into the care of adults who are in loving control of the situation. In the process, the infant comes to know that human contact is the great good that ensures his continued existence. As a byproduct of caring for the most basic bodily needs, the parents call out the child's longing for human contact. The longing for human contact ultimately develops into a longing for the deeper attachment we ordinarily call love. It is the unconditional love of the mother for the child that creates this first, most basic attachment between the child and the rest of the human race. This attachment provides the foundation for the conscience and for reciprocity. It is no exaggeration to say that civilization depends on a good first year. This is why the free society needs the family. And in turn, this is why your marriage is important to the free society.

In addition to the psychological importance of the basic attachment, the time spent with mother does something else for the infant. The connection between the baby and his mother helps the child's brain to continue developing. In fact, the conscience development is probably in part related to the brain development that I am about to describe.

Neurodevelopment

The human brain has three parts, the proto-reptilian brain, the limbic brain, and the neocortical brain. The proto-reptilian brain controls the most basic, primitive bodily functions needed for survival. As its name suggests, it is the part of the brain we have in common with our remote reptilian ancestors. The limbic brain is the part of the brain that controls emotions and connections between people. The neocortex is the part of the brain that is capable of logic, abstraction, and language.[7]

The reptilian brain is the most primitive. This part of the brain regulates our basic bodily functions. We can live without the other parts of the brain, but without the reptilian brain, the basic brain stem, we will simply die.

The limbic brain is unique to mammals and allows us to have the kind of social life typical of animals whose young are born dependent. The limbic brain controls our bodily responses to other people and allows us to respond to touch, proximity, and others' emotions.

This is the part of the brain that makes ~~makes~~ watching a movie in a crowded theater a different, more intense experience than watching it at home by yourself. Close contact with all those other people makes the scary parts scarier, the funny parts funnier, and the exciting parts more thrilling. The responses of the limbic brain make physical contact with others a healing experience. This is why bringing pets into nursing homes and hospitals can help sick people get better.

The limbic brain allows us to "read" other people's feelings. We can look at each other and sense whether another person is angry, happy, or fearful, for basic facial expressions are remarkably consistent across cultures. We can read many of the same cues in other mammals.[8] This is why we prefer other mammals for pets, and hardly ever bring lizards or tarantulas to the Pets in the Hospitals programs.

The human brain is so large compared with the rest of the human body that it is not fully developed before birth. If our brains were fully developed in utero, our heads would be too big to make it out of the birth canal without killing our mothers. Much of the development of the limbic brain, therefore, takes place after birth, in response to the child's being in a relationship with his mother.[9]

We can see the physiological impact of the relationship between and infant and his mother by looking at other mammals, as well as at the behavior of humans. Infant mammals have a predictable pattern of reactions to separation from their mothers. They first go through a "protest" phase, and then a "despair" phase, after a prolonged separation. Each of these phases can be easily observed, and the physiological attributes associated with these phases can be readily measured.[10]

Anyone who has tried to wean puppies or kittens will recognize the behavior of a baby in the "protest" phase: it has some similarities to a toddler's objections to the arrival of a babysitter. The youngsters cry out, run around, and search for their missing mommy. A scientist can measure more subtle but hardly surprising responses. The baby's heart rate increases; so does his body temperature. His little body produces elevated levels of cortisol, the body's stress hormone, and elevated levels of catecholamine, an adrenaline-like hormone that increases alertness.[11]

If his mother goes away, an infant, whether human or some other species of mammal, will cry out in anxiety for her to return. Now, in an evolutionary setting, this response is at first puzzling. How could a helpless creature increase his chance of survival by calling attention to itself? Screaming can have survival value only if it obtains some genuine help from somebody who cares, namely, the parent. But if no one comes, the baby stops crying out.

The baby cannot sustain this heightened level of alertness and tension indefinitely. If the mother is absent long enough, the infant enters the "despair" phase. He stops running around crying for his mommy. He may slouch, huddle himself, and look sad. The infant's heart rate and body temperature decrease. His consumption of oxygen decreases, his immune system is impaired, and his sleep rhythms change.

His little body produces less growth hormone. This is why children raised in orphanages or who have prolonged hospital stays lose weight and fail to grow, no matter what their caloric intake. This is the physiological source of the "failure to thrive" syndrome, also called "hospitalism" by its discoverer, Rene Spitz.[12]

A few years ago, there was a spate of books about creating baby geniuses. These books claimed that parents could increase their children's IQ by proper stimulus to the brain. *The Mozart Effect*, which claimed that playing Mozart's music for babies would stimulate their brains, was only the most celebrated of these books. These books were obviously sensationalized, and they over-dramatized the ability of parents to influence their children's development.[13] Yet the grain of truth in these books was that the development of the brain does depend in part on what goes on in the child's environment.

The human child is neither so maleable or so vulnerable as the "baby genius" hysteria suggested. The truth is that most babies achieve their optimal brain development in the most ordinary of ways, from being in a relationship with a responsive parent. The give and take of the response seems to be what stimulates the development. But it is not so much the neocortex, the part of the brain that gets good grades in school, that develops in this way, but the limbic brain. A child deprived of human contact is most stunted in his emotional growth, in his responsiveness to other people's emotions, even in his ability to notice or care about other people.[14]

This is a "good news, bad news," situation. The good news is that most people can be reasonably good parents, just by doing the ordinary things that—literally—come naturally. Rocking the baby, feeding the baby, looking at the baby, imitating his little noises, bouncing him on your knee: all these things are part and parcel of developing the limbic system of the brain.

The bad news is that, precisely because so much of child care is ordinary and natural, many modern parents seem to want to pass off the care of their infants to day care providers. Modern parents are too busy to do the important work of completing the child's development, so they hire a substitute. In my judgment, this accounts for the enthusiasm for *The Mozart Effect* and similar books. They can be read to imply that the modern, busy mother can delegate the care of her baby's developing brain to a well-trained, well-instructed substitute, while she herself goes back to work.[15]

But the mother-business of creating a relationship with the child never really takes place in the same intense way. A relationship is in part, a physiological event. In the process of rocking the baby, feeding the baby, looking at the baby, responding to the baby, the mother is helping the baby's limbic brain to continue its development. This is probably why the problems of the little orphanage children are so persistent. These children are completely deprived of a mother, or even a mother substitute. Not only are they psychologically damaged, but their brain development has been hampered as well.

Indeed, physicians have defined a new syndrome to describe the complex of symptoms these children have: "institutional autism."[16] Autism is now understood to be a neurological disorder, not normally caused by poor parenting or distant mothers, as used to be thought. But in extreme cases where children receive no mothering at all, some institutionalized children develop symptoms of autism.

A Challenge to Our Individualism

The experience of the infant shows us that both self-interest and interdependence are central to the human condition: they are both "natural" and have survival value. A baby has an instrumental need for other people: he becomes attached to the adults in his life because it is literally a matter of life and death. Deeper connections with others flow from the satisfaction of these most basic needs of the body.

A baby's neediness calls him out of his own little world and into the world of the other person. The infant's neediness is resolved, not by his calculated negotiating skills or his independence. Rather, his neediness is resolved by trust and dependence. Infant helplessness and the adult response to it is the most basic socialization experience: it introduces the child to human social relationships.

From the perspective of a free-market individualist, the role of reciprocity in the infant's life is paradoxical. The reciprocity of the marketplace presupposes and uses our self-centeredness. The market channels self-interest in a constructive direction, allows us to pursue our own self-interest without bothering others too much, and even allows our natural self-centeredness to be helpful to others. The reciprocity of the nursery does something more profound. It allows us to notice other people in the first place. In bonding with his mother, the infant has his first experience of sociability. This early experience lays the groundwork for later social experiences, including participation in the market, in political life, and in building a new family.

Unlike those who participate in market exchanges, the infant and the mother cannot realistically refuse to participate in an exchange with each other. Voluntary transactions are central to the moral case for a free market: a person can walk away from any economic transaction that he believes will not benefit him. Indeed, the ability to walk away defines free exchange. Most economists are highly suspicious of economic transactions with some form of compulsory participation. Of course, mothers can abandon, neglect, or abuse their infants. But given the demands that newborn infants place upon their caregivers, it is surprising that so few mothers do abandon them. The willingness of an exhausted new mother to attend to a crying baby in the middle of the night is a challenge to any naïve theory of self-interest.

The modern, sociobiological theory of self-interest offers a partial explanation of the mother's willingness to endure pain for the sake of her child. A strong maternal attachment has survival value for a species with a long period of infant dependency. The mother's body cries out to respond to the child's neediness. Her breasts become sore if she doesn't nurse. When the baby wakes up crying, the mother cannot sleep as deeply as others, or even as well as she herself used to be able to do. The distinctive howl of the newborn baby cuts through a woman's body like a knife. Men, as well as women who have never had children, might be able to recognize that there is something especially piercing about a newborn's howl, but a new mother can't ignore this sound. After having given birth, a woman can identify that newborn howl, even when it comes from someone else's child.

Men and women alike find babies appealing. Thousands of generations of evolution have conspired to make us think these noisy, messy little creatures are cute, so that we will nurture them through their early dependency. Obviously, there is survival value in all this responsiveness. And babies somehow know how to be cute and attractive. They learn to smile, to look at us, laugh, and make us laugh. In some primal, evolutionary period before humans had developed cultural norms about how to treat infants, an obnoxious baby surely had a lower probability of survival than a cute baby.

All this may well be an accurate evolutionary account of the physiology of human attachments. But no intelligent sociobiologist would claim that such a mechanism is foolproof, in the sense of offering a guarantee that every mother will take care of every child. The sociobiologist can simply aver that those mothers who nurture their children to the age of reproduction are those most likely to have their own genes reproduced. Those children that have sufficient cuteness to keep adults attached to them have a higher probability of survival.

What the sociobiologist cannot tell us is how we ought to behave. Here is an example that illustrates the kind of problem I have in mind.

I once had a friend whose son was colicky as an infant, a real screamer. This young, inexperienced couple lived in a second-floor apartment. One afternoon, after the baby had screamed for an eternity, his father took him by the feet and held him upside down outside the second-story window. An act of frustration, certainly, but also a strategy for diminishing the irritation caused by a screaming child: the father places the screams at a further remove, so they aren't as loud.

Now, a sociobiologist might say that only a father would think of such a thing. His reproductive strategy is to impregnate as many women as possible, as often as possible, knowing that some of his children will survive to reproductive age. The mother, on the other hand, would be more concerned about the child's safety, since her reproductive strategy tells her to nurture each of her relatively few children to adulthood.

This particular mother demolished that sociobiological forecast. She looked at her husband, holding the infant upside down, outside a second-floor window, turning his face away, trying to tune out the sounds of the baby howling and yelled, "Drop him!"

My conjecture is that a variant on the evolutionary insight might still apply. Generations of evolution have made the mother's physiology more attuned to the child's screaming. Most of the time, this is a long-term survival strategy. The irritation caused by the baby's fussing induces her to respond to his needs and take care of him. But that very same characteristic can also push her over the edge more easily than someone with less of a connection to the baby, so the baby's screaming bothers her more than it bothers her husband. A mere irritation to the man can be an intense agony for the woman.

(Needless to say, my friend did not drop his baby out of the window. Neither he nor his wife regretted his act of self-control. The little boy grew up to be quite a nice kid.)

Evolutionary psychology and sociobiology can tell us who is more likely to respond to certain types of pain. But it cannot tell us how we ought to define, or redefine, pain. When is it something to be avoided, and when is it worth bearing. It is our culture that in various ways supplements the physiological pleasure-pain calculus with a more subtle set of indications of how we ought to behave.

But sociobiology is not the only account of human nature. Christianity also offers an account. Although there are differences among the various Christian religions about the details of human nature, Christians agree that human nature is something specific and that it is not infinitely malleable. Likewise, sociobiologists disagree among themselves on various points, but all agree that human nature is something stable enough to be studied. Like evolutionary psychology, Christianity has something to say about the tension between individualism and self-interest on one hand and interdependence and altruism on the other. But Christian teaching adds a few things that the purely scientific view cannot address and unabashedly tells us something about how we ought to behave and why.

Christianity, of course, recognizes the helplessness of the infant and its extreme dependence on its mother, seeing in this a metaphor for every human being's continual and complete dependence upon God. Christianity encourages mothers to take pleasure in their newborns, just as God, our loving father, takes pleasure in each of us. Our initial period of dependency gives us a template for relaxing into the care of a loving God.

The mother naturally gives of herself to her child, according to the sociobiologists, because this behavior has survival value. According to Christian teaching, she does so because the human person is made for love. We are most fully human when we love and are loved. Pope John Paul II puts it this way: "Man cannot live without love. He remains a being that is incomprehensible for himself, his life is senseless, if love is not revealed to him, if he does not encounter love, if he does not experience it, and make it his own, if he does not participate intimately in it."[17] This statement is completely consistent with the discoveries of neuropsychology, as we can see from those little orphanage children

who bang their heads, turn their faces away, and never develop consciences or relationships. Their lives make no sense to them unless
they encounter love. But for them, love is not an abstraction. They
must encounter love in the person of their mothers, or someone who
will take personal, individual care of them.

Christianity insists that our initial period of dependency is not
something we ought to entirely outgrow. It is both a template for our
continual dependence on a loving God and a model for our own vocation to love other people. Our parents' love for us demonstrates our
vocation to love those who need us and are legitimately dependent
upon us. Watching our parents love each other as they care for us
teaches us how to love those who are our equals in competence and
capability, but who may complement us in our specific areas of weakness and strength.

The interdependence of mother and child may be dismissed by
some as being only marginally relevant to the larger business of society. Some individualists more or less dismiss discussions of children
and their rights as being peripheral to the main business of building
a free society. I used to say this myself, for instance, when giving talks
introducing people to libertarianism. I would always delay the discussion of children and their rights for a more advanced lesson.[18] Needless to say, the right time for that more advanced lesson never quite
arrived. The issue of children's rights causes libertarians discomfort
because it seems to undermine the general presumption in favor of
self-interest, as well as the general presumption against any notion of
obligatory self-sacrifice.

Ayn Rand, one of the most radical individualists of the twentieth
century, dismissed what she called "life boat ethics," as being a kind of
cheap trick to induce people to sacrifice themselves for others.[19] Suppose three people are shipwrecked. They have a lifeboat big enough for
two. Allowing the third person to enter the lifeboat would endanger all
three lives. This situation presents a moral dilema. Altruism suggests

that a good person would sacrifice himself to save the third person unfortunate enough to be outside the lifeboat. The lifeboat situation is supposed to demonstrate that an ethic of individualism is inconsistent with our deeply held moral intuitions. Ayn Rand dismissed the entire thought experiment, arguing that lifeboat morality bears so little resemblance to the actual world we inhabit most of the time that it is improper to draw general conclusions from it.

She was, of course, correct about the lifeboat. But the society around the infant is not a bizarre or unlikely situation. It is the story of every human life. The experience of dependency and helplessness is in some sense the only truly universal human experience. It is my considered opinion that Western liberalism and libertarianism would be greatly strengthened by facing up to this fact, not continually postponing the subject for a later lesson.

The issue is not whether a free society consisting of free markets, participatory limited government, and rule of law is more desirable than its major competitors. Democracy and free markets have defeated their competitors. In this sense, Francis Fukyama is correct: the important institutional question has been decided by History.[20] We now have a different question before us: how should we define our understanding of self-interest? I maintain that we can build a more appealing society by redefining self-interest to include the good of others in an explicit way.

Many of us in the West have "live and let live" inclinations. We have focused on the "free" part of the free society and neglected the "society" part. What motivates people to form themselves into groups? Is there something that keeps these groups together, beyond explicitly political structures? The answers to these kinds of questions can help us provide the social glue for the non-governmental and non-market parts of our world. It is the family that provides the foundation for a truly free society.

The Child with an Incomplete Family

What does any of this have to do with marriage in general—and your marriage in particular? From what I have said so far, you could conclude that children with a conscience are women's gift to a free society. But that is only part of the story. Children are more likely to thrive in a two-parent, married-couple family than in any other living arrangement. Kids do best living with two parents who love each other. This is why children with a conscience are not only women's gift, but matrimony's gift, to a free society.

It was once customary to refer to divorced families as being "broken homes." That term has fallen into disfavor, but it captures a poignant reality from the child's perspective. Every child has two biological parents, one mother, one father. No matter how the post-modernists try to parse the situation, this underlying biological fact remains. From the child's point of view, divorce breaks his family.

The child whose parents never marry may not have a "broken family," since no family ever formed around him in the first place. But he does have an incomplete family. He may never know his father, or may not have the opportunity to cultivate much of a relationship with him. But from the child's point of view, the loss of his father counts as a loss, no matter what the parents say or think about it.[21]

By now, social scientists have accumulated an impressive body of evidence showing the difficulties that children in single-parent families, and even stepfamilies, face. Let's take a look at some of this evidence.[22]

A recent study from Sweden showed that children of single-parent households are twice as likely to attempt suicide or to abuse drugs as children from married-couple families. This study made sure that the results were not simply a result of single-parent families, having less money, or of some underlying genetic tendency toward mental instability. Sweden is famous for its provision of a generous social safety net. Yet even in Sweden, the absence of a father produced these sad results.[23]

A review of studies performed through the 1980s found that children from mother-only families obtain fewer years of education and are more likely to drop out of high-school.[24] They have lower earnings in young adulthood and are more likely to be poor. The daughters of single mothers are more likely to receive welfare when they become adults than daughters from two-parent families. Children from mother-only families are more likely to marry early and have children early, both in and out of wedlock. Those who marry are more likely to divorce.[26] Offspring from mother-only families are more likely to commit delinquent acts and to engage in drug and alcohol use than offspring from two-parent families.[27]

One might think that the income differences between single-parent and two-parent households might account for some of these differences between the children of the two types of households.[28] But income differences account for only a portion of the differences between mother-only families and two-parent families. The problems remain to a somewhat lesser degree, even when the fact that single mothers have lower income is taken into account. Nor does the relatively large number of non-whites among single-parent households account for the whole constellation of problems. The effects of single-motherhood are consistent across a large number of racial and ethnic groups.[29]

A comprehensive study performed on 1988 data found that children raised in disrupted or never-married families are at increased risk of health, academic, and behavioral problems, in comparison with children in intact families with both biological parents present.[30] Children from disrupted marriages were over 70 percent more likely than those living with both biological parents to have been expelled or suspended: those living with never-married mothers were more than twice as likely to have had this experience. Children with both biological parents were less likely to have repeated a grade of school.[31]

A recent study of academic performance using a nationally representative sample of over twenty thousand eighth-graders from 970 schools collected information about the family characteristics of the students, as well as characteristics of the school they attend. The study takes account of parental income and education, and the mean level of socio-economic status of the families attending the school. The most striking finding has to do with the effects of having a peer group composed of lots of single-parent households. Students who attended schools with a high concentration of students from single-parent households had math and reading achievement scores that were 10 percent lower than students who attended schools with a higher concentration of two-parent households. This suggests that mother-only families create spill-over effects to other children in the schools.[32]

Children living in single parent households are also more likely to have emotional and behavioral problems. The children outside of traditional families had 50 percent to 80 percent higher scores for indicators of anti-social behavior, peer conflict, social withdrawal, and age-inappropriate dependency. Such children also had 25 percent to 50 percent higher scores for indicators of anxiety, depression, headstrong behavior, and hyperactivity.[33]

Children of divorce are statistically more likely to be depressed than children in two-parent families. Parental divorce increases a boy's probablity of depression, regardless of the quality of parenting or level of parental conflict. The impact of divorce on girls' depression seems to be indirect, generated by poor parenting and increased parental conflict. Looked at from the opposite perspective, the negative impact of divorce on girls' depression can be mediated by high quality parenting and low levels of parental conflict. For boys, on the other hand, nothing seems to compensate for the sense of sadness that boys experience at the loss of their fathers from the home.[34]

One might think that replacing the absent father with a new man would alleviate some of the children's difficulties. A stepfather typically does bring additional income to the family. The stepfather at least has the potential to increase the amount of adult time and attention the children receive. But introducing a "new father" into the picture does not necessarily solve the child's problems, and may add some new ones.

Children in stepfamilies show more developmental difficulties than those in intact nuclear families. The adjustment of children in stepfamilies is similar to that of children in one-parent families.[35] For instance, children with stepfathers have approximately the same high risk of repeating a year of school as do the children of never-married mothers, around 75 percent. The increase in risk was 40 percent for children of divorced mothers.[36] A recent study showed that when a stepfather enters the home, children exhibit more behavior problems compared to their peers who live with both biological parents, and the impact is slightly stronger for boys than for girls.[37]

Another study found that more involvement by any type of father, including a stepfather, reduces both problems at home and in the school. That is, the more involved any father is in the life of his children, the fewer behavior problems they exhibit. However, the study showed that stepfathers are less involved with children. The presence of a stepfather is also correlated with less involvement by the mother in her children's lives. Since the mother's involvement also correlates with fewer child problems, the presence of a stepfather effectively delivers a double blow to the children. It is no surprise that the study found that children who live with stepfathers have more behavior problems than children who live with two biological parents.[38]

This study gives a hint as to why the difficulties of mother-only children persist even after the arrival of a stepfather: the stepfather and children can easily become rivals for the mother's attention. The introduction of a new parent disrupts established loyalites and creates conflicted loyalties.[39] A certain amount of conflict over child-rearing is inevitable, even in the best of marriages. An intact marriage has one major advantage over blended marriages. Raising children is a shared project from the beginning, rather than one person's project that the other person joins mid-course.

Many parents have difficulty surrendering authority to the new parent, and the new parent usually does not feel entitled to demand equal decision-making. Families resolve this issue in a variety of ways. In some families, the child can successfully triangulate the parents, pitting them against each other. Although some children become very skillful at triangulating and seem to take pleasure in it, it is seldom in their best interests.

Sometimes the parents can agree to something akin to a "property rights" solution, in a kind of a hands-off arrangement for the stepparent.[40] "These are my kids, not yours. I take responsibility for them. Our relationship and my discipline system doesn't concern you." In that case, the addition of the new man doesn't really add much except rivalry for the mother's attention. Or the mother may spend less time with the child because she is eager to establish her relationship with her new spouse. In all these cases, the child becomes a wedge between the parents, rather than a focus of their unity.

These problems can translate into lowered academic acheivement. One study specifically examined the relationship of family structure, time spent with children, and academic acheivement.[41] Children in two-parent families got the highest grades of any family structure. In all types of families, the time fathers spent with children had a positive impact on their grades. But the effect of father's time did not entirely offset the negative impact of family structure on grades.

The most striking finding did not concern the subject directly under study: stepfathers spend less time with children than do fathers in two-parent families, on average. While extra time from stepdad could offset some of the loss the child feels, the fact is stepfathers are unlikely to spend as much time with children as biological fathers are.

Finally, studies have shown that children whose parents divorce have greater difficulty entrusting themselves to others. A study of sixty college students found that students from divorced homes trusted their dating partners less than their peers who came from intact homes.[42] The ability to empathize with others is, obviously, a crucial social skill. A person who cannot empathize with others is doomed to a life of isolation. The involvement of the father in a child's care is the biggest single factor in predicting how empathetic a child becomes.[43]

Childhood Needs and Parental Freedom

I began this chapter with a startling claim: Children with a conscience are matrimony's gift to society. All the evidence that I have cited points to this conclusion. The development of conscience requires relationship building, which requires time, time, time, between the baby and parents. A mother needs to be there to nurse and rock. A mother's attention to the baby helps develop his conscience, as well as other forms of responsiveness and attentiveness to the needs of others. A father needs to take care of many of the material and financial needs of both the mother and the baby, so they can be together for the extended, intense period of time that is truly necessary. A mother and father need to be together so they can renew and replenish their love for each other, as well as for their child, who is their common concern.

The information about family structure points to a similar conclusion. Children need to have a relationship with their parents. They need for their parents to love them and to love each other. Absent that love, children have a much more difficult time developing the qualities of self-command and self-care that society needs for them to have.

Virtually all researchers accept the correlation between higher levels of child well-being and living with both biological parents, because it shows up in so many studies. The debate centers on how much of the difference in child welfare can be accounted for by the disparity in resources typically found between two-parent and single-parent households. But the debate is so intense, the arguments so passionate, it is hard to believe that people are getting that worked up over t-statistics,

R-squares, standard deviations, and omitted variables. Something else, something more personal, is generating all the heat.

I believe the real issue driving the "marriage debate" is the question of what we owe to children. Do we owe them material resources, provided by society at large? Or do we owe them personal relationships, provided for them by the particular people who brought them into existence? If children truly need a two-parent, married-couple family, this would place obligations upon adults to get married and stay married. Many adults are reluctant to accept these particular obligations. So they, along with their allies in high policy-making places, try to minimize the importance of the evidence or to reinterpret it to mean that children really need more material support from government and business.

From this perspective, the questions are: What is the minimal set of human relationships that a child can have and still turn out tolerably well?[44] What is the least adults have to do in relationship terms for their kids to get by? How much money does society have to pump in from outside the family to make up for the loss of relationship, so that I won't have to give up my belief that parents are entitled to any lifestyle choices they want?

This minimalist mentality shows up in the conclusions people draw from these studies. For instance, people reinterpret the studies showing that a stepfather who spends enough time with his stepchildren can ward off some of the problems often seen in divorced families. At one level, this is undeniable. Of course children benefit from more time and attention from their fathers and stepfathers. But we are not justified in drawing the conclusion that there is no reason to be concerned about family structure as long as stepfathers spend enough time with their stepchildren. The very same study also shows that stepfathers, on average, spend much less time with their wives' children than do biological fathers.

Many people seem to believe it is unreasonable to expect or even encourage people to get married and stay married. But asking stepfathers to behave like biological fathers may be every bit as unreasonable. Stepfathers behave systematically differently from biological fathers. It is unrealistic to expect men to work as hard on a relationship with another man's child as he would with his own child. It is more straightforward, as well as more sensible, to expect men and women to work together to maintain their marriages in the first place.

Some people argue that the children of single and divorced parents would do fine if only society would increase the resources available to the children. The government should provide some combination of subsidized day care, housing allowances, and income supplements to increase the standard of living of the children of single-parent households. This position is unpersuasive because most studies show that problems remain even after accounting for differences in economic resources. The resources that two parents can provide are not likely to ever be fully replaced by a single parent, no matter how heavily subsidized.

I believe that children are harmed by the loss of relationship itself, not simply by the loss of resources. The primary business of parenthood is relational. Parenthood is much more than a process of transferring resources from Big People to Little People. If that were true, resources from outside the family could possibly make up the losses that children experience from the loss of a parent.[45]

The primary responsibility of parents is to build relationships with their children and prepare their children to build relationships on their own when they mature. The whole attachment process, upon which conscience development depends, is a relationship-building process. Replacing a father with a paycheck is not a service either to the child, who misses out on the father's love, or to the father, who becomes reduced to a combination sperm donor and wallet.

I propose that we confront these relationship issues with more generosity toward children. Instead of asking how little we have to do, we should ask what children need from their parents in order to thrive. Instead of asking, how much money it takes to substitute for the presence of both parents, we could ask what parents can do to keep growing in love and regard for each other. We should not embrace a collective responsibility for financial support for children when we could embrace the personal obligation to nurture and cultivate loving relationships between spouses. We should be asking how we adults can support each other in maintaining our marriages.

A free society needs a civil society composed mostly of people who can control themselves and take care of themselves and others. The future of freedom depends on people with a conscience. People with consciences do not emerge out of thin air, but are created inside a loving family. And families are created by love and marriage.

In short, free government and a free economy need a robust civil society. Civil society needs the family. The family needs marriage. This is the number one reason why your marriage matters to the rest of the world.

2

The Gift of Sex

IN THE PREVIOUS CHAPTER, I showed that society begins with the family. In infancy, our neediness compels us to be involved with other people. Yet infants are inevitably self-centered. They have to be: growing up is a full-time job. But the very neediness that makes them so focused on themselves also draws them out of themselves to be in relationship with their parents, who have the ability to give them the help they need so much.

In sexual activity, too, there is an interplay between our self-centeredness and our need for others. Sex is the foundation of community. Our desire for sexual satisfaction draws us out of ourselves, and into relationship with others. The sexual urge provides a motive force for sociability.

Sociability Beyond Infancy

Once beyond infancy, neediness fades as a motivation for human connectedness. In the normal course of development, we acquire more and more independence. We become more able to take care of our own needs, but we still need the assistance of others. We learn to feed and dress ourselves, but we continue to need some help figuring out what to eat and wear. We learn to move around by ourselves, first to walk, then to ride a bike, and later to drive a car. We don't learn a single one of these skills for independence completely on our own. In these experiences, we can come to know that self-care is a good thing, and so is being willing to accept help. Gradually, our dependency fades, and our relationships with our parents become based more upon equality of power, strength, and ability.

As we stumble and swagger into adolescence, we enjoy our new powers and abilities. We are eager to prove that we no longer need anyone, that we can manage on our own. We aren't quite ready to earn a living, but we are anxious to be independent consumers. We discover how ignorant, limited, and downright foolish our parents are, and always have been.

What is it that draws a person out of his self-absorption? In infancy, we pay attention to others because our lives depend on it. Once we no longer need other people, our self-centeredness returns to the surface. To be sure, some teenage boys become Eagle Scouts, and some teenage girls volunteer at nursing homes. But by and large, adolescents are wrapped up in themselves, their own feelings, thoughts, and plans. Teenagers need to pay some attention to themselves, of course, because they need to figure out who they are. But most of us skirt the edges of excessive self-absorption, at least some of the time during our adolescence. It is the feature of adolescence that can be alternately the most charming and the most maddening.

Is there some impulse universal enough and powerful enough to lure people out of themselves, even when they are capable of independence? The most reliable instinct I can think of is the sexual urge.

The Sexual Urge as a Motivation for Sociability

Sexual desire has the potential to make adults aware of another person and able truly to be concerned about the good of another person.

Instead of leading us into a relationship of dependency, sexual desire attracts us to another person who is our approximate equal in age. We aren't ordinarily looking for a sexual partner who is weak and needy, nor are we exclusively looking for someone to take care of us, as though we were babies. Most people, most of the time, are attracted to someone comparable to themselves in strength and abilities.

Because the relationship is between people who are approximate equals, the way the attraction and neediness play out is quite different from the attachment between an infant and his parents. Adults are drawn to one another, but they are not bound to each other by any natural or necessary connection, as a baby and mother are. There is something automatic and axiomatic about the relationship between the mother and the baby. Not quite so between two potential lovers: they must win each other's love.

That means they have to pay attention to each other. They each must develop a genuine concern for the other—what he or she likes, wants, feels. Part of the purpose of courtship is to discover who the other person really is. In the process of developing the relationship, the lovers come to know the unique little quirks of the other person, some attractive, some irritating. But it is sexual desire and sexual attractiveness that make that other person interesting and initiate the relationship.

We do not automatically become genuinely interested in the person to whom we are sexually attracted. It is certainly possible to view another person simply as a means to satisfy our sexual desire. We can view him or her as interchangeable with a variety of other potential sex partners. We can think of sexual activity as just another recreational activity, something fun to do on a Saturday night. We can reduce the other person to an object, a sexual object, to be sure, but an object just the same.

Of course, in a relationship between two adults of approximately equal ego-strength, neither will tolerate being used in this way. Each will insist on being treated, not as a means, but as an end in himself or herself. The Kantian Imperative, "always treat other people as ends in themselves," or the Christian Golden Rule, "do unto others as you would have them do unto you," operates as a behavioral norm. This norm tells us that a good person will neither want to use another person nor allow himself to be used.

In this way, the sexual urge has the potential to make us more sociable than our natural self-centeredness might suggest we could be. We have to become aware of the other person as a person in order to win his or her affection and his or her willingness to be sexual with us.

The Natural, Organic Purposes of Sexual Activity

Sexual activity has two natural, organic purposes: procreation and spousal unity. The procreation part is pretty obvious. Babies are the most basic and natural consequences of sexual activity. But the idea of "spousal unity" may require some explanation. Spousal unity is the feature of human sexuality that distinguishes it from purely animal sexuality and that makes "morally indifferent sex" so problematic.

I just wish your idiocy was just as obvious to you...

Spousal unity as one of the natural functions of sex means simply that sex builds attachments between the husband and wife. Shakespeare described the sexual act as "making the two-backed beast." Both the Hebrew and the Christian Bible describe the sexual act as uniting the spouses in the most literal sense: "the two become one flesh." The two, dissimilar bodies become unified; what were once two people become, if only for a short while, one flesh. Evolutionary psychology explains the survival value of spousal cooperation. Men and women who attach themselves to each other and can cooperate have a better chance of seeing their offspring survive long enough to produce grandchildren.

These natural, organic purposes have something in common. They both build community. Procreation literally builds the community of the family by adding new members. Spousal unity builds the community of the family because it contributes to the stability of the marriage.

Men and women connect to each other in a powerful way through the sexual act.

We have mixed feelings about this connectedness: we are vexed by our dependency upon the Other. The very fact of sexual reproduction underscores our essential limitation. We need a mate in order to reproduce. Genetically and biologically, nobody is going anywhere alone.

At the same time, this interdependence charms and thrills us. We love the connection: our bodies cry out for it. Together with a spouse, we can do what neither of us could do alone: participate in bringing a new person into existence. Not to mention that we really enjoy one another in the sexual act.

Because reproductive technology has made it possible to separate sexual activity from procreation, we have lost sight of the community-building features of sex. We seem to think we are entitled to have sex without babies simply because we can. We can do a technological end-run around the procreative function of sex, so we think we can bypass the spousal unity function of sex as well. But neither our bodies nor our souls will allow us to completely undo the connections between sexual activity, spousal love, and babies. And our ability to build a community or a society worthy of the name depends more upon these connections than we are always willing to admit.

Building bonds between sexual partners is every bit as "natural" a consequence of sex as procreation is, though it may be a less obvious consequence. The connection between spousal unity and sexual activity is imprinted on the body just as the procreative function is. These natural connections undermine the very idea of "morally indifferent sex." We are not really capable of being indifferent to our sexual partners, nor are we really capable of calculating and recalculating our attachments to our partners.

Modern physiology is discovering that the attachments we feel to our sexual partners are more than mere feelings and cultural conditioning. A relationship is a physiological event.[1] There are slightly different aspects to the physiology for men and for women, which I will discuss in turn.

Oxytocin: The Touch Hormone

Women need help in raising their young through a long period of dependency. We need help in obtaining resources for survival, and in providing protection. It is easy to see among primates. Males help provide food, territory, and protection for the mother and her young. The social structure of the troop has survival value. Therefore, the parts of primate physiology that nurture and support the social structure contribute to the survival of the group.

We sometimes imagine that we are exempt from the biological rules of survival. After all, a woman and her offspring can physically survive in a modern economy without the help of a man. A woman can get herself artificially inseminated and have a child without even performing a single sexual act. However, the chemistry of the body works against our attempts to be completely independent of a mate.

Women connect to their sex partners, and to their children, through a hormone called oxytocin. This hormone spikes during orgasm and is involved in the birth process and breast feeding. Oxytocin rises in response to touch, and promotes touching. It also promotes other forms of affectionate and parenting behavior.[2]

Let's pause on this fact and look at what the hormones of touch do for us. A woman's oxytocin level surges during orgasm, labor, and breast feeding. The title of one of the early important papers on this subject tells the story, "The Role of the Oxytocin Reflexes in Three Interpersonal Reproductive Acts: Coitus, Birth and Breastfeeding."[3] A woman's body responds to these community-building acts. The flood of oxytocin increases her desire for further touch with both her mate and her child. The hormone itself connects her to her child and her child's father.

This physiological reality helps explain a couple of otherwise puzzling bits of social science data. First, despite our protests to the contrary, cohabitation is not really a substitute for marriage. Couples will sometime move in with each other to "test the waters," thinking that they can avoid the commitment of marriage, but still have many of the benefits of marriage.[4]

Few such couples realize that their hormones may create an "involutary chemical commitment."[5] The very acts of spending time together, touching each other, having sex, and sleeping next to each other night after night create a powerful bond between them. Touching itself increases oxytocin levels and promotes bonding.

Cohabiting couples are sometimes reluctant to get married because they are unsure whether they are really right for each other. Unfortunately for them, living together does not encourage sensible decision-making because it can itself create a commitment. If the person was not right in the first place, cohabitation may reveal this fact. But cohabitation can also make it more difficult to break off the relationship. This may account in part for the surprising finding that divorce is more, not less, likely among couples who lived together before marriage.[6]

The effect of the bonding hormone can also illuminate the remarkable propensity of battered women to return to the very men who have abused them. Our hormonal response to touch, to sex, and to proximity is so powerful, that it can trump our better judgment. Battered women's shelters are filled with women who against all common sense return to abusive men.[7] Moreover, oxytocin is known to decrease a person's cognitive ability and impair memory.[8] So the touching hormone delivers a double blow. These hormones attach a woman even to an abusive lover, while impairing her judgment about what is good for her. This combination of factors may also explain why domestic violence is so much more prevalent among cohabiting couples than among married couples.[9] Some advocates claim that women return to their abusers because they have no economic options. But a lack of material resources is not sufficient to account for this. Biochemistry is surely a part of any complete explanation.

Finally, the oxytocin factor may explain something otherwise inexplicable to the modern mind. Arranged marriages, so far distant from the experience of most educated Westerners, sometimes work reasonably well. We assume that couples in arranged marriages stay together because they have no culturally acceptable alternative or because they have low expectations for emotional fulfillment within marriage.[10]

While this may be true in part, we should be cautious about dismissing too quickly so many marriages in so many different cultures. People today who come from cultures in which parentally arranged marriages are common will tell you otherwise. They grow to love their partners. This may be a tribute to the wisdom of their parents' choice. It may also, in part, be due to the biochemical impact of being in close, physical, and intimate relationship. The relationship itself often creates its own hormonal glue. Our scepticism may well be no more than our cultural and chronological snobbery talking.

Attachment for Men

What about men? It is a commonplace both in sociobiology and in ordinary life that men are less attached to their sex partners than are women. Can we make an argument that, even for men, the sexual act builds up the relationship between the partners?[11]

While oxytocin helps to bind women to their sexual partners and their babies, something slightly different is at work in male physiology. Vasopressin, primarily a male hormone, has sometimes been called the "monogamy molecule." Less is known about vasopressin than about oxytocin, but the preliminary research suggests that vasopressin helps to counteract the male tendency to "play the field."[12]

Jealousy: The Dark Side

Jealousy appears to be so common among men that we may safely call it "natural." At least one psychologist argues that jealousy helps men to connect with their sexual partners.[13]

Evolutionary psychology argues that men and women have distinct mating strategies. Men seek to impregnate as many women as possible and invest as little as possible in each child, while women seek to nurture each child to full maturity. Men must compete for women, and women prefer men who will be faithful providers for them and their children. The woman's strategy compels men to be more faithful than they would otherwise like to be. The man's strategy places him at war with himself.[14]

The evolutionary payoff for men to settle down with particular women is the assurance that the children he invests in are indeed his own. Therefore, feeling jealous or possessive toward a woman turns out to have survival value. A man is more likely to be angered by perceived sexual infidelity than by emotional infidelity.

A man doesn't feel jealous or possessive toward every woman he sees, or even toward every woman he finds attractive. He feels jealous about a woman with whom he is engaged in a serious relationship, particularly if he has had sex with her. This feeling of jealousy is in some ways a nuisance for the woman. She might feel that the man is trying to control her activity, or even her thoughts and feelings. It is, of course, possible for a man to become obsessively jealous, even dangerously jealous. But a woman knows that she matters to a man who is jealous. Some women even find a moderate amount of jealousy attractive and would be worried about a man who didn't feel any at all.[15]

The fact that a man feels jealous toward a woman he has sex with makes it all the harder for him to have sex with her and just walk away from her and her offspring. The naïve strategy for a man is to just impregnate as many women as possible, with as little investment of his own as possible. A more sophisticated strategy takes account of a woman's ability to make choices as well. She doesn't want to be abandoned by the father of her child; she wants a man who will stick around and contribute. She is less likely to choose a man who literally follows the naïve strategy of philandering. This means that it is advantageous to a man to overcome his tendency to play the field. Jealousy is one thing that helps him to do this.

If a man is going to be successful, he needs to find some way to be attractive enough to a woman that she will let him have sex with her. While it is advantageous to him if he can overcome his desire to have indiscriminate sex, it is even more helpful if he can credibly commit himself to the woman, if he can convince her that he will be a stable mate who will be a good provider for their children.[16]

Notice that none of this argument is vitiated by allowing the man access to multiple partners, as in polygamy. A woman may agree to a polygamous marriage, provided she believes that the man will provide adequately for her and her children. And a man's access to multiple wives does not mean that he will necessarily be less jealous or possessive of any of them. In fact, the opposite may be true. The man who has a harem may very well guard it all the more jealously than the man who is true to one and only one wife. The monogamous man has made a greater commitment to the single, particular wife, and is therefore highly credible to her without elaborate or passionate displays of jealousy.

The man's body tells him that having sex with a woman puts that particular woman into a new and different category. This is not merely an attractive woman: this is a woman who may give birth to his child. She is, therefore, different from other women. The sex act has changed her from a potential sex object to the potential mother of his children, with all that this implies. No matter how sophisticated we think we are, our bodies continue to respond to the sexual act in this way.

Loyalty: The bright side

The sociobiological perspective covers male physiology, but does not do justice to the male psyche. While it is true that jealousy is a way that men attach themselves to women, it is the "dark side" of the attachment. The more positive way to view the attachment is this: men are capable of heroic loyalty to women and children.

Men will work for a lifetime at jobs they don't like in order to support their families. Even after divorce, men go to heroic lengths to support their children. Despite the common image of divorced men as "deadbeat dads," most men meet their child support obligations, sometimes at tremendous cost to themselves. Even when they lose their jobs, divorced men continue to make child support payments.[17] Sanford Braver has shown that divorced fathers who have regular contact with their children pay close to 90 percent of the child support payments required by their divorce settlements. In fact, Braver contends that the regularity of fathers' contact with their children is highly correlated with their compliance with the terms of their divorce decrees.[18]

Fathers can be jailed for failing to meet their legal obligations to support their children financially. But mothers are rarely penalized for denying children their court-mandated rights to see their fathers. In spite of this imbalance in the legal system, many men continue to make payments to support children they may never be allowed to see and make valiant efforts to visit children whose mothers badmouth them regularly.[19]

Warren Farrell observes that the male "fathering instinct" tends to be more transferable to children other than his own than does the "mothering instinct" to non-biological offspring.

> Maybe the "instinct" isn't a fathering instinct per se, but an instinct to protect, provide and take responsibility in whatever form it takes—with the reward being to give and receive love. This male instinct seems to be triggered when needed by someone who loves him, and when trusted by someone who loves him.
>
> This male instinct to protect and provide can be called upon on behalf of a beloved country or a beloved child. For war, or for love. It is adaptable and transferable. As long as it's for what he loves and he loved for what he's doing. . . .

It is common for a man to marry or live with a woman whose children are living with her, have no new biological children with her, continue to work full-time earning more money than she does, and contribute both time and money to his wife's or womanfriend's children, receiving nothing but his wife's or womanfriend's love and the hope of her children's love in return.

Now reverse the situation. Think of how many women you know who married or lived with a man whose children are living with him, who had no new biological children with him, and who continued to work full-time earning more money than he, contributing both money and time to him and his children, receiving nothing but her husband's or boyfriend's love and the hope of his children's love in return. Almost always, a stepmom also has biological children of her own, or plans to have one with her new husband, or receives some financial advantage in being a stepmom, including the abilty to cut back on her hours at work.

A difference between male and female parenting then, seems to be that a woman's is both more specific to her biological child and more dependent on being coupled with financial support, either from a husband or the government. The man's is more transferable, less conditional upon receiving money, but quite conditional upon his ability to give and receive love, to feel needed and wanted.[20]

The view that most men, most of the time, have no attachment to their sex partners is a caricature, a cartoon version of reality. While it may be true that men attach to their sex partners less than women do to theirs, men are not simply looking for sexual release, but attach to their partners somewhat differently than women attach to theirs.

To illustrate this point, I will ask my male readers to perform a thought experiment. Imagine that you go to bed with a beautiful woman who is attractive to you in every way. She invites you to do whatever you wish, but she just lays there without responding. She doesn't resist, but she doesn't encourage, either. In fact, she gives no sign of feeling anything. You successfully ejaculate, and she quietly asks you if you are finished.

Why isn't this satisfying? What is missing? You had your orgasm, your sexual release. You had the experience of bedding an attractive woman. But there is something wrong, and it is obvious what is missing. Her response matters. She isn't just a sperm receptacle, or an instrument to help you masturbate. You want her to at least pretend that she felt something.

Take a different example. The woman is very responsive, very passionate. But when it is all over, she tells you casually that she was fantasizing about her high school sweetheart the whole time. She even looks at you funny, as if she doesn't know who you are. Why does this feel all wrong?

In the first case, you are using her; in the second case, she is using you. But that doesn't make you feel any better.

So even for men, who are supposed to be indifferent to emotional nuance and relational affect, the relationship matters. A man might be able to talk himself out of expressing his feelings of connection, neediness, and attachment—or perhaps more accurately, a man might not feel any particular need to talk about his feelings.[21] But I dare say it would be almost impossible for a man to suppress a feeling of revulsion at a completely unresponsive or totally manipulative woman.

In short, men have feelings about sex beyond mere lust. They have feelings about the quality of the relationship, though these feelings are somewhat different from women's. We should not let the element of truth in the sociobiological perspective blind us to this fact.

Sex and Sociability

All of this means that sexual activity is necessarily related to our sociability. Sex is especially germane to our ability to create and maintain the most basic of social groups, the family. Our bodies ensure that we enjoy sex so that we will engage in it and keep the species going. Our bodies help us to connect to our mates so we will stick together long enough to raise our young to maturity and independence. We respond to our emotions as well as to our reason.

The ability to create community is biologically based. Reptiles don't bother. They lay their eggs, perhaps help incubate them, and then walk (or slither) away. It is the part of the brain that is uniquely mammalian that actually cares about offspring, and about specific mates.

Of course, humans are far beyond any evolutionary period in which our bodies operated on autopilot to help weed out unfit genetic changes and preserve the adaptive, survival-enhancing ones. Our culture enhances the basic physiological structure that our bodies give us to work with. Women don't need to rely solely on the biggest, meanest male to provide protection against predators. We have an entire legal structure that performs that function. Women don't have to rely on males physically to find food. The modern economy makes it possible to exchange money for products that supply our needs.

But the human tendency to attach to our sexual partners is built into our biochemistry and is more than simply cultural conditioning. Cultures may differ in how they support spousal attachments, and indeed, how they define the spousal relationship. But the basic desire to connect to one's sexual partner has deep physiological roots. We can construct, deconstruct, and reconstruct our cultures all we want. It is our privelege as thinking creatures. But we are more likely to be satisfied with the outcome if we work with our biology rather than against it.

This is the sense in which we can say, as I did in the opening of this chapter, that one of the natural, organic functions of sexual activity is spousal unity. Our bodies cry out for connection with our sex partners, quite apart from any cultural structures or strictures we may have. By having sex, our bodies attach themselves to each other.

The second organic purpose of sexual activity is conceiving and bearing children. This, too, is a community-building activity. And, not surprisingly, our bodies cooperate with us in this part of community creation. Our bodies help us attach to our children, so that, in spite of their neediness, we will stay with them long enough to raise them. These attachments show up in a mother's body chemistry through oxytocin which helps connect a nursing mother to her baby.

I won't bore you with the obvious fact that people want to have babies and that babies are the natural result of sexual activity. Nor will I recount in detail the newest findings showing the psychological pull of women's "biological clock." I won't recount the evidence, anecdotal and empirical, that hard-charging career women sometimes find themselves up against the physiological reality that they are no longer as fertile as they once were, or that women who are unable to have a child are often bitterly disappointed. Many women have found that they wanted children more than they ever expected, and certainly more than anything in their education prepared them for.[22]

The natural, organic result of sex is not only a baby, but a little community. The baby is at the center of that community. The community is formed around the parents' attraction to each other and is sustained by their love for each other and their child.

Community is the gift of sex to the world.

PART II

THE PROBLEM WITH
CONSUMER SEX

The Problem with Consumer Sex

ERHAPS I SHOULD SAY, community is the gift of rightly ordered sex. It goes without saying that for many people in modern America, sex has little or nothing to do with building community of any kind. Sex is a purely private matter, in the narrowest sense of private. Sex is a recreational activity, a consumer good. My consumption of this good, my enjoyment of this activity, is a completely private matter that should be viewed as any other good and activity.

I don't agree with that position. The sexual revolution has been disappointing because it has been profoundly anti-social. By uncoupling sexual activity from both of its natural functions, procreation and spousal unity, we have capsized the whole natural order of sexuality. Instead of being an engine of sociability and community building, sex has become a consumer good. Instead of being something that draws us out of ourselves and into relationship with others, our sexual activity turns us inward on ourselves and our own desires. A sexual partner is not a person to whom I am irrevocably connected by bonds of love. Rather, my sexual partner has become an object that satisfies me more or less well.

I call this modern approach to sexual behavior "consumer sex." It has also been described as "morally indifferent sex." Judge Richard Posner uses this term in his arguments that decisions about sexual activity are and ought to be made on a rational choice basis.[1] Posner argues not only that people do, but that they ought to, calculate what is in their best interests to do or refrain from doing, quite apart from any traditional moral prohibitions. He suggests that society would, generally speaking, be better off discarding the traditional prohibitions, and encouraging such calculations.

Posner uses the rational choice, utilitarian approach because he believes it is the most reasonable. I, too, believe in rational choice. Nevertheless, I disagree with Posner's application of rational choice theory. I believe Posner misunderstands both the science of sociability and the purpose of morality. He views the sexual urge and sexual activity as something that pertains only to the individual. Yet the underlying biology, as well as long-standing experience of the human race, points to a more social interpretation.

Moral codes exist both to govern our behavior toward other people and to tell us what to value. An ethical code that tells us that sexual activity has no more moral significance than eating falls short on both counts. Our sexual behavior has directly to do with how we treat other people. Therefore, there must be at least a tacit moral code at work in defining our sexual ethics. I propose to make that implicit moral code explicit. What does our sexual behavior imply about how we may justifiably treat other people?

A moral code should tell us what we ought to value. Economists assume value neutrality as an analytical device for predicting how people will behave, given their preferences. But the point of an ethical code is not to predict our behavior, taking our values as given, but to help us shape our values and the behavior that flows from them. We implicitly demonstrate what we think is important by the kinds of sexual activity that we praise, put up with, criticize, or outlaw. I propose to make explicit the values that are now implicit in our sexual behavior.[2]

The view I laid out in the first section is an outline of the alternative view: human sexuality is about building up the community of the family, both through bringing new children into being and through unifying the spouses in heart and soul as well as body.

I believe this difference in world view is at the heart of the culture wars. One side believes that the meaning of human sexuality is primarily individual. Sex is primarily a private activity; the purpose of sex is to obtain individual pleasure and satisfaction. The alternative view is that sex is primarily a social activity. The purpose of sex is building up the community of the family, starting with the spousal relationship and adding on from there.

My aim in this part of the book is to show that the modern view of human sexuality is mistaken. The predominant modern view of sex is a limited, and limiting, stingy, narrow view of sexuality. So much so, that I feel safe in saying to those who hold this view: you don't know what you are missing. Here is the outline of the argument.

Implicit in the modern view is that sexual activity without unwanted pregnancy is an entitlement. Put another way, sexual activity is not only a good, but such a great and important good that curtailing it in significant ways constitutes an unacceptable infringement on personal freedom. There are two value judgments implicit in this view. First, separating sexual activity from reproduction is an entitlement. Second, voluntary sexual activity without procreation is always and everywhere a great good. Notice that neither of these statements is "value-neutral." Both contain powerful moral judgments, as well as tacit empirical claims.

Notice also that the argument for consumer sex requires that both statements be true. The argument collapses if it is contrary to reason or morality to claim that persons are entitled to have sex without pregnancy. There would automatically be a potential Third Party present to every sexual act with entitlements of his own. It would therefore be false to claim, as a matter of principle, that every voluntary sexual act is a morally indifferent act.

Moreover, if it turns out that voluntary sexual activity is not always and everywhere good, then it follows that sexual activity is not an absolute good, but only a partial good. If sexual activity is a partial good, we need to specify the contexts in which it is good. If it is only a partial good, then it is no longer plausible to assert that we ought to treat sexual activity as morally indifferent. Even if we have no government regulation whatsoever of sexual activity, we still can not treat it as a matter of moral indifference.

I propose to make these arguments in the chapters that follow. First, I argue that reproductive freedom is an illusion. Second, I show that sexual activity is only a partial good by showing why recreational sex is not fun.

For these reasons, the idea of morally indifferent sex is irrational. (When an economist says that something is irrational, you really have to sit up and take notice, since "irrational" is the only word economists have that means "bad.") It is irrational to engage in sex as if it were a matter of moral indifference. Treating sexual activity as if it were a baseball game or an ice cream cone will not make you happy. It is irrational to believe that such a thing as morally indifferent sex is even possible. Our sexual ethics have everything to do with how we treat other people. Only if how we treat others is a matter of no moral consequence can we sustain the idea that morally indifferent sex is possible.

Moreover, consumer sex is anti-social. Engaging in sexual activity as if it were no different than going shopping breaks down the bonds of sociability, which human sexuality quite properly can and should be building up. In short, there is a huge missed opportunity associated with treating sex as a private consumption good.

Finally, the sexual revolution itself proposes its own form of sexual morality. The revolutionaries hide behind the claim that they are proposing a morally neutral approach to sexuality that accepts everything and rejects nothing. But a closer look reveals that the radicals have a moral code of their own, which they are imposing on others without admitting it. We can see this by using a variant of the cost benefit approach from utilitarian moral theory: a moral code tells us what kinds of costs are worth bearing and what kinds of outcomes we ought to regard as beneficial. This is why I believe we have been kidding ourselves that there even is such a thing as morally indifferent sex, much less that we ought to engage in it.

I am not now, nor have I ever been, a member of any governmental legislative body. I have never run for elective office, lobbied for legislative change, or brought a highly leveraged lawsuit before the courts as a means of social change. I have no wish or power to "impose my morality" on anybody. The only kind of power I have or seek to have is the power to persuade. If I come up with an argument that persuades you, it is your own integrity that will compel you to change your mind. If you do change your mind, it is your own integrity that will compel you to change some of your behavior, and possibly to repent of past behavior.

And why should I go to the trouble of trying to persuade you, a complete stranger? I have found through my own experience that it is extremely difficult trying to figure out the meaning of human sexuality on your own. By the time you have conducted enough trials and errors to to figure out that your initial premises were false, you've lost a lot of time. In fact, you can waste all of your prime years of peak sexual enthusiasm trying to figure out what it all means, what type of partner to look for, how to treat that partner, and what are reasonable expectations from that partner. You may be menopausal by the time you figure it out.

This is part of what older people ought to offer to younger people: the benefit of experience and hindsight, so you don't have to make it all up as you go along. I am willing to share some of what I have learned in the hope that my experience will be helpful to you. I believe that people have been sold a moral bill of goods by the sexual revolution fundamentalists. If you don't agree, you've lost nothing by listening. Take it, or leave it.

And that is why all of this matters to you and your marriage. Without challenging the moral premises of the revolution in sexual attitudes, you and your spouse are going to have a lot of trouble sustaining life-long love. And most of that trouble is unnecessary and avoidable.

3

Why Reproductive Freedom
Is an Illusion

"REPRODUCTIVE FREEDOM" IS A MISNOMER AT BEST, and at worst an impossibility that leads to irrational expectations. Yet the claim that reproductive freedom is not only possible, but an entitlement, is a necessary component of "consumer sex." I aim to show that reproductive freedom can never be a freedom of the same sort as older, more modest kinds of freedoms.

Requiring people to marry before they have sex, or requiring people to accept the responsibilities for any children that might result, used to be commonplace. These were considered norms for the protection of children, women, and the future of society. But now, both these presumptions are considered unacceptable infringements on personal liberty. Sex with or without marriage and without any children resulting is almost considered a constitutional right. If the contraception fails, abortion is available as a backup.

Gloria Feldt, former president of the Planned Parenthood Federation of America explicity made this argument. Shortly after the U.S.-led coalition had liberated Iraq, Feldt issued a statement which read in part, "if we are fighting for freedom in Iraq, then most surely that freedom should extend to women globally and in the United States. The most fundamental freedom is the freedom of reproductive self-determination. . . . Reproductive health care is an essential part of any health care package—to address sexual violence, HIV prevention, maternal and neonatal moratality and morbidity, and to provide basic reproductive health services," this last being the code word for abortion.[1]

"Freedom of reproductive self-determination" as the most fundamental freedom? More fundamental than the right to a jury trial, the right to confront your accuser, the right to be free from cruel and unusual punishment? This will surely surprise those Iraqis who were released from Saddam's prisons and torture chambers.

Likewise, the relatively sensible feminist Joan Williams stated, as something she believes "with absolute certainty: Without access to abortion, equality is impossible for women. . . . Like most women of my class, I view an active sexual life as an entitlement."[2]

An active sexual life as an entitlement? Strong language. Having an "entitlement" to something implies that somebody is required to provide that something. Not everyone can obtain the sexual partner he wants or the amount and kind of sexual activity he desires. Who, exactly, is required to provide women with an active sexual life? Only a rapist literally believes that he is entitled to sexual activity on his own terms. So Williams and other feminists can't really mean that an active sexual life is an "entitlement." Once we start asking what the entitlement actually does consist of, we find that it is neither as appealing or as reasonable as it first sounds.

Gender Equality and Reproductive Freedom

First, look at how new this notion of freedom really is. Was no one ever free before the invention of The Pill? Did the Minutemen at Lexington die for the ability to control their family sizes? The Marines raising the flag at Iwo Jima, were they fighting for the freedom to be completely unburdened by any kind of family obligation?

Even to pose these questions is to see their absurdity. Those men risked their lives precisely because they were bound up in their family and human commitments. Military personnel, today as well as yesterday, view themselves not only as fighting for the abstractions of "liberty" and "freedom" and "the American Way." They also view themselves as fighting for very specific people, their parents, husbands, wives, and children.

In fact, it may well be that no one truly dies for an abstraction. People die for particulars, for particular people, living in a particular home on a particular street in a particular town. This is no denigration of their valor or their values. It is simply to say that we are creatures of the particular, as well as of the general; of the specific and earth-bound, as well as the ethereal and the abstract. To cut loose the abstract noun "freedom" from its context of specific people and places is to rob freedom of its connection with the ordinary course of human affairs.

Some of my feminist interlocutors might, at this point, observe that it used to be only men dying in battle. These feminists might say that reproductive freedom was not especially valuable to the Minutemen at Lexington or the Marines at Iwo Jima. The burden of reproduction falls in a special way on women. Ask women what they would fight for. Reproductive freedom is a much more salient issue for women than for men.

I believe this objection is misleading for two reasons. First, ask the women of Iraq: is the right to an abortion really the highest political and social priority? It strains the imagination to think that mobile abortion clinics are the greatest contribution to women's lives in a country where people used to be whisked away to prison for failing to be sufficiently enthusiastic about Saddam. It is misleading even in America, because it overlooks the way that men and women must cooperate in rearing children. That cooperation changes both of them, and it imposes obligations on both.

When a couple have their first child, both of their lives are turned upside down. The mother may feel trapped at home, unable to enjoy the mobility she used to take for granted. She can't go anywhere without a car seat, diaper bag, and baby carrier. If fact, she can't go anywhere completely on her own. She either has to bring the baby with her, or arrange for someone else to care for the baby while she is gone. In either case, her movements are entangled with other people.

But the father may feel just as trapped. Perhaps his wife worked before the baby came. Now, she is not working, at least for a while. He went from being financially responsible only for himself to being financially responsible for three people. He went from being free to come and go as he pleases to being connected to the new mother and baby. He's connected by strands as callous and calculating as the wallet and the law to the tenderest strands of his heart. Men's and women's lives are both altered irrevocably by the arrival of a new child. The fact that their lives are changed in different ways does not refute this basic fact.

The father may be required to support the child, even if he is not married to the mother. The child may not have been entirely his choice. In that case, his body and his freedom of movement are very much at stake in the future of the child. He will be required to work for eighteen to twenty-one years to support the child. It is seriously misleading to say, "a woman's body, a woman's choice," as if a man's body were somehow not at stake in the requirement that he pay child support.[3]

In many couples, the man is the one who insists on postponing pregnancy. It isn't unusual for a middle-aged woman to hear her biological clock ticking and feel a greater desire for children than her husband does. She has to persuade and cajole her husband into having a child. Why should this be, if all the burden of caring for the child falls exclusively on the woman?[4]

Men as well as women fear the responsibilities of a child. They fear the prospect of changing the character of their spousal relationship from "couple" to "parents." As it happens, men are often more realistic about this aspect of parenthood than women are. The woman may assure him that nothing will change, but when the baby comes, she can easily get absorbed in the new baby's care. The father feels left out, just as he predicted. For both men and women, a new baby creates new complications. Neither a mother nor a father can ever again see herself and himself as completely autonomous as she or he was before.

Behind the description of reproductive freedom as a "woman's issue" is a desire for particular kinds of equality or symmetry between men and women. If parenthood creates systematically different kinds of opportunities and obligations for men and for women, then they cannot be equally free. Joan Williams made this case succinctly: full equality for women is impossible without access to abortion.

What kind of equality could this mean? The most superficial meaning is income equality. If women have babies and leave the labor force to raise those babies, the lifetime incomes of women will be lower than the lifetime incomes of men. Let us concede this point: if this is what the feminists mean by equality, they are correct. The presence of children is the single most salient factor in the income differences between men and women.[5]

Of course, very few sensible people literally maximize their income. Most people, men and women alike, sacrifice some income for other things that they value. Since most women want children at some point in their lives, there will always be some income differences between mothers and others. Access to abortion allows women to manage that income difference to their own satisfaction. They can postpone or completely forgo having children, if income maximization should happen to be their goal. Access to abortion allows women to achieve income equality, or at least as much income equality as they can stand.

So the more subtle sort of freedom is the symmetry between male and female roles. Since pregnancy and childrearing affect men and women differently, equality is impossible without somehow removing the sting of that difference. Allowing every pregnancy to be explicitly chosen, exclusively by the woman, is a way of leveling the playing field between men and women. Insisting that men take on a greater role in household chores is another. And so, finally, is attempting to equalize the income earning possibilities of men and women at every point in their lives.

This is what all these features of the modern feminist agenda add up to: making men and women equal, in income, social status, and mobility, requires that the differential impact of childrearing on men and women somehow be equalized or at least neutralized. In effect, women are to be autonomous in the same way as men. Men can earn their own living; women should be able to as well. Men can expect to be in the labor force, more or less uninterupted, for a lifetime; women are entitled to this as well. Freedom for women means having the same freedom of movement, choices, and autonomy as men do.

But there is another way to manage the differences between men and women that flow from parenthood. That other way it to enhance the cooperation between the parents so that their different life paths become an opportunity to build one another up, rather than to exploit one another. Instead of focusing on the size of their paychecks, which has to do with their relationship with the outside world, we could focus on the cooperation between them, which goes on inside the household. This cooperation has the potential for opening up opportunities for both of them and enriching both of their lives.

Nowadays, the feminist Left speaks for a relatively small number of women. Few women are motivated primarily by a desire to maximize their income. Fewer still are driven by some psychological need to be literally equal with men. Nor do most women view reproductive freedom as more basic than freedom of speech.

So let us continue, not by looking at the defenses of reproductive freedom offered by the feminist Left. Let's look at the concept of reproductive freedom as it might be intuitively understood and applied by the ordinary person. My purpose here is to show we have been sold a bill of goods. I want to unpack the idea of reproductive freedom, to see what it actually means, why it is appealing, and why it is ultimately both impossible and inhuman.

Suspending Cause and Effect

The first thing to observe about the concept of reproductive freedom is its irrationality. Richard Posner's analogy between sex and food makes this case quite clearly, contrary to his intention to harness it in defense of consumer sex.[6] He suggests that our relationship with food is and ought to be morally indifferent, not freighted with lots of taboos and laws. He concedes that we ought not to allow our lives to be dominated by food. But we can prevent this domination without creating a lot of unreasonable moral fussing around eating. Likewise, we ought to calm ourselves about sex, and rid ourselves of the taboos surrounding it: "So while eating is not a moral subject except to vegetarians and to persons who adhere to religious dietary restrictions, neither is it a free-for-all; it is guided by aesthetic and prudential considerations. So would sex be in a society in which it was a morally indifferent subject. An intelligent person understands that one is dealing with a strong desire that must be kept in place, not allowed to dominate or endanger one's life."[7]

But here is an aspect of the food analogy that Posner doesn't consider. One can argue that eating is a good and necessary thing, that everyone is entitled to eat, or that gourmet eating is one of life's great pleasures. But it does not follow from any of these statements that each and every person is entitled to eat anything he wants with a guarantee that he will never get fat. No one has a constitutional right to eat as much as he wants, without ever getting heart disease or high blood pressure, or suffering other natural consequences of overeating. You cannot coherently claim that every person has a constitutional right to eat without getting fat, and call it "gastronomical freedom."

Likewise, no one has an entitlement to eat as little as possible, with a guarantee that he will never succumb to anorexia. You are free to purge yourself after every meal, but you are going to create a whole string of negative consequences for yourself. The state cannot reasonably promise to suspend the laws of cause and effect to provide its citizens with the gastronomical self-determination that would allow them to eat or not eat, as much or as little as they want, without any negative consequences.

By analogy, it doesn't make sense to argue that every person has a right to unlimited sexual activity with a government guarantee that no one will never become pregnant. Calling it "reproductive freedom" doesn't alter the underlying biology.

This is not an ideological argument, because it does not depend on any particular view of the proper role of the state and the proper scope of its guarantees. Advocates of the welfare state might well argue that everyone has a right to food, at state expense if necessary. Advocates of more minimal government might argue that people have every right to such food as they can obtain through fair market exchanges and gifts. But no libertarian would claim that people have a right to eat without consequences. No legislator in his right mind would attempt to pass a law guaranteeing such a thing. (The very idea is reminiscent of a state legislature's notorious attempt to pass a law declaring the value of "pi" to be an even 3, rather than that irrational number with lots of pesky decimal places.)

The supposed right to sexual activity without pregnancy is really a demand to suspend the laws of cause and effect in order to obtain what we want. We don't usually think of freedom in this light. We don't think of freedom of movement as meaning the right to jump off the Golden Gate Bridge and not die. Freedom of assembly doesn't mean an entitlement for an entire fraternity to actually fit inside a telephone booth, however much they might enjoy trying. Freedom of speech can't mean the right to shoot off our mouths any time we want, and still have friends. No court of law could grant such a right.

Nor do we normally think of freedom as an entitlement to be successful at something we have chosen to do. Economic freedom doesn't mean the right to succeed in business, only the right to try. We don't think of political freedom as the right to have our preferred candidates always win elections, only as the right for our candidates to compete in any election.

Likewise, no sensible person thinks of freedom as synonomous with "being in possession of all good things." Central heating and air conditioning are wonderful inventions that have greatly improved people's comfort and well-being. That doesn't mean that being without air conditioning is a deprivation of freedom. It is an inconvenience if the heat goes out, but it is not the equivalent of slavery. You may regard contraceptive devices as great advances in technology. That doesn't mean that the right to use them without failure constitutes freedom.

This is the sense in which "reproductive freedom" is different in kind from the more basic economic and political freedoms. These older freedoms guarantee that people have the opportunity to participate in the economic and political systems under a set of transparent rules that apply to everyone. Political and economic freedoms are not guarantees of getting the particular outcome we want.

Changed Probabilities, Not Guarantees

The Supreme Court case *Griswold v. Connecticut* was one of the stepping stones toward creating this illusion of a new freedom. In this 1965 case, the Supreme Court held that states could not constitutionally prohibit the flow of contraception information or the sale or use of contraceptive devices.[8] The Court held that such prohibitions are unacceptable invasions of marital privacy. Contrary to widespread belief about this case, however, the Court specifically declined to find a right to use contraceptives. Instead, the Court simply held that the many goods of marital intimacy are damaged by exposure to others. The enforcement of the prohibition on marital contraception would expose the married couple to the scrutiny of outsiders, which would harm the relationship in ways the Court thought excessive.[9]

Obviously, *Griswold v. Connecticut* does not, and cannot change the ultimate connection between sexual intercourse and pregnancy. That relationship is what it is, due to nature's design, not any human design. The link between pregnancy and sexual intercourse, while straightforward, is and has always been a roll of the dice. Improved contraception information and technology just allow people to roll the dice on slightly different terms.

Notice that I don't say, "on more favorable terms." Contraception changes the probability of pregnancy, of course; that is its purpose. But no contraception reduces the probability of pregnancy from a given sex act all the way to zero. Moreover, the use of any contraceptive method potentially changes other things about the couple's relationship and the sexual act itself. Some kinds of contraception interrupt the spontaneity of the sexual act. Some contraceptive methods have medical side effects, usually for the woman. If the use of contraception unambiguously improved the terms of sexual activity, everyone would use it all the time, for every act of intercourse. But some people decline to use it, for a variety of reasons that seem good to them. Therefore, if we say that contraception allows people to "roll the dice on improved terms," we are prejudging the situation to assume that reducing the probability of pregnancy is always and everywhere people's overriding concern. It is more neutral, and more fair, simply to say, contraception "changes the terms," rather than "improves the terms."

If allowing people to change the terms on which they have sex is all that we held about sex and contraception, it would be an intellectually defensible position. But the social norms and constitutional interpretation around sex and conception have morphed into something quite different. We now believe that we are entitled to have sex without getting pregnant.

The 1972 case *Eisenstadt v. Baird* disaggregated the married couple into an association of two individuals and found an individual right to obtain and use contraceptives: "Whatever the rights of the individual to access to contraceptives may be, the rights must be the same for the married and unmarried alike." It was this decision that created the illusion of reproductive freedom. The Court said, "The marital couple . . . is an association of two individuals each with a separate intellectual and emotional makeup. If the right of privacy means anything, it is the right to be free from unwarranted government intrusions into matters so fundamentally affecting a person as the decision whether to bear or beget a child."[10]

This statement by the Court exaggerates what any government is in a position to guarantee. Legal impediments to the flow of information may amount to "unwarranted government intrusion" into an admittedly very personal decision. However, allowing people full access to information is not the same thing as completely removing all barriers to the personal decision of "whether to bear or beget a child." All the information in the world about the most sophisticated forms of contraception does not assure that a person, either married or single, will be able to fulfill his reproductive plans. Contraception sometimes fails. People sometimes use it incorrectly, or intermittently. In these cases, the person's "decision" to avoid conception will not be fully realized. It is not any state interference, warranted or unwarranted, that thwarted the person's "decision," but simply the probabilistic connection between sexual activity, contraception, and conception.

So it does not follow that we have a "right" to sexual activity without conception. Nor did the Court discover such a right, although its language in *Eisenstadt* might mislead people into drawing the conclusion that such a right exists. It is a "right" that the state is not in a position to guarantee. The only way avoiding unwanted pregnancy while being sexually active is to have unlimited access to abortion. More accurately, this is the only way the state could guarantee the right to have sex without having a live baby. Perhaps it is not surprising that *Roe v. Wade* followed a mere year after the *Eisenstadt* decision.

And this, really, is the entitlement that Joan Williams was referring to at the beginning of this chapter. She isn't entitled to "an active sexual life," in the sense that somebody is required to provide her with a partner if she wants one. What she means is that an active sexual life, without the complication of unwanted children, is a good and desirable thing. She feels herself cheated if her desire for sexual activity is compromised by the undesired outcome of pregnancy. The "entitlement" is that the law should permit her to eliminate unwanted pregnancies for any reason or no reason.

Many people who consider themselves pro-life have no objection to contraception. That's fine, as long as they understand what they are saying. A person can be pro-life and pro-contraception, as long as he does not think that successful contraception is an entitlement. You may well believe that contraception has been a great boon to the human race, that the ability to limit and time one's pregnancies has been an unmixed blessing. But you don't have to move from that belief to the belief that you are entitled to be completely successful in acheiving your reproductive plans, whatever they might be. If you go that route, you will have to support an unlimited abortion license: any abortion, any time, for any reason or no reason.

If you consider yourself a pro-life, pro-contraception person, you might meditate on this observation: only eight years elapsed from the discovery of a Consitutional right of marital privacy to the judgment that this right required an unlimited right to abortion. This suggests the possibility, that the distinction between the right to use contraceptives and the right to an abortion is not very stable, as a political, legal, and social matter.

The Libertarian Ethos

I have this challenge for my libertarian friends in particular: in our current cultural situation, people don't just think they are entitled to use contraceptive technology to change the probability that conception will result from a particular act of sexual intercourse. Our culture now encourages people to believe they are entitled to get what they want.

We should not be surprised if people who think this way also regard themselves as entitled to a whole host of other things that the state has no real power to offer.

The American political system has manufactured a whole series of illusory entitlements. We think we are "entitled" to goods like "free" medical care, "free" education, or "free" retirement benefits. But these benefits are not really free. The state has simply disguised their cost, by transfering it to politically concealed third parties. A democratically elected government may very well offer people a variety of tax-supported benefits. But it is fundamentally dishonest to describe those benefits as "entitlements." What the state has done is to create a positive obligation on the part of one set of citizens to provide an ongoing set of benefits for another set of other citizens.

I don't think we should be surprised to find the champions of "reproductive freedom" concentrated overwhelmingly on the political Left. It is quite true that people from across the political spectrum take full advantage of contraception, and even abortion. But it has been the Left that has taken the lead in promoting these things as somehow central to personal liberty.[11] The Left believes that educational and athletic equality means equal numbers of men and women in college sports programs. (Never mind that women prefer dance to competitive sports as their means of getting exercise.) The Left believes unlimited state intervention into the economy is justified in the name of creating equal economic outcomes. (Never mind that people differ tremendously in their talents and ambitions, and that these differences thwart attempts to generate equal incomes.) This is the same Left that believes people are entitled unlimited sexual activity without a live birth resulting.

The Left has redefined freedom to mean achieving particular outcomes. No amount of state intervention is too much, no amount of manipulation of individuals and circumstances is too much, if it will make progress toward this end. The Left believes that achieving equality is worth any damage that the rule of law might sustain.

It is the Right, broadly defined to include conservatives, libertarians, and traditionalists, that defines freedom as having rules that apply equally to everyone. We have been fighting an uphill battle for the rule of law for a long time. We believe that a relatively small number of carefully crafted rules that apply equally to everyone has the best chance of enhancing human happiness. We take this minimal position regarding law in part because we have reasons to believe that other parts of the social order can contribute significantly to creating a really decent society in which people would enjoy living and would prosper. The market is part of that self-sustaining social order. So is the family.

A functioning market order requires a relatively small amount of regulation. It certainly does not guarantee anybody particular outcomes, such as meeting his economic goals or acheiving equality with any particular person or class of people. The decentralized nature of the market precludes such assurances. Yet the system works reasonably well most of the time, because it harnesses the energies, knowledge, talents, and motivations of more people, more of the time than any other economic system known to us.

We libertarians and free market economists have tried to encourage people to accept that a certain amount of risk is inherent in markets. Meanwhile, the Left has systematically attacked every kind of economic risk as being intrinsically unfair. While we have tried to argue that equality of opportunity is the only kind of equality that is either rational or sustainable, the Left has tried to convince people that any inequality across racial or ethnic groups is automatically suspect. The Right believes freedom means the opportunity to make choices and accept the consequences of those choices. The Left thinks freedom means getting what you want.

So is it really any surprise that in the hands of this same end of the political spectrum the right of access to contraceptive information evolved into a right to acheive the particular reproductive outcomes we desire? Convincing people that they are entitled to completely control their reproductive lives creates an illusion of control that is quite unsustainable. It creates an image of freedom that is really the opposite of freedom, because it requires continuing interventions in private choices.

For instance, many doctors don't really like doing abortions, and make a practice of not performing abortions. But the abortion rights advocates hold that the limited number of available abortionists creates an undue hardship on women's reproductive rights. So the state of California requires that all hospitals provide abortions on demand, even religious hospitals. This places the right to reproductive freedom on a collision course with religious freedom.[12] The state of California holds that reproductive freedom requires all doctors in Ob-Gyn residencies must take training in providing abortion, even doctors who have every intention of never performing an abortion.[13] Something is plainly amiss with somebody's notion of freedom.

The Assymetries of Reproductive Freedom

Having made the case that the concept of reproductive freedom is irrational, I have to concede that it is easy to see its appeal. Our families are extremely important to us. How many children we have, the spacing between them, these raw demographic facts create the texture of our daily lives. These kinds of facts are the most basic facts of our childhoods as well. How many brothers and sisters do we have? Where do we fit into the birth order? How old were our parents when we were born? Were our parents married to each other? Are they still? The modern idea is that by taking control over the timing and size of our families we have more control over these large facts of our lives. Taking control means taking responsibility, the definition of responsible parenthood.

There is a truth to this idea, but there is a deep untruth to it as well. Responsible parenthood is better than irresponsible parenthood. (In fact, it is a major premise of this book that getting married and staying married is essential to being a responsible parent.) But there is a difference between responsible parenthood and taking control of our families. "Taking control" of our families can easily lead us into a mindset in which genuine interdependence is impossible.

Other people resist being controlled. If we are going to be involved in a relationship of any duration or intensity, we will have to surrender some of our desires to the other person. We are likely to have desires and wishes for them that they might not want for themselves. We have to relinquish either those particular wishes or our control of the relationship. In either case, we will have to give up something important to us. If we define freedom as getting the outcomes we want, we can't remain in the relationship and still be free. This definition of freedom places freedom and relationship in opposition to one another.

I believe this is one reason for the appeal of defining freedom as autonomy. We are free if we are independent of and autonomous from other people. This definition of freedom can be applied in a reciprocal fashion by both people in the relationship. Neither of us has a right to control the other: you do your thing and I'll do mine.

In spite of its apparant reciprocity, it is a one-sided definition of freedom. It places a higher value on autonomy than on relationship. The only way to resolve the conflict between autonomy and relationship is to end the relationship. Thus does the definition of freedom as autonomy reinforce itself.

Moreover, defining freedom as the ability to acheive specific desired outcomes sets people up for disappointment. The perfect control we had envisioned inevitably fails to materialize. Then we instinctively look for someone or something to blame for that failure.

Likewise, reproductive freedom is a one-sided kind of freedom. It is a right only to refuse children; it is only the power to say no. There is not, and cannot be, a right to "pregnancy on demand" that would correspond to "abortion on demand." Even with the most sophisticated reproductive technology, no one can have a guarantee of a pregnancy exactly when and how she wants it. This language invites us to think that our freedom depends upon the development of such a technology. We won't really be free until we completely master both the giving and the taking of life, with or without the messy intervention of actual sexual contact with a person of the opposite sex.

Reproductive freedom really only means the right to say "no" to more children. You can't make more children happen. Infertility can be one of the great tragedies of a person's life. Many women planned to have children after their careers were established, and then found that those children didn't arrive according to schedule. These women found that birth "control" is an illusion.[14]

My husband and I had this experience of infertility. As I mentioned earlier, I was one of those career women who thought I would wait until I got tenure and then have a baby during the summer. I'd just pop those kids into day care in the fall and get right back on the career track. Imagine my surprise when a year went by with no baby. We went to the doctors. We followed their instructions and took their tests. And then another year went by. No baby. No explanation.

For me, infertility provoked a spiritual crisis. This was the first time in my adult life that I couldn't acheive my goals by working harder and longer. In fact, as every sensible Old Wife knows, trying harder to conceive is counterproductive. Yet I couldn't suppress the desire for children. I couldn't bring myself to believe that motherhood didn't matter to me. I couldn't avoid knowing that this was a plan that I was not going to bring off on my own terms.

This turned out to be the tip of the iceberg. For I then had to confront other ways in which my plans might go awry. My husband had plans and thoughts and feelings of his own. From the start, he wasn't as keen on having children as I was. He couldn't relate very well to my frenzy. He was satisfied with our child-free lifestyle.

This baby project was our first truly joint project, and we weren't really doing very well with it. Up until now, our lives were built on our separate identities. That was the reigning paradigm of marriage, after all. No self-respecting modern career woman could allow herself to lose her identity in marriage. Two distinct, independent people: two last names, two jobs, two cars, two bank accounts, one house, one bed and a few shared activities. Even the dog was privately owned: Newton was my dog. I was becoming dimly aware that parenthood couldn't be like that, although I didn't have a clue what the alternative would look like. I had to admit that our "married-singles" lifestyle was based on the fact that we truly didn't know how to be interdependent.

Then we found that we did have a possible explanation for not being able to conceive: his low sperm count. He was devastated. All at once, I was concerned about him and his feelings in a way I had not been before. He was vulnerable in a way I had never seen. I felt like an idiot for being hysterical because I finally saw the impact my grief had upon him.

My husband was lukewarm about adoption, which for me had always been the fallback position. But he was willing to support me in a sperm donor pregnancy, if it would finally shut me up. Through our infertility support group, I had a phone conversation with a woman who had had sperm donor pregnancies. She was an ecstatic stay-at-home mom. I could hear the chattering of her children in the background. But in the course of the conversation she said, "my husband loves the kids, but he is still sad. Every once in a while, he says wistfully, 'the kids don't look like me.'" She resolved her infertility issue, but her husband hadn't.

I didn't like the sound of this. Was having a baby all about me and my plans? Or did it have something to do with my husband and me as a couple? I could satisfy my desire to become preganant and have a baby, but for my husband, the child would be adopted. I had to ask myself: Am I using my husband to get what I want? I am the one pining for a baby; he is trying to accomodate me. He is perfectly content with our current lifestyle.

One thing was clear: I had a negative, visceral reaction to the idea of sperm donation. It wasn't even a decision. I recoiled from the thought and never looked back.

I couldn't articulate it at the time, but in the years that have passed, I have come to a better understanding of my visceral reaction against sperm donation. Having a baby through sperm donor would have changed the relationship between my husband and me in a fundamental way. Instead of being a joint project, the baby would be my project with my husband along for the ride. He would be offering support, just like a good Sensitive New Age Guy ought to do. But on what basis could I ask that of him? He doesn't owe me support for the child of an anonymous sperm donor. He'd be a wallet and an assistant mom.

And what about the baby? Do I have a right to treat a baby as a project of mine? This is another person; she will have the right to be loved and wanted as an independent and ultimately separate being. I was reducing a Someone, the baby, to a Something, a project that satisfies and gratifies me.[15]

As we went through the infertility process together, my husband and I met a number of other couples who were struggling with the same issues. It was becoming clearer to me, from watching the others, how tight a rein I had been keeping on my life. (Unappealing behavior is always easier to recognize in other people than in oneself.) You might say, I had a death-grip on the reins of my life. I saw women who were obsessed with pregnancy, and who in the process became obsessed with themselves. Instead of being drawn out of themselves into concern for a new baby, their thwarted desire for a baby turned them inward: they had to have their own way.

At every support group meeting, they would share with the group the details of every test, every doctor's appointment, every injection. We saw women use up all their insurance pursuing infertility treatments. We saw couples get divorced. One of our dearest friends ultimately committed suicide.

I became dimly aware of how my "self-actualization" and "self-esteem" were really just garden-variety selfishness. My self-esteem depended on getting my own way, to a far greater extent than I had ever realized. I wasn't much fun for my husband to be around. Every disagreement took on life-and-death dimensions, because my self-worth was always on the line.

For the first time in my adult life, I had to accept that I was not in complete control of all the important outcomes in my life. I suppose that being an economist helped me out here. I could wrap it up in language I was used to: I can control the inputs, but I can't control the outputs. Forces outside my control play a role in how my efforts will finally work out in the world. A business can do a fine job of making plans and hiring workers and buying materials and still not succeed because a competitor appears out of nowhere or an unforeseen market force causes consumers to lose interest in the product. There is no help for it but to pick up the pieces and try again.

Likewise, I can do my part in making my marriage relationship what I want it to be, but I can't completely control the outcome. I can't control my husband, what he wants, what he values, what he thinks is important. I don't even have the right to try to control him. I have the right to walk away from him, but not to control him.

Looking at it this way raised a whole new set of questions for the radical individualist that I was. What would be a better way to see myself in relationship to him? What kind of philosophy is it, anyhow, that can only come up with an exit strategy, but not with an engagement strategy?

The baby's not arriving on schedule is just one example of a larger problem for individualists trying to manage a life together with others. Other people have minds and lives and plans of their own. We have no right to be in command and control of the other people in our lives. We can't allow freedom to mean this, or we will either be domestic tyrants or complete hermits.

I know libertarians of both sorts. I have known radical individualists who were abusive to their families, and I have known those who lived essentially alone, not just single, but radically single. They were people who couldn't accomodate others intruding on their plans and goals. I know people with no definable political orientation who fit both these categories. I have no doubt that plenty of leftist individualists do too. This particular form of personal individualism is so deeply engrained in our culture that it cuts across political lines.

I have often felt that infertility was excellent preparation for parenthood. Entering into parenthood with the expectation of being in control is a foolish. Infertility helped me to see that I really needed a broader repertoire of ways of dealing with people, besides demanding my own way and walking away if I didn't get it. Freedom couldn't possibly mean control in this context. Being free had to mean something other than getting my own way.

This is the sense in which reproductive freedom is empty. It is based on a misunderstanding of the amount of control that is reasonable or desirable in a fully lived human life. We convince ourselves that we are entitled to control the timing and arrival of children. If that is so important, isn't it equally important to control who those children are, what those children do, whether those children please us? But this is plainly both impossible and inhumane. Yet that is what we set ourselves up for, when we begin to think in terms of "family planning."[16]

This may be part of the reason that family sizes have fallen so dramatically that the populations of industrialized, developed countries are not replacing themselves. It is not credible to believe that people in the richest countries the world has ever seen cannot "afford" more children. I believe we have reduced our family sizes more out of fear than out of necessity. By reducing the number of people we have intimate relationships with, we reduce the number of people who can legitimately make demands on us. We limit the number of people who have the power to disappoint us or hurt us.

Autonomy, Freedom, and Fear

If freedom doesn't mean getting my own way, what does it mean? If freedom doesn't include an entitlement to suspend the laws of cause and effect, what logical meaning can reproductive freedom have?

I wouldn't be surprised if some of my readers find themselves very uncomfortable at this point. An entire generation has grown up taking low risk, high reliability contraception for granted. This same generation has grown up assuming that any woman can have an abortion, any time, for any reason. In fact, the Supreme Court said as much in the *Casey* decision, by way of justifying the continuation of the unlimited abortion license.[17]

So I would not be surprised if some readers are angry and fearful. And though they are angry at me for raising questions about matters that shouldn't be questioned, the fear is probably even more basic. What is it about these matters that makes even raising a question seem threatening?

I am not advocating any change in law whatsoever; I am not telling you to throw away your diaphragm. I am simply arguing two things: that reproductive freedom is different in kind from other freedoms, and that embracing this understanding of freedom is almost certain to result in serious disappointment. I am not particularly interested in whether you choose to use or not use any particular form of contraception. I am more interested in the consequences of the public arguments we make to defend our contraceptive practices.

I have no power at all, except the power of argument. If you think I am mistaken, my arguments will have no effect on your behavior and you can simply dismiss me. But if my arguments have some merit, you might have to change some of your ideas or some aspect of your behavior. You wouldn't "have to" because I am going to make you. You would have to because your integrity would demand that you keep your intellect and your behavior in some sort of correspondence with each other. With this in mind, let's look at what might be frightening about my arguments. What would you have to give up, if I'm right, that would be hard for you to give up?

Having sex without babies implicates two separate sets of behavior. I am free to have sex, and I am free to not have a baby. Obviously, I can retain my freedom to not have a baby by not having sex. It is the confluence of these two things that modern people value so much. Only the first is, properly speaking, "sexual" freedom. I will deal with sexual freedom *per se* in another chapter. Here, I want to take up this question of the impact of a baby on freedom.

The freedom to not have a baby is a freedom from a particular set of responsibilities and experiences. Without children, I am free to come and go as I please, free to make my own life plans without the responsibility of caring for a dependent person. It is the freedom to be unencumbered by that dependent child.

The responsibility of caring for a dependent person, a child, seems like a huge burden. Your life would never be completely your own again. You could not pursue your education, career, and hobbies on your own terms. You would have to compromise these other goals if you had responsibility for a child.

You would, as well, almost certainly have some kind of relationship with the child's other parent, whether or not the two of you were married. There might be legal and financial entanglements with that other parent. You might have to negotiate visits and responsibilities with each other. You may eventually have grandchildren in common. You will be involved with the child and the child's other parent for the rest of your life.

We tell ourselves that reproductive freedom is all about independence and autonomy. That is one way to look at it. The other way to look at it is that "reproductive freedom" is about fear: fear of relationship with the child and the child's other parent; fear of the responsibility for the care of a dependent child; fear of entanglement with that other parent; fear of being disappointed or hurt by the other parent, by the child, and maybe even fear of being disappointed in your own performance as a parent.

So the freedom we now call "reproductive freedom" is a freedom from other people. We think ourselves unfree if someone may legitimately place demands upon us. We can't do what we want, when we want, how we want, if other people need us the way a baby needs us.

We also think ourselves unfree if we need other people. New mothers often feel themselves trapped if they are dependent upon a spouse for financial support, while staying home taking care of a baby. But notice that the interdependence is inherent in the situation of having a baby to take care of. The new mother who depends on a husband for financial support for herself and her baby is no more dependent than the unmarried mother who relies on her employer for financial support and her babysitter for child care. The modern arrangements transfer the mother's dependence from a personal relationship with a husband to a commercial relationship with an employer and babysitter. This creates an illusion of independence, but not a reality of independence.[18]

This particular fear of dependence has created a whole set of social demands. New mothers are entitled to the same access to career advancement as men, in spite of the substantial, if temporary, demands on a mother's time. New mothers are entitled to low cost, high quality child care, so they can pursue their careers, even when their children are very young. Women's freedom and economic equality requires that women not be dependent upon their husbands at any time. Instead of making it easier for women to move in and out of the labor market at different times, the feminist mainstream has insisted on a series of regulations that create more equal outcomes for men and women at all times. Instead of strengthening the lifelong bonds between mothers and fathers that would support flexibility in moving in and out of the labor market, society has allowed the institution of marriage to be deconstructed into a non-binding, entirely private, contract.

It is as if we have substituted the labor market for marriage. Instead of having permanent marriages, we have highly structured, highly regulated labor markets. Instead of relying on a husband, a mother relies on an employer who has been constrained by these regulations. Instead of constraining the husband to stay married and fulfill his obligations to his wife and child, the law constrains the employer to provide a work environment that meets the needs of mothers of small children. The modern mother has more employment stability, and less marital stability, than her foremothers.

We have redefined freedom as autonomy, without realizing what a unique period of our lives actually fit the description of the kind of autonomy we seem to have in mind. The only person who truly meets the modern standard of autonomy is the single person, of fully sound mind and body, who has no family responsibilities. We are autonomous only during that period of our lives when we are old enough to take care of ourselves, but before we have children of our own, when we aren't suffering from any illness or injury.[19]

We have conflated freedom and autonomy. We have put our notion of freedom on a collision course with our ability to be in sustained human relationships. This understanding of freedom does not, and truly cannot, make us happy. Let me state my position as a prediction that you can test for yourself: anyone who defines his own freedom as being in necessary opposition to human relationships is going to bring misery on himself and those around him.

Conclusion

No sensible person can believe that freedom means getting your own way. No one can possibly believe that he is entitled to get a particular outcome from a process that is as inherently probabilistic as that linking pregnancy to intercourse. So if that can't be the freedom that reproductive freedom creates, what is it?

It is the freedom to limit the number of people who can legitimately place demands on us. Fear is at the heart of the sexual revolution: fear of other people, fear of relationship, fear of permanence.

I believe this is how we have created that new definition of freedom I described at the beginning of the book. To be free is to be completely unencumbered by human relationships. Other people make demands upon us, that is certain. Choice is a good thing, that is certain as well. But it is a vapid and empty kind of freedom to insist on complete control over personal and family relationships. If freedom means having complete control over personal relationships, then only a hermit can be free. It is weak-hearted and stingy to insist that we never be in a position in which other people may make legitimate demands upon us.

Yet reproductive freedom is an essential step in the argument for morally indifferent sex. We believe that it is possible, permissible, and even desirable to take control of our reproductive lives. But if this kind of "reproductive self-determination" is either not possible or not desirable, then we are mistaken in believing that sexual activity can be matter of moral indifference.

If reproductive freedom is not really possible, but only an illusion, then every sexual act has the potential to involve a third party, the baby. That third party needs to be taken into account. If the attempt to take control of our reproductive lives is not as desirable as we think, if it brings other problems in its wake, then we need to consider those potential problems as part of the moral calculus in evaluating particular sex acts in particular contexts.

This brings us to the second part of the argument in favor of morally indifferent sex: voluntary sexual activity is always and everywhere a great good. If this isn't true, then we need to specify the contexts in which it is a good.

I have what may be a surprising method for spelling out these contexts: I propose to show situations in which recreational sex is not fun. From there, we'll be in a position to see something about what makes sex one of the great goods of a human life.

4

Why Recreational Sex
Is Not Fun

REPRODUCTIVE FREEDOM IS AN ILLUSION: there is always some risk that one's reproductive plans will not be fulfilled. There is one straightforward way of avoiding the difficulties involved in having responsibility for a child: don't have sex. But that seems impossible. And in fact, our notion of sexual freedom is that we are entitled to sexual activity, which we have come to see as a variety of self-expression.

The issue isn't whether we are entitled to sexual activity, but under what terms we are entitled. Neither is the issue what should or shouldn't be legal. To my mind, the issue is: what ought we to do with the broad freedom given to us by our society?

I dispute the widespread belief that mutual consent is the only criterion for judging the morality or appropriateness of sexual activity. We cannot credibly say that our sexual activity is a matter of no moral consequence, even if both adult parties give their complete consent to it. We can give our consent to acts that are harmful to us and others. To make consent the only standard of morality robs us of our ability to reflect on our past mistakes. In fact, it comes very close to saying we can never make moral mistakes. If we agreed to it, then it must have been ethical or, at least, acceptable.

But some things, in retrospect and on reflection, do seem to work out better than others. It isn't very helpful to exonerate oneself after the fact by remembering that one consented to something. Nor is it helpful to reinterpret every unsatisfactory experience as having been, in some sense, coerced. Yet if consent is our only criterion for distinguishing good sex from bad, the definitions of consent and coercion is likely to become pretty fluid, to accomodate the wide variety of negative sexual experiences a person might have. It is more helpful to have a broader range of possible candidates for "bad sex" than simply coerced sex. Then, when things do go badly, we can try to remember and understand why it seemed like a good idea at the time.

In this chapter, I offer evidence that sex in some contexts is recognizably no fun. Once we see that some contexts for sex are objectively and predictably better than others, we will be in a position to see whether morally indifferent sex is possible. Ultimately, we'll be able to figure out the context for sex that has the most potential for really making people happy.

The Date Rape Crisis

We are said to have a date rape crisis on college campuses. Date or acquaintance rape is said to be reaching epidemic proportions. What exactly is date rape, and why is it a problem?[1]

Date rape is unwanted sexual activity that can be distinguished from ordinary rape by the absence of overt violence. If a woman's date violently attacks her and literally forces her to have sex, then what we have is rape without adjectives, not "date" rape. In some cases of date rape, a female college student claims she was raped by her date, while the male insists that the sexual act was consensual. Sometimes, alcohol consumption has clouded the picture of who did what, said what, and meant what. She didn't say no clearly enough; she wasn't clear in her own mind what she wanted. Or maybe she was clear in her own mind that she didn't want it, but she allowed herself to be talked into it and then regretted it later. That process of "talking her into it" becomes the act of aggression that justifies the description of the act as a rape.[2]

Perhaps date rape crisis centers are nothing more than political fronts. Maybe radical feminists invented the concept of "date rape" as a means of badgering male students into submission. Individual women can play out their vendettas against men they have decided they don't like, for whatever reason. Women as a group can keep men as a group on the defensive, knowing that a charge of date rape can be lodged against them with little in the way of corroborating evidence. There might be a completely cynical, economic explanation for the existence of date rape crisis centers: these centers are essentially a means of funnelling grant money to professional activists.[3]

But even if this argument is true, it overlooks one crucial point: why is the claim of unwanted sexual activity a plausible vehicle for this kind of power grab? Even if we assume the very worst about the activists and their motives, there must be something at least superficially plausible about the idea of date rape. Otherwise, it would not serve the alleged political purpose.

The Walk of Shame

I once had a college student describe to me something he and his fraternity brothers called the "Walk of Shame." This is when a guy slinks back to his frat house or dorm room, early in the morning after an all-night sexual encounter. He doesn't want anybody to see him. He can't quite put his finger on what is so embarrassing about staying out all night with this particular woman. Sometimes the woman is a loser that he'd be embarrassed to be associated with. But more often than not, his embarrassment has nothing to do with the particular woman. In fact, that's the problem: she isn't a particular woman at all. He has had sex with a woman he isn't especially connected with, or doesn't know especially well. He has had sex with a woman more or less at random.

In any case, he doesn't want to have to explain himself to the other guys. He'd prefer to just slip into his room unnoticed.

Now, what is this all about? He can't be afraid of the moral disapproval of his roommates: American college campuses are about the least judgmental places on the earth. Presumably, the sexual encounter was consensual, so he didn't violate anybody's rights. Presumably, he and the lady in question used appropriate contraception, so there isn't any concern about pregnancy. Presumably, he was able to acheive orgasm. So he satisfied the Big Three criteria for moral acceptability of a sexual encounter: it was voluntary, it avoided pregnancy, it caused an ejaculation. Yet, for whatever reason, this young man and others like him desire not to be accountable for particular sexual acts. They do not want to have to explain why they had sex with a particular woman at a particular time.

Why would he be reluctant to give an account of himself if the decision to have sex had no more significance to him than the decision to go to a movie that turned out to be a dud? He might complain loudly if he had gone to a restaraunt with crummy food and lousy service. But the disappointing sexual encounter is a source of embarrassment that he is reluctant to divulge.

The Cohabitation Puzzle

The Census for the year 2000 reports a 72 percent increase in the number of cohabiting couples since 1990. Unfortunately, research shows that cohabitation is correlated with a greater likelihood of unhappiness, instability, and domestic violence. Cohabiting couples report lower levels of satisfaction in the relationship than married couples.[4] Women are more likely to be abused by a cohabiting boyfriend than by a husband.[5] Children are more likely to abused by their mother's boyfriends than by her husband, even if the boyfriend is their biological father.[6] If a cohabiting couple ultimately marry, they tend to report lower levels of marital satisfaction and have a higher propensity to divorce.[7]

Why should this be? Most of the researchers who have studied cohabitation expected that living together prior to marriage would improve the quality of married life. One suspects that many of the cohabiting couples themselves shared the hope that their trial marriage would reduce their likelihood of divorce. As a matter of fact, we might expect that outcome just as a statistical artifact: those couples most likely to divorce would end the relationship without ever getting married. Yet even researchers favorably disposed toward pre-marital cohabitation consistently find these unfavorable results.

These three situations, date rape, the walk of shame, and cohabitation, have two things in common. They all involve sexual activity that is unsatisfactory in some way to the participants themselves, even when they have consented under the ordinary understanding of consent. And in these three situations, the commitment between the partners is limited to non-existent.

To get an understanding of the problem, let's start with cohabitation. In cohabitation, there is no serious doubt about whether the relationship is voluntary: nobody is coerced into moving into a new apartment. This is the situation of the three in which the parties know one another the most intimately. It is longer term than a one-night stand that might lead to the Walk of Shame, or the dating situation that might lead a woman to feel she has been manipulated into something she doesn't want.

There are two puzzles to the cohabitation phenomenon. First, why does cohabitation produce such disappointing outcomes? Second, given this record, why do people keep moving in together?

Why Not Take Her for a Test Drive?[8]

Most recent reports and commentaries on cohabitation reveal its difficulties but tend to downplay them. I suspect this is because people do not know how to make sense of their findings. Many people imagine that living together before marriage resembles taking a car for a test drive. The "trial period" gives people a chance to discover whether they are compatible. "You wouldn't buy a car without taking it for a test drive, now would you?" This line, usually delivered with a chuckle, seems so compelling that people are unable to interpret the mountains of data to the contrary.

Here's the problem with the car analogy: the car doesn't have hurt feelings if the driver dumps it back at the used car lot and decides not to buy it. The analogy works great if you picture yourself as the driver; it stinks if you picture yourself as the car.

Yet this is the implication of the "test drive" metaphor. I am going to drive you around the block a few times, withholding judgment and commitment until I have satisfied myself about you. You are not permitted to have any feelings about this trial run. Just behave normally. Pay no attention to my indecision or my periodic withdrawals to evaluate your performance. Try to act as you would if we were married, so I can get a clear picture of how you're likely to behave as a spouse. You pretend to be married; I'll pretend to be shopping.

Some economists, libertarians, or others influenced by laissez-faire thinking might make a consent argument: living together is fine as long as both people agree to it. The consent argument might be adequate if the only question is what ought to be legal. Cohabitation is not rape, case granted. But the consent argument doesn't buy much help if the question is, "Is it in my interest to agree to live with this person to whom I am not married?"

The agreement amounts to this: "I am willing to let you use me as if I were a commodity, as long as you allow me to treat you as if you were a commodity." This is a bogus bargain. We can say at the outset that we agree to be the "man of steel" or "woman of steel." But we can't credibly promise to have no feelings of remorse or pain if the relationship fails. In order to keep this agreement, a person would have to be steeling himself or herself against certain kinds of feelings.

The desire for commitment or permanence will most likely surface from time to time. This desire will sometimes emerge as a desire to make certain kinds of demands on the other person. Can I count on you to be here for me, on this occaision, for this purpose? Can I count on you to not get mad and walk out on me if I object to something you are doing? If I ask for certain kinds of help, will you feel entitled not only to refuse, but to ridicule me for not standing on my own two feet? Will you interpret my requests as illegitimate demands, or as part of the normal give and take of a long-term relationship?

Since the tacit cohabitation agreement stipulates that the desire for permanence be suppressed, I might be reluctant to make these kinds of requests. I may end up distorting my own knowledge of myself, my feelings and my desires, in order to maintain stability in a relationship that is basically not stable. I may hold back on the self-revelation that is at the heart of intimate relationships.

Barbara Dafoe Whitehead reports from her interviews with unmarried women that men and women often have very different views of the nature of the cohabiting relationship. The woman is more likely to view cohabitation as a stepping stone toward marriage. The man is more likely to view cohabitation as a perfectly acceptable end-state and feel no particular urgency toward marriage. The relationship proceeds under a tacit misunderstanding. The man has little interest in bringing the subject up. Women who might wish for clarification feel great reluctance to bring it up for fear of rocking the boat.[9]

Here is an analogy that reveals a different aspect of living together than the test drive analogy. Suppose I ask you to give me a blank check, signed and ready to cash. All I have to do is fill in the amount. Most people would be unlikely to do this. You would be more likely to do it if you sneaked out and drained the money out of your account before you gave me the check. Or, you could give me the check and just be scared and worried about what I might do.

When people live together, or sleep together, without being married, they put themselves in a position that is similar to the person being asked to hand over a blank check. They either hold back on their partner by not giving the full self in the sexual act and in their shared life. Or they feel scared a lot of the time, wondering whether their partner will somehow take advantage of their vulnerability. Think about it: What do you have in your checking account that is more valuable than what you give to a sexual partner?

Cohabiting couples are likely to have one foot out the door throughout the relationship. The members of a cohabiting couple practice holding back on one another. They rehearse not trusting. Social scientists who gather the data do not have an easy way to measure this kind of dynamic in the relationship. In my view, this accounts for the disappointing results of cohabitation. I am sorry to say that I learned this from experience. My husband and I lived together before we were married; it took us a long time to unlearn the habits of the heart that we built up during those cohabiting years.

Accounting for the disappointing results of cohabitation is the first of the two puzzles I set out to solve. The second is accounting for the fact that people keep moving in together in spite of cohabitation's poor record. The solution to this second puzzle lies in something I alluded to in a previous chapter: the involuntary chemical commitment.

When people have sex, their bodies try to get them to attach to each other. The body has ways of conveying to us that this person has moved from one category to another. When a person moves from being a friend to a lover, the body knows that this is no longer a person at random, but a person who may be a partner in the life-long business of raising a baby. The sexual act builds upon itself.

The woman's body cries out for attachment through oxytocin. The man's body generates a jealousy that pushes him toward a desire for exclusivity, at least on her part if not on his own. For both men and women, the sexual act itself drives the couple toward permanence.

A date with sex can turn into a sleep-over. A few sleepovers can turn into a habit. And the habit of sleeping over can turn into cohabitation, all without much thought or planning. The daily living together, sleeping together, snuggling up to each other create an attachment. It isn't accurate to describe this as a trial marriage, as if the two people were dispassionately considering the pros and cons of living together. Our bodies create the attachment, whether our reasoning faculty is engaged or not. (And, to be quite honest, it usually isn't.)

Once, after I had given a talk on this subject, a priest in the audience offered the following observation: "I have noticed that engaged couples don't break up like they used to." He told me that he gives engaged couples a pretty intensive list of questions to work on together during marriage preparation and used to notice that a certain percentage of the couples would conclude that they were not right for each other and call off the wedding. ("We were going along fine, Father, but question thirteen, here, well, we just don't think we can work that one out. That's a deal breaker.") But now, he said, nobody breaks up any more. He speculated that cohabiting, or even copulating but not cohabiting, couples are too attached to each other. They are not able to make the judgments needed to end a relationship that might not really be strong enough for a lifetime.

This is why living together is not just a glorified roommate relationship. Adding sex to the mix changes the roommate into a lover. The body knows the difference between sexual activity and other forms of activity. We have a deep longing to be cherished by the person we have sex with, a longing that is not fooled by our pretense of indifference.

"We're living together" is a way of avoiding a decision. Once a couple begins asking themselves if they should get married, they bring the intellect more fully into the decision-making process. People can't slide into marriage in quite the same way they can slide into cohabitation. People decide to get married. They offer an account of themselves; they tell people what they are doing and why; they invite people to come and celebrate. A person doesn't quite do any of that when moving in with a partner a few possessions at a time.

A recent report, jointly commissioned by the Independent Women's Forum and the Institute for American Values, shows how this process of gradual cohabitation can take place in co-ed dorms on college campuses.[10] The report interviewed college women at a variety of campuses across the country. The women described a type of relationship that could be called, "joined at the hip" relationships, or cohabitation, college style. These are relationships that develop quickly from initial sexual encounters. Student couples, who typically live in the same co-ed dorm, find themselves studying together, eating all their meals together, and, of course, sleeping together.

Students reported that these relationships sometimes developed as early as freshman orientation week. Couples pair up early and stay together throughout their college years. In some cases, students viewed these relationships as a defense against the uncertainties and stress associated with living in co-ed dorms. Having a permanent partner protects a student both from loneliness and from some of the more predatory sexual behavior that occurs on college campuses.

Many students had serious reservations about these "joined at the hip" relationships. Some who had been in cohabitation relationships vowed never to do it again. As one student said, "It convinced me that I never want to live with someone unless I plan to marry them because you are so confined by living with a person into making relationship decisions that you might otherwise have made differently."[11] Some reported that breakups were particularly painful if the boyfriend lived in the same dorm: they would still see the guy every day. Others thought the constant presence of the boyfriend would be stifling. Despite these reservations, many students are coasting into cohabitation.

The Hook-Up

This same report also had something to say about the women's perspective on the Walk of Shame. The researchers found that the "hook-up" is a common pattern among college students. The researchers, Norvell

Glenn and Elizabeth Marquardt, defined "hook-up" as when a girl and a guy get together for a physical encounter and don't necessarily expect anything further. Ninety-one percent of the students reported that hook-ups were very common at their schools.[12]

Only a minority of the women students admitted that they themselves actually hooked-up "frequently." But the reports of this minority are interesting because their reasoning reveals fears that are probably common to many students. Some students stated that it is easier to have sex than to talk with a guy: "People just get really weirded out by each other . . . neither of the people are willing at all to talk about their feelings . . . [that's] why it is easier to like hook up with someone as opposed to . . . talking to him."[13] Others reported that they wanted to hook up as a way of avoiding a commitment and painful breakup. Many women feel awkward and empty after these encounters. Some feign indifference to commitment, but still hope the guy will call them.[14]

Another feature of the hook-up is that sometimes it is associated with drinking. Often, students will go to a party, get very drunk, and then find themselves in a sexual situation. Some of the students were honest enough to admit that they sometimes placed themselves into these party situations because they wanted sex, but didn't want romantic entanglements. The "binge drinking" problem on some campuses may be more closely related to the sexual environment than people are prepared to admit.[15]

But there is something peculiar about this apparent pledge of allegiance to the credo of the sexual revolution. If it is really perfectly normal to have morally indifferent sex, that is, to have sexual intensity and release without any commitment or connection to the other person, why bother to get drunk? Why not stay sober to enjoy the full pleasure of sex? If the heart, soul, and body really believe the mind's article of faith about sexual activity being an entitlement, the need to get drunk doesn't make any sense.

It almost seems as if the students are anesthetizing themselves with alcohol in order to diminish the bad feelings they associate with this non-committal, indiscriminate sexual activity. In other words, these features of university social life have made sex not fun for college students. You wouldn't think such a thing would be possible.

Strangely enough, 83 percent of the one thousand women surveyed agreed that "being married is a very important goal for me." The overwhelming majority, 63 percent, reported that "I would like to meet my future husband in college." Yet neither of the common patterns of sexual behavior at college, the "hook-up" and "joined at the hip," is consistent with the goal of marriage and life-long love.

Co-ed dorms facilitate both of these destructive patterns. Students could certainly find ways to have casual sex without the co-ed dorm, but is there any doubt that this living arrangement makes it easier? Likewise, the co-ed dorm makes it possible for a couple of eighteen-year-olds to slide into living together without actually making a decision or without even giving it much thought.

Whose bright idea is it to put teenagers into such a compromising situation? Students believe that college administrators provide co-ed living arrangements because it "prepares them for real life." But there actually aren't many real-life situations in which a large number of unrelated men and women live in such close and intimate proximity to each other. As Glenn and Marquardt observe, "if co-ed dorms offer 'real life' training, it appears to be an early training in hooking up and cohabitation, but little else."[16]

Back to the Date Rape Crisis

Drinking as a prelude to the hook-up brings us back to date rape. For doubtless the combination of intoxication and sexual ambivalence is a large factor in date rape allegations. The man thinks his date wanted sex; the woman insists she did not. Maybe the reality is somewhere in between. Both wanted sexual release; both have conflicted feelings about what they actually did. Under the confused circumstances surrounding college sex, it is easy to see how a couple of young people could be confused themselves.

But the real puzzle is why unwanted sexual activity is a problem of crisis proportions. How does a bit of confusion turn into a crisis? When people go on dates, they let themselves get talked into doing many things they don't especially want to do. Why is it a crisis when you let yourself get talked into sex, but not a crisis when you let yourself get talked into eating Chinese food when you really wanted Mexican? Likewise, students don't normally have to get completely plastered with alcohol to face the question of whether they want to go to a basketball game or a movie. Why don't we have "basketball game date crisis" centers, where students go after being traumatized by being talked into going to a basketball game they didn't really want to go to?[17]

Posing this absurd comparison between unwanted sex and unwanted activities of other kinds helps us to see that there really is something unique about sex. The whole premise of the sexual revolution is that sex is just another recreational activity. But the proliferation of date rape crisis centers demonstrates that no one really believes this. If sex were really no big deal, just another activity, then being talked into unwanted sexual activity shouldn't be any bigger deal than being talked into going to a ball game when you would have preferred a movie.

An advocate of consumer sex might reply that the distress college co eds feel about this unwanted sexual activity stems from vestigial moral codes that still cast unreasonable judgments and condemnation upon sexual activity. This seems implausible, given that college campuses are among the least judgmental sexual environments. Students have pretty much unlimited opportunity for sexual encounters in their co-ed dorms. Some college courses are thinly veiled pornography classes.[18] It seems unlikely that the students go to the date rape crisis centers out of some sort of vestigial prudery.

In addition to the kind of date rape charge that results from mutual ambivalence, there are undoubtedly a number of cases that are actually assaults. In this kind of case, why call it "date rape" instead of an assault? What makes a violent attack by a guy you know seem so much worse than a random attack by a stranger?

Being attacked by someone you considered your friend is more than an attack: it is a betrayal of trust. All the complications that make this kind of date rape or acquaintance rape a special case have to do with the difficulties people feel in managing the relationship. Can I really call the police on this guy in my American Lit class who mauled me on a date? How many of my friends and his friends do I tell and enlist on my side? Do I really want to send him to jail? How do I deal with my own feelings of being betrayed by someone I cared about, and who I thought cared for me?

If this kind of assualt were really only about violence and power, and not about sex, as many feminists insist, these questions wouldn't be so complicated. If an acquaintance knocked me down and stole my purse, I wouldn't have a problem calling the cops, and I wouldn't be plagued by a sense of self-doubt, betrayal, or shame. I would just be angry.

It is the sex that makes it all feel different. The level of the assault is more intense because it is an assault on the interior of the person. The mistrust and betrayal a person feels from being assaulted by an acquaintance is far deeper than she would feel from an assault that was physically identical but committed by a stranger. The fact that a sexual assault by a presumed friend can be worse in some respects than a similar assault by a stranger demonstrates that sexual activity cannot be evaluated without considering the relationship in which it is embedded.

Either sex is a big deal, or it isn't. If it is really no big deal, then "unwanted sexual activity" shouldn't be particularly traumatic. Colleges ought to save themselves some money, shut down the date rape crisis centers, and tell the co-eds to grow up and get over it. If sex really is a big deal, then we can't very well say that sex is just another recreational activity. And every serious person knows which these is true.

The Limitations of the "Consent" Standard

Date rape points to the one of the underlying problems with the notion that all voluntary sexual encounters are morally acceptable. We are asking the concept of "consent" to carry all the weight of evaluating our sexual experience. Since "wrong" and "right," "good" and "bad" are no longer useable terms in our post-moral, post-modern world, we don't have very many adjectives to describe a negative sexual encounter. Yet, as any experienced person knows, some rendezvous feel all wrong. But if the sex was voluntary, and appropriately contracepted, there aren't any socially acceptable grounds for telling yourself and your friends that it felt icky. (Sorry, there's no other word.)

When we reflect on this, of course, we can imagine all kinds of things that might be unpleasant, even unpleasant enough to describe as "wrong," or at least "wrong for me." Having sex makes a person uniquely vulnerable, both physically and emotionally. We could get beat up by a date, but the more subtle emotional injuries are much more common.

After all, we don't just give our bodies to the other person during sex. Our whole spiritual, emotional, and psychological being is bound up in the body. We can afford to be nonchalant about how we use our bodies only if we believe the body is an empty shell and the soul of the person resides elsewhere.[19]

Look at the variety of non-physical harms we might experience during a voluntary sexual encounter. We might feel used or manipulated. We might feel ignored while the other person attends to his own orgasm. We might feel like a fool because the experience mattered more to us than to the other person. The more it means to one person, the more vulnerable he or she is to the other person's indifference. If we allow it mean a lot, we leave ourselves more open to being hurt. We might resist letting sex mean very much by holding back on the other person and focusing only on the physical pleasure of the act. This strategy might protect us from the bad feelings that flow from vulnerability. But in the process, we've become a kind of perpetrator ourselves, a person who uses others.

So we may well have very sound and understandable reasons for judging our own sexual actions to be wrong. Even if we grant the premise that all consensual sex is morally acceptable (which I don't), it doesn't automatically follow that all consensual sexual acts are morally indistinguishable. Because our moral vocabulary is so limited, we have a lot of trouble seeing the difference between morally acceptable and morally superior or inferior. It is in principle possible to judge that among the set of morally acceptable acts some are morally inferior to others. But our ability to describe these unsatisfactory, but voluntary experiences is extremely cramped by the initial premise that all voluntary sex is acceptable. We've collapsed all the possible delineations or categories into rape, which is bad, and consensual sex, which is good. If these are the only categories, then all consensual sex is essentially the same, every voluntary sexual act is indistinguishable from all others.

This may account for some of the date rape charges that seem to be frivolous. The encounter was unsatisfactory, but voluntary. This category is not supposed to exist. It is difficult if not impossible to say, "I feel cheap, or I feel used, or I feel as if this was all wrong." The words will be incomprehensible to a listener with the stunted moral vocabulary of the post-modern mind. So in order to make sense of the very powerful feeling that something was dreadfully wrong with what happened, the woman reinterprets the act as an assault.

This is the sense in which the term "consent" is doing all the moral work. We aren't supposed to object to consensual sex. So if the experience was somehow objectionable, the sex must not really have been consensual.

The Marriage Angle

I have tried to show that there are some situations in which "recreational sex" is not really much fun. All these situations involve unmarried couples. I want to change focus for a moment and look at the question from the opposite perspective. What do married couples do to make their sex lives more fun? "Recreational sex" means something quite different for a married couple. They can put aside a whole set of fears around the question of commitment and just enjoy each other. The recent raft of advice books have quite a different focus from old-fashioned sex books like *The Joy of Sex* and *Kama Sutra Sex*.

Michele Weiner Davis has been counseling couples for twenty years.[20] In one of her groups for women, she encouraged those with "hubby trouble and poor sex lives" to go home and seduce their husbands for two weeks, even if they didn't feel like it. The result? The women came back in two weeks, giggling and whispering. "I couldn't believe what happened. My husband started reading the kids bedtime stories. He never does that.·He was talking to me more often. He was putting grout between the tiles."

Weiner Davis explains, "All good marriages are based on the notion that people who love each other take care of each other. It's a very simple principle, but when you are caring about your spouse's needs and desires, there's almost always reciprocity. What happened with those women is that, rather than wait for their husbands to be more of the men they were hoping they would be, they took responsibility for their own role in the marital stalemate and decided to tip over the first domino. And in this case, that was being more physical, more sexual."

Weiner Davis's book, *The Sex-Starved Marriage: A Couple's Guide to Boosting Their Marriage Libido*, has been a bestseller.[21] And what is the simple message of this book? The amount and intensity of sexual desire is not something that is a given. A couple can increase their desire for one another by going through the motions of love: touching one another, initiating sex, and most important, responding to each other's sexual initiative, even if they don't feel like it.

A couple's relationship and sex life mutually build upon one another. Since touching itself can increase desire through the hormonal rush of oxytocin, a person can influence the amount of desire he or she feels. When people start to invest more energy in their physical relationship, it triggers feelings of closeness and connection. Weiner Davis emphasizes that the "low-desire" member of a married couple needs to make a decision to touch his or her partner, to be available to his or her partner and to respond positively to his or her desires. Quite often, the "low-desire" partner enjoys sex quite a bit, once it gets going. The level of desire is, in part, a decision.

Likewise, Dr. David Schnarch in *Passionate Marriage* argues that what couples often perceive as sexual difficulties are really relationship difficulties.[22] Problems in the relationship surface in the bedroom. Sexual problems often offer a key to other kinds of problems. People have trouble being sexually intimate because they have been having trouble being intimate in other areas of the relationship.

One of his suggestions is for people to learn to do something he calls "self-soothing." He defines self-soothing as "turning inward and accessing your own resoures to regain your emotional balance and feeling comfortable in your body. . . . Self-soothing is your ability to comfort yourself, lick your own wounds, and care for yourself without excessive indulgence or deprivation."[23] The idea here is that it is not my partner's problem to relieve me of my uncomfortable feelings. This is particularly important when my partner has something to "communicate" to me that I don't especially enjoy hearing. I can take in what he has to say, accept it as helpful information or not as the case might be. But I am not required to insist that he see me as I see myself. I can calm myself even if the truth about myself is upleasant, or if he sees me differently than I see myself.

According to Schnarch, the ability to self-soothe and to differentiate one's own feelings from the partner's contributes tremendously to improving a couple's sex life. They can be honest with each other because they are not expecting or insisting on total validation at all times. They each can have opportunities to say things that are important to them, without their partner being overwhelmed. They can each have the opportunity to hear what their partner has to say, knowing that they are not required to agree with every last word that comes out of the other person's mouth. In short, they can be genuinely intimate. Schnarch finds that this kind of improvement in emotional intimacy greatly contributes to an increase in sexual intimacy.

None of this makes any sense if sex is really nothing more than a recreational activity or an interaction of plumbing parts. It really shouldn't matter much whether a couple communicate a lot or a little, or whether they are mad at each other or not. Both Schnarch's observations and Weiner Davis' suggestions are much more consistent with the idea that sexuality is primarily about building up the relationship between the couple. Trying to take the relatedness out of the sexual activity makes for less enjoyable sex.

Conclusion

We have identified several situations in which sexual activity is not fun. We have the testimony of therapists, as well the experience of ordinary people, that the quality of the relationship outside the bedroom largely determines the quality of the relationship inside the bedroom. This tells us something we should have known all along: it simply cannot be that sexual activity is always and everywhere a good. We have to ask ourselves what circumstances and conditions make it a good, or prevent it from being a good. It is clear that neither using other people nor being used feels very good.

This is only a preliminary step in developing a conherent and useable moral code around sexual conduct. We will take a few more steps in the next chapter.

$\backsim$ 5 $\backsim$

Why Consumer Sex
Is Anti-Social

NOT ONLY IS RECREATIONAL SEX NO FUN, but consumer sex is profoundly anti-social. The sexual revolution has retarded people's ability to create community life and to relate to one another. Even worse, our modern sexual moral code does not cultivate an attitude of respect for others, in spite of our elaborate schemes of equality and our hypersensitive habits of speech. To the contrary, our modern sexual ways have led us to believe that we are entitled to use people.

Public, Private, and Social

The terms "private" and "public" are often treated as if they were exhaustive categories. But these terms come from economics and politics and are not entirely applicable to either sex or the family. When we describe something as "private," we usually mean that it concerns only a particular, discrete set of individuals and has no effect on other people. When we describe something as "public," we usually mean either that it takes place in an open, accessible location or that it is somehow under the jurisdiction of government authorities.

We are understandably reluctant to classify sexual activity as public in either of these senses. We don't do it out in public, nor do we want to give the government jurisdiction over it. So if the only analytical categories are public and private, that means that sex is private. As a result of that designation, all voluntary sexual acts are treated as "victimless crimes," to use the libertarian term. No act of voluntary sex is presumed to be wrong, not by the legal system, not by public opinion, not by the media, not by many mainstream churches, not even by your Great Aunt Sally, who could otherwise be counted on as an enforcer of informal social norms.

But this is odd for a couple of reasons. First of all, just as a political observation, it is peculiar that a doctrine championed primarily as an economic philosophy should be adopted by leftists for whom "laissez-faire," "freedom of contract," and "atomistic individualism" are obscenities. The people who argue that the right to privacy includes the right to any form of sexual conduct are not, as a rule, the same people who would defend the right of an employer and an employee to strike a deal (a fully voluntary, completely consensual deal, mind you), paying the worker two dollars an hour for twelve hours a day.

Secondly, it simply isn't true that sex meets the technical definition of private, since one person's sexual activity potentially has significant consequences for other people, and some of those consequences can be very negative. This suggests there might indeed be "victims" involved in some forms of sex, even sex to which adults have consented. But no one, from anywhere on the political spectrum, really wants to give others jurisdiction over it, or a vote on it, or veto power over it.

The previous sentence, in a way, captures the oddest fact of all. "Jurisdiction," "voting," and "veto power" are all political terms. We don't normally think of family relationships in such impersonal, political terms. Nevertheless, it doesn't really make sense to ignore the interests that other people might legitimately have in our sexual activity, despite the awkwardness of these terms. This suggests that contrasting "private" with "public" does not do justice to the inner workings of the family.

There is another possible category for sex: a social good. This is not a distinct category that we use in economics, nor even very much in politics. In fact, "social" is sometimes used as a sub-category of "public." When an economist or policymaker starts talking about "social" effects of private activity, he is usually working up to some justification for government regulation or jurisdiction. But the word "social" can be used to mean a sphere of activity that is properly outside the scope of government yet still concerns a group of people beyond the individual. Sexual activity is social in exactly this sense.

Many thinkers have come to recognize the importance of a robust social sphere, as opposed to either a strictly private or strictly public. Theologian and philosopher Michael Novak describes the three spheres of a free society: the free market, free political institutions, and a cultural and social sector that is compatible with those other, more formal free institutions.[1] Richard John Neuhaus and Peter Berger invented the term "mediating institutions" to describe the organizations that stand between the individual and the state, protecting the individual from the state and providing the framework for civil society.[2] Charles Murray talks about the "little platoons" of civil society, the small, voluntary associations of people who band together to accomplish important objectives that are more limited than those of the government and more extensive than an individual could achieve.[3] From the more liberal end of the political spectrum, Robert Putnam, who gave us the phrase "bowling alone," mourns the loss of community and points to the need for a robust social sector.[4] Amitai Etzioni makes a communitarian argument for the importance of putting the "social" back into "society."[5]

The two natural, organic purposes of human sexuality, procreation and spousal unity, are both social in exactly the sense I mean. Both of these natural purposes build up the community of the family. When these two natural purposes are disconnected from sexual activity, one of the most important motives for building community is undermined.

Sexual activity can be destructive of community if people become focused inward, exclusively on their own desires, rather than on the building up of the community of the family.

In this chapter, I hope to convince you that we ought to treat sex as a social activity, not as a private or public activity. I will give some examples to illustrate what I mean by social and anti-social sex. I will show some of the problems associated with treating sex as if it were a consumer good. But first, I will tell you something about myself that will show that sex can not possibly be a genuinely private good.

A Modest Confession

Let me illustrate the social aspect of sex by making a little confession. During my student days, I more or less did the whole sexual revolution. On one level, I was a highly focused, hard-charging career woman: I got my doctorate in economics from the University of Rochester, did a post-doctoral year at the University of Chicago, had my first teaching job at Yale. On top of all that, I was already an iconoclast by being a committed free market economist. I enjoyed my self-image as an economic and political libertarian. I was proud of my intellectual consistency. I looked like I had it all together.

But beneath the surface, I was giving a new meaning to "having it all." My first book, *Love & Economics*, had as its subtitle *Why the Laissez-Faire Family Doesn't Work*. I got to be an expert on what doesn't work by trying most of the things I write about. I committed just about every sexual sin in the book: adultery, fornication, cohabitation, group sex, same-sex sex. I had an abortion; I was married and divorced.

It was not actually such a jolly time. I hurt myself and others, and it was my fault. I can't credibly blame the man I married or anybody else. I'm sorry for the harm I caused to others, harm I can never fully repair. I'm not here to complain, but to accept responsibility for what I have done.

I bring all this up for two reasons. The first is purely defensive. I don't want somebody trying to prove me a hypocrite. Don't bother: I confess in advance.

But I plan not to give a full confession. The reason why has to do with the theme of this chapter: the social aspect of sex. I could tell the whole story of every sexual encounter I have ever had. I maintain I don't have the right to do that because *the other people involved in have feelings of their own about them.* Every person I ever had sex with, casually or intimately, has their own relationship to what happened. They might not want me telling "my" story, as though they were mere props in my private drama. The kid I fooled around with in the dorm is now a grown man. He might be chagrined by what he did. Even if he isn't ashamed of what he did, he might be embarrassed to have done it with me. He might have political and religious ideas that would make him embarrassed to have been associated with me, even so long ago. Perhaps he has his own version of events that he is attached to and would prefer not to have challenged. And even if he didn't mind, he has relatives who might very well mind. His wife and kids might mind. Maybe his elderly parents would be mortified if I spread their family name all over the place.

I had the idea that my sex life was my private property. I needed that idea: it gave me permission to do what I did. But I was wrong. My sex life is not really my private property.

We moderns are tempted to reduce the sex act to a species of contract. As long as the two people agree to it, no third party has any right to an opinion. We would like to believe that every social feature of the sexual act can be captured by this implicit contract to which the two people agreed. But the contract metaphor can't address this particular problem.

Every sexual act I have ever had has been fully consensual. I never raped anybody; nobody ever raped me. Yet it would be presumptuous to claim that those I had sex with tacitly consented to me telling my version of our story any time I choose to do so.

In case you are not convinced, let's say that sex really is private. The implicit understanding of a casual sexual coupling, the default mode, if you will, is that there are absolutely no obligations between the parties. Only explicit agreements bind the parties to do or not do certain things, to say or not say certain things. We do what we want, with no further constraints on or expectations of each other.

If I want to hang a banner outside my dorm room window, with a score sheet announcing your performance, I'm allowed. That's a chance you took when you went to bed with me. You think it's tacky? Tough luck. If we really believe that only explicit agreements constrain this type of behavior, then morally as well as legally, there is no difference between a lifetime of discretion and a full-page ad in the *New York Times*, describing every detail of our encounter.

This "buyer beware" position is exactly where the logic of the consumer-based, private-property approach to sexuality leads us. This sexual encounter is mine, for me to do with as I please. In the absence of an explicit agreement to share information about our relationship only by mutual consent, I am entitled to share anything I want, on any terms I choose. If you don't like it, you should have chosen somebody else to fool around with.

To be sure, full page ads in the *Times* are not all that common. But it is certain that people do exploit the vulnerability that sexual intimacy creates. That exploitation is particularly noxious, because sexual vulnerability is, or at least can be, more intense than any other kind. Think of couples going through nasty divorces who say the most embarrassing things in an effort to hurt and humiliate each other. Think of people who talk about their short-term sex partners with little regard for their feelings. The more one person talks, the more the other feels justified in doing so. In a perfect example of the unraveling of mutual cooperation, one person's defection from an implicit agreement of discretion can quickly lead to the destruction of the relationship.[6]

The only thing that prevents people from running off at the mouth is their regard for the other person and a sense of common decency. But why do we consider that kind of reticence to be "common decency?" I think it is because we know that the sexual act does create a shared space between two people. We even know that the shared space has the potential to become sacred space. The sexual act creates a "we" out of two "I's." The sexual story becomes "our" story. By exposing the encounter to third parties, one person has effectively appropriated all that common good for himself. In the process, he has damaged or even destroyed it, because this was a good that existed only by virtue of its being shared.

Of course, people sometimes have legitimate reasons for wanting to tell something about a sexual encounter. Their partner might object to sharing some of those things. As long as their association is an ongoing, working partnership, it is reasonable to think that people ought to consider the other person's preferences seriously before revealing information to a third party. In fact, if a person completely disregarded the other person's feelings about this, it might well destroy their friendship.

This isn't any kind of enforceable right or claim against the other person. It isn't something we could sue each other over. No reasonable person would want the "right to privacy" defined in this way to be an enforceable claim. Nonetheless, this connection to the other person and this regard for his or her feelings are key parts of what restrains people from indiscriminate talking. This widely shared understanding of the need for restraint is what allows us to say that discretion is a matter of "common decency."[7]

If sex partners marry each other, that sense of connection and regard for the other person extends over their lifetimes. The married couple, in effect, make a commitment to at least consider, if not respect and honor, one another's feelings for the rest of their lives. Their sexual relationship can be properly understood as private with respect to the rest of the world. But between the two of them the sexual relationship is social. Their sexual intimacy, the private space between them, belongs to them both. One person cannot take full possession of it for himself without destroying it. Nor can they attempt to divide it between themselves, without destroying it. The "good" of their sexual intimacy is a social good, a public good, a non-rivalrous good. They have created a small society between themselves.

By contrast, the members of an uncommitted couple have not quite created a society between themselves. Each is vulnerable to the other person's revelations or indiscretions. As the relationship comes to have meaning for both of them, they begin to create a society between themselves. It no longer makes sense to think of it as "private," in the same way as they initially did. They have created something that belongs to both of them and cannot be parcelled out between them as individuals. Either party might be devastated if the other treated the relationship as if it were his to talk about and to share with others. This couple's lack of commitment keeps that shared good continually at risk. That is one of the things that creates the "edge," the uneasiness, so common in cohabiting relationships.

I think most people would agree that something precious would be lost if one's sex partner shared information indiscriminately. This is a powerful corroboration of my claim that sex is a social act, not a private act. Both people have an interest in what happened. Each has claims on the other. They cannot, of course, compel each other to see it or to interpret the events in the same way. But each has a claim upon the other to at least refrain from making a unilateral decision to tell a story. That we regard this as "common decency" supports the view that the organic view of sexuality resonates more deeply with our experience and our intuition than the consumer-based view of sexuality.

I think, by the way, that this is why "tell-all" memoirs, confessions, or revelations so seldom do any credit to the person who initiates them. People have a lurid fascination with intimate details, so these stories often find a ready market. But ultimately the audience is left wondering why the person is telling the story. You know he is leaving something out (like, for instance, the other person's side). You have to scratch your head and ask, "Who really cares?" But finally, most of us conclude that there is something twisted about somebody opening his life up to the inspection of strangers, without the slightest concern for the impact it might have on the other people involved.

Hollywood and the Two Meanings of Privacy

This difference between the "private" and "social" views of sex helps us to understand Hollywood's commitment to the politics of the "lifestyle Left." For the entertainment industry, all sex is a private good. Anything I choose to do or not do is acceptable. My sex life is all about me and my desires and has nothing to do with community of any kind.

But Hollywood presents us with two, seemingly contradictory positions. On the one hand, many stars seem to delight in taunting the public: "My sex life is my private business; how dare you utter a word of criticism." On the other hand, this same group of people readily make their sexual activity public. In addition to the fictionalized sex produced for movies and television, many entertainment figures share the details of their love lives with the public—every marriage and divorce, every affaire and rumor. As the stars age, and their biological clocks start ticking, we are treated to every facet of their pursuit of a baby, whether conceived artificially or naturally. Yet when some members of the public object either to the content of the films or the tasteless self-display of the stars' private lives, the entertainment world pretends to be shocked.

This apparent contradiction can be resolved with one word: narcissism. Privacy in the sense that "this is my private business" is really an implicit claim that I am entitled to do what I want without having to answer to anyone. People express this position by saying, "Your rules don't apply to me. I am entitled to adapt the rules to my personal needs and desires." A cynical observer might offer a less charitable interpretation: these people are really saying "I am entitled to make up the rules as I go along." At the same time, the lack of discretion that seems to be the opposite of privacy allows a person to expose himself (literally and figuratively) to an anonymous public. "Look at me! Pay attention to me!" Pathological narcissism, the worship or idealization of the self, is the thread common to both of Hollywood's interpretations of privacy.

Privacy as unaccountability has crowded out privacy as discretion. Indeed, these two notions of privacy cannot really coexist. A person who accepts accountability for his actions is probably not the sort of person who will simultaneously parade his sexuality in front of an anonymous public. So privacy in the sense of modesty or keeping to oneself has become passé. Hollywood has replaced modesty privacy with a self-display of one's sexuality.

This is the ultimate transformation of human sexuality into a consumer good. A movie star's sex appeal is part of his image, persona, and product. The star's sexiness is a continual advertisement because sexual stimulation is what the star is selling. Everyone understands the reason that stars and studios package sex along with some other commodity: sex helps sell the product. But we also realize that there is something revolting about the whole process. We consumers understand that we are being manipulated. With a subtle mixture of cynicism and all-knowing hipness, we allow ourselves to be manipulated.

At the same time, it is no secret that many of our most highly paid entertainers have miserable lives, in spite of their fabulous, almost surreal, level of material wealth. The drug problems, the instability of relationships, the public lovers' quarrels, the legal and even criminal problems: these are not the sorts of things that mark people as deleriously happy. Perhaps some of these stars have made themselves miserable precisely through their chosen method of acquiring wealth. By displaying their sexuality as a commodity, they have diminished and dehumanized themselves. It is hard to imagine being genuinely intimate with a person who exhibits his sexuality the way so many of our entertainers do. So the mutually contradictory meanings of "private" come back to haunt those people who enact the most extreme versions of both. Looked at from this point of view, it is sad to think of how many people treat entertainers as role models.

In a milder way, narcissism is potentially a problem for us all. Everyone enjoys being the center of attention; everyone wants to be noticed. Yet that desire can easily lead to a milder form of the destructiveness so common among the stars.

There is, for instance, a narsissistic quality to many of our thirty-something singles, so focused in their work and so intense in their play. Some of the men among them are unwilling to commit themselves to marriage and family, despite their success at their high-powered jobs and their expensive hobbies. Other thirty-something men drift, not only among women, but even among jobs, seemingly content to let women support them, or to accept whatever jobs happen to present themselves. Both types have in common an excessive focus on themselves, a focus that makes it difficult to involve themselves with other people.[8]

Thirty-something women are surprised when love and romance, endeavors which are every bit as intense and passionate as work and hobbies, do not work out the same way.[9] Some go so far as to use business techniques for finding romance. For instance, one highly successful businesswoman (who earned $21 million in eight stressful years) offered to pay $100,000 to an associate if he introduced her to a man she ultimately marries. She calls it, "incentiving her sales force."[10] She seemed surprised to find that these techniques don't work very well in finding and cultivating relationships.

The reason for these women's frustration is the same as the reason for the men's lack of commitment. They are looking in the wrong direction: a person has to direct his attention outside himself in order to succeed in relationships. The exhilirating, child-free endeavors in which they have succeeded so spectacularly reward an intense focus on oneself: training, discipline, and drive. But these same qualities do not serve nearly as well in the creation and sustenance of relationships. And often, the person who has succeeded very well in work finds it difficult to generate genuine interest in and attention to another person.

Anthropologist David Gutmann observes that any society is sustained by the efforts of its adults. The very young are pre-productive, and the very old are post-productive. These groups can be allowed greater freedom and self-indulgence. It is the prime-age adults, both male and female, who must "define its values, fight its wars, take responsibility for its governance and do its routine but necessary work—all this while turning out enough physically and mentally healthy children to keep the whole enterprise going across the generations." But, he continues, in modern American, the next generation is being called, but "many do not muster at the usual assembly points. Or, of those who do mobilize, too many quickly desert: . . . in too many the capacity for commitment to either love or work is stunted; and far too many attempt marriage but defect to divorce when the early passions cool down."[11]

Professor Gutmann attributes this problem to narcissism. America's young have great difficulty finding a focus for the universal human need for awe, worship, and idealization. These needs can be focused inward or outward. In an immature or pathological narcissism, the "claims of the individual trump all others' and the personality is mobilized to defend, justify and achieve these self-priorities."

There are striking similarities between this immature narcissism and the consumer-based approach to sex. When we engage in consumer sex, we do not fully consider the impact of our actions upon others: our priority, and sometimes our only motive, is self-gratification. Consumer sex is focused inward, on personal pleasure, not on the building up of the community of the family.

By contrast, acquiring a mature moral identity involves discovering the "ideal self outside the self." The young person recognizes some group, vocation, religion or nation as being worthy of his loyalty and commitment. "We can say that adulthood has been acheived when narcissism is transmuted, and thereby detoxified, into strong lasting idealizations and into healthy narcissism. . . . Instead of himself, the true adult venerates the ideal versions of his community, his vocation and his family."[12]

Likewise, a mature sexuality is directed toward the spouse and any children the couple might create. It directs the person away from himself or herself, and allows a healthy attention to other people. This approach to sexuality is mature, and not only because it helps to overcome our natural self-centeredness. It is also mature because it is grounded in reality, the reality of the organic purposes of human sexuality.

These are some of the reasons why I say that sex is neither private nor public, but social. Every sexual act involves another person. Once we see the social dimension of sexual activity, we can start to see that some sex is more social than others. Some sexual behavior has significant negative consequences for others, and hence can be considered, in fact, anti-social.

Let me offer some examples that will support my claim. Then, we can begin to make some reasoned judgments about which kinds of sexual activity are appropriate and life-enhancing choices that we really want to make.

Social Sex

Suppose a young couple decide to get married. Their decision to marry means that each is deciding to direct his or her sexual urge exclusively toward the other. Their families have reason to celebrate this new relationship. The marriage draws one new member into each of the existing families.

The marriage might produce children. Everybody is excited about those children, sometimes years in advance of their birth. They will be somebody's grandchildren, nieces, nephews, and cousins. The children will be born into a pre-existing social network, with pre-established, ready made relationships.

The father and the mother will be the child's primary relationships, of course. The new parents will work together to build up their own new little family with love. They will do their best to get along with the other relatives, on both sides of the family, even though some of those relatives will present challenges of various sorts. But everyone understands that the man and woman have privileges and responsibilities with regard to each other. All of those understandings, both implicit and explicit, lie behind their new community.

For the married couple, sexual activity is linked to its natural purposes, enhances the love between them, and may result in a child. The child becomes their joint project. Their love for each other helps them to work together for the sake of their child.

Their sex life is not public: They don't do it out in the open. They don't need a government permit for it. They don't report on it to their family members. But at the same time, it is not exactly private. Their sex life has social ramifications across the generations. If they live close to their relatives, those relatives might even notice if things aren't going well between them.

Now a jaded modern soul might scoff at my depiction of the young married couple: "This is certainly a idyllic picture you've created. But it is not very realistic. Some of those relatives are going to be a net drain on this happy couple. The bride's father can't stand his new son-in-law and glares at him constantly. The groom's parents are divorced, and the kid hates the stepmother. His mom takes the bride aside and tells her to be sure she keeps her job, in case her darling son ends up walking out, just like his father did to her. The bride's big brother has a couple of kids out of wedlock, and won't be exactly a role-model for responsible fatherhood. The bride's Uncle Louie is a drunk in denial. The groom's Aunt Nettie is an impressive career woman, but she is single, talks incessantly about herself and her accomplishments, and is a real bore. The only decent relatives merely seem decent because they live a thousand miles away and nobody actually has to put up with them for more than three days at a time. Get real."

I have seen some unpleasant families and relatives myself. And they are an argument for what, exactly? Because we have difficult, disappointing relatives, we should have sex outside marriage? How will this improve things? In fact, reflection on the troubled souls that every family seems to have strengthens the argument for sociable sex.

Anti-Social Sex

Unmarried Parents. So now imagine another couple about the same age. These two people chose to have sex with each other without getting married. No one in either of their families necessarily knows or approves of the relationship. In fact, it is understood that their sexual relationship is a private matter only between the two immediate parties. No one, no matter how close to them, has the right to express an opinion about it, short of unlimited approval.

Perhaps a baby results from this sexual activity. Maybe the relatives are excited. More likely, they put on a good face about being excited, but they are secretly worried about the fate of the baby and the baby's impact on the rest of the family. They might be concerned about the demands the new baby will place on the unmarried parents, and on them, the members of the extended family. Will the father stick around and support the baby and the mother? Will the mother accept a relationship with him? Will the mother be making demands upon the rest of the family for support, financial and emotional, and for perpetual babysitting?[13] With no commitment between the parents, the baby is a potential drain on the rest of the family.

This scenario of unmarried sex solves none of the problems cited by our cynical critic of marriage. Uncle Louie is still a drunk. Aunt Nettie still can't shut up. The in-laws are still pains in the neck. This young couple surely doesn't have an ideal support network. But instead of contributing something positive to the family, their actions add to the cycle of destructive self-absorption: "I don't have to get married.

I don't want to and you can't make me." "The bitch wants the baby. It's not my problem. Why should I care?"

When a young couple get married, having sex and having a baby are the key facts in their lives that help them grow up. Perhaps the young mother has the primary responsibility for caring for the baby and the young father has the primary responsibility for earning a living to support his wife and child. Perhaps they combine their roles in more complicated, less specialized ways. How they allocate these parental responsibilities between them doesn't matter as much as their commitment to work cooperatively and each one's appreciation of the other's contributions.[14] By getting married, this young couple makes a decision to take their place in the adult world. Marriage creates a context in which their sexuality contributes to their process of maturing.

By contrast, the couple that has a baby without marriage has embarked on a whole series of decisions that avoid adult responsibility. Many discussions of the public policy consequences of unmarried childbearing focus on the consequences to the child: an unmarried mother is not able to care for the child as well as a married mother, for a whole variety of reasons. Without taking anything away from that analysis, I want to focus on something that isn't talked about as often: The unmarried couple are not accountable to one another in the same way they would be if they were married.

The unmarried father is only vaguely committed to paying child support. It isn't unusual for an unmarried woman to assure the father that she doesn't want any child support, or that she won't make any demands upon him. He will have a legal obligation only if the mother goes through a series of steps to create one. If the mother names him as father, if she insists on child support, if she uses the courts to force him to pay, then he will have a legal obligation. He might be saddled with a huge, lifetime responsibility. Or he might not. He might choose to live with his child's mother and love her and work together with her. Or he might not.

For him, this is the appeal of not getting married. He can have sex, father a child, and then do what he wants about it after that. He does not have to be accountable to the mother or the child, unless she jumps through all the legal hoops necessary to make him accountable. Until and unless she does that, he does not have any particular obligation to her that is legally, socially, or morally enforceable. There is no social or cultural template to channel his actions or expectations into any particular direction.[15] He gets to do what he wants, until he is compelled to do otherwise.

This man may become a "dead-beat dad," who irresponsibly fathers a child and then refuses to support the child. The "dead-beat dad" has become a familiar image, particularly in discussions about family policy. We are less accustomed to thinking about the woman's contribution to such a situation. Yet unmarried motherhood offers the woman a lack of accountability that is every bit as anti-social as the more familiar male variety.

The unmarried mother is not accountable to the father for maintaining any kind of working relationship with him. If she wants to kick him out of her life, she can. If she wants to be so obnoxious that he doesn't want to have anything to do with her, she can. If she wants to go after him for child support, she can. If she wants to make visitation impossible or unpleasant for him, she can. For her, this is the appeal of not getting married. She can have her baby without being answerable to the father for anything.

Mind you, neither of these unmarried parents has a very realistic perspective on his or her responsibilities to the other. They enter into the non-marriage relationship with the idea that this gives them more control over the situation than they would have if they were married. They evidently do not realize that the other person can make life quite difficult for them in a way that would be far less likely to succeed if they were actually married.

The unmarried father can find himself with a long-term legal obligation to pay child support, despite his girlfriend's assurances that she will never make such demands. That legal obligation might or might not allow him to have a relationship with his child, or even to see his child. If he were married, he would be more likely to have a relationship with the child, even if the marriage turned sour.

Likewise, the unmarried mother may believe that she can have her baby without being tied down to the father. She may seriously underestimate the amount of interaction she will end up having with the father. She may misjudge the complications she will endure from having to deal with a man she didn't like well enough to marry. She probably didn't really think about having children and grandchildren in common with this man for the rest of their lives.

Nonetheless, both the woman and the man may enter into the situation thinking they are more free than if they were married. The unmarried parents are often operating under the illusion that it is possible for a single person to take care of a child for a lifetime without any need for the other parent, without any help from the other parent, without any conflict with the other parent. By underestimating the difficulties and overestimating the benefits, young people can convince themselves that unmarried parenthood is a good deal.

They are mistaken, because the marriage commitment creates a series of obligations, benefits, and understandings for both of them. Marriage provides a context of stability in which those needs can be met, that help can be provided, and those conflicts can be worked out. Marriage blends the couple's actions with the two natural purposes of human sexuality. Sexual activity, love of the partner, and procreation: instead of these three things being in three separate compartments of a person's life, marriage has harmonized them. Because I love my husband, I direct my sexual energy exclusively toward him. Our love produces a child whom we both love. Our sexual desire draws us closer to each other and builds up our mutual love. We work together to support each other and our child.

Sex outside the context of marriage deprives the person of the opportunity to integrate these parts of his life. Consumer-based sex fragments the self, by placing these three things into separate compartments. My sexual activity has no necessary connection to the love of a partner. I do not expect the sexual act to enhance my love of my partner, and in fact I may actively resist loving him. I have no intention that my sexual acts should produce a child. If I really want to have a child, I can obtain one in some way other than through a committed relationship with this particular person. I can have an uncommitted relationship with this man, and inform him after the fact that he is going to become a father. I can have an anonymous encounter with another man, or with a sperm bank. I am entitled to have a child, if I want one, but I need not have any relationship whatsoever with the father of my child. In the most extreme of these combinations, I can have sex or a child or both, without being burdened by a relationship with a troublesome man.

The superficial appeal of this arrangement is that I am totally free to fashion my combination of sexual activity, relationships, and children in any form or fashion I choose. The downside of this arrangement is that I am alone, and I have deprived my child of a relationship with his father.

Adultery. Adultery is another example of anti-social sex. Two people who are married to others have sex. Instead of this sexual activity building up a new community of love, it tears down an existing one. Nobody is excited for this couple and the offspring they might produce. Their relationship is a source of pain to their spouses and their children. Their relationship may disrupt two households, and may have consequences that will reverberate down through the generations.

In our divorce culture, this couple are entitled to throw their existing families into upheaval. We are forbidden to pass judgment upon whether their unmarried sexual activity is better or worse than their married sexual activity. They are free to enjoy their new relationship, break the old one, and start a new family with each other, leaving the children of their previous relationships behind. Their sexuality is not directed toward anything beyond themselves. The responsibilities they previously assumed are only as important as they choose to make them.

They are not required to maintain a relationship with their children or with their children's other parent, because any legal requirements to the contrary can be thwarted by a lack of good will on the part of either parent. The custodial parent can move so far away that the other parent has little realistic prospect of visiting his child.[16] If he has no sense of personal responsibility, a father can evade child support. Even if he pays the money in full and on time, that money cannot take the place of his time and attention to his child.

Likewise, without some sense of good will toward the father, a mother can undermine his efforts to be involved in his child's life. According to one study, 42 percent of all children of divorce who are living with their mothers say their mothers tried to prevent them from seeing their fathers after the divorce.[17] The legal system tries to replace the personal accountability a married couple routinely imposes upon itself, but it is a pathetic substitute for an working relationship between the parents.

Indeed, a vindictive parent can use the legal system to harass the other parent. Fathers can wear down mothers with repeated legal challenges to the divorce decree. Mothers can have fathers arrested for failing to pay child support. Mothers can eliminate all contact between their children and the father by accusing him of child abuse.[18] Mothers can use restraining orders to prevent their children from seeing their father. All she has to do is say that she feels threatened. In many jursidictions, she does not even have to show why she feels threatened.

Some social commentators talk about "good divorce." It is possible, they say, for couples to divorce on amicable terms. They can work together for the good of their children; they can avoid quarreling and squabbling and drawing their kids into their quarrels. Joint custody or shared parenting time should be the norm for divorcing parents so that kids have the chance to have a relationship with both parents. Counseling prior to divorce can help everyone understand the negative impact of these conflicts.[19]

I call this "happy talk," because it ignores one crucial question: if the parents can work that hard at their divorce, why can't they work that hard at their marriage in the first place? If we are going to argue for a rebuttable presumption in favor of shared custody (which I actually think is a good idea), we could just as well argue for a rebuttable presumption in favor of staying married. The current state of divorce law allows divorce for a new partner or for no reason at all. It makes more sense to reform the unilateral divorce law, so we have fewer divorces in the first place, than to try to make better divorces.

When a married person has sex with someone other than his spouse, this is an anti-social act. Our society no longer admits this, even as a probable fact, much less an indisputable fact. The law applies the most extreme version of libertarianism to an arena in which it least applies. Family courts treat adultery and divorce as if they were victimless crimes.

But this is simply untrue: both adultery and divorce can impose long-lasting and heavy costs on other people. The kids are harmed, as are the other spouses. The family court system is burdened by trying to resolve the problems generated by the disrupted marriage. The school system is taxed by having to deal with the stressed-out children of parents preoccupied with their new lovers or their contentious divorces. The police and criminal justice system are taxed by continual "Amber Alerts" for missing children, who all too often turn out to have been kidnapped by their own parents. Nobody thinks freedom means being allowed to impose costs on other people. But in our "no-fault" divorce environment, we are barely able to acknowledge that both extra-marital sex and divorce typically impose costs on other people.

Irresponsible Sex

It is possible to have irresponsible sex, as well as anti-social sex. This is sexual activity that does not directly disrupt social or community relationships, but which does impose significant costs on other people.

Perhaps this term "irresponsible sex" sounds strange to our ears. In our post-moral age, we have come to believe that responsible sex is synonomous with successfully contracepted sex. If we use birth control, we are being responsible. If a child does result from a sexual encounter, we need only know whether the mother chooses to have the child. As long as "every child is a wanted child," we have no grounds for criticizing a woman's choice. We need not ask ourselves any other questions to evaluate a sexual act.

This is a deception. There are plenty of other ways to be irresponsible in sex. These ways have to do with the impact of our sexual activity on other people. I think most people will recognize the following cases as candidates for irresponsible sex.

A homeless couple gives birth to child after child. This family (let's assume the couple is married), has no means of supporting their children, no job, no home. But they keep on having babies. Most people would consider these people irresponsible. Probably many would argue that they should be forcibly sterilized, or otherwise compelled to cease and desist from further procreation.

Here is another case. An unmarried woman has unprotected intercourse. She becomes pregnant. She has an abortion. She repeats this process, a couple of times. By the time she is out of her childbearing years, she has had four abortions.[20] A large marjority of Americans find this behavior irresponsible. Many Americans find this revolting, and would prefer that it not be legal.

Some might argue that what both of these women need is better access to more reliable forms of birth control. But that doesn't really solve the problem. The woman having repeated abortions presumably can find out about contraception at the Planned Parenthood clinics where she has the abortions. She has a reliable form of birth control: abortion, safe, legal, but in her case not so rare. Likewise, the homeless woman can presumably learn something about contraception from the various public agencies with which she undoubtedly has contact. She could obtain either contraception or a legal abortion if she really wanted to limit her family size. For whatever reason, she chooses not to do either. In some sense, she has chosen to have each one of her children.

These two women have something important in common, despite the difference in the number of live births they produce. They have a similar attitude toward sexual behavior. They both believe that sexual activity without consequences is an entitlement. To be precise, both these hypothetical women believe they are entitled to have sex on their own terms and to bear only the consequences that they specifically choose to bear. The woman using abortion as a birth control method believes she is entitled to have sex without a live baby resulting.[21] The homeless mother of many believes she is entitled to have sex and to give birth to a baby if she chooses, regardless of the consequences for that baby and for the society around her.

In my view, these women are irresponsible in the same way. They both believe they are entitled to have what they want, regardless of the consequences for others. Choosing not to use ordinary contraception is not really the problem for either of them. As a matter of fact, the contraceptive mentality is exactly the problem. One woman believes she is entitled to the outcome that perfectly functioning contraception would provide.[22] The other woman takes very literally the old Planned Parenthood slogan, "every child a wanted child." The fact that she wants these children is necessary and sufficient justification for her to have them and to engage in the sexual activity that brought them into being. By definition, she is entitled to have as many "chosen children" as she chooses.

A Politically Incorrect Observation

Both men and women sometimes behave badly. Men are capable of using and exploiting women; women are capable of using and exploiting men. As libertarian feminist Cathy Young puts it in one of the chapter titles in her book, *Cease-Fire*, "Women are from Earth, Men are from

Earth."[23] The fact that women use men in different ways than men use women should not blind us to the fact that people of both sexes are more than capable of imposing harms on others if they think they can get away with it.

This is not a male or female problem; this is a human problem. People, male or female, are capable of reinterpreting the facts to favor their own side of a dispute. People, male or female, have a tendency to describe any situation in terms that put their own behavior in the best possible light. Most people, men and women alike, are fully capable of exaggerating the other person's offenses while minimizing their own. Both men and women are fully capable of understating the other person's contributions and overstating their own in an effort to build up their own image.

I say this because the modern women's movement has consistently emphasized the transgressions of men against women. This line of argument has helped the women's movement erect legal structures and inculcate social norms that favor the woman's side in many kinds of disputes. It stands to reason that women will take advantage of these legal structures and social norms. And some of the women who use them will push the limits of good taste, justice, and legality to get their own way. This is not a tendency unique to women, of course.

The examples I gave of irresponsible sex are exactly situations in which women have made the primary decisions. It is no good saying that all would be well with either of these women if only the men would shape up and act differently. It is the women who have chosen to have multiple abortions or multiple live births. Some women use their legal and social power in ways that are harmful to themselves and others.

In addition to the harms women can inflict on their children through irresponsible sex, women can also impose substantial costs on men. It has become so politically incorrect to treat women as anything other than victims that few people are willing to point out this possibility. But the very fact that women can, if they so choose, operate under the "cover" of the institutions created by the modern feminist movement has allowed them to take advantage of men. Women who do this create a whole string of serious negative consequences for the men they use and for the children who result from these unions.

Let us take it as a moral principle that it is always a serious wrong to use another person. It is not necessarily a criminal offense, for which one might be arrested, or a civil wrong for which one might be sued. Nonetheless, using people is wrong. No serious moral philosopher explicitly denies this principle, even though virtually every human being violates it regularly.

Let's look at a perfectly legal way in which women can use men: paternity fraud. A woman wants to have a baby. She doesn't want to have a relationship with any particular man. She has a sexual encounter with a man and doesn't tell him she is planning to have a baby. She sues him for paternity. He is required to pay child support for eighteen to twenty-one years. He may or may not be permitted to have any contact with his child.

Here is a slightly less egregious case. A woman has a relationship with a man, not a one night stand, but an actual relationship. She gets pregnant. She wants the baby; he doesn't. He tries to talk her into an abortion. She refuses. They break up. She sues him for paternity. He is required to pay. He may or may not have a relationship with the child.

Here is an even worse case. A woman has sexual relations with more than one man. She gets pregnant. She sues the richest one for paternity. Or she picks out members of the Armed Services as sex partners, because she knows their wages can so easily be garnished.[24]

Here is another. A married woman has an affaire. She gets pregnant. The baby is presumed to be her husband's child, and the birth certificate says so. The husband discovers the affaire. He insists on DNA testing. He finds he is not the father, but still has to pay child support under the presumption that he is the father of his wife's children.[25]

In these cases, the woman is using the man as a combination sperm bank and wallet. She is exploiting him to get what she wants, namely a child and financial support for that child. The feminist mantra "a woman's body, a woman's choice," rings hollow in these cases. Her body has the baby all right. But his body has to work for two decades to support the results of her choice.

All of these are cases of paternity fraud. In some cases, the man is legally required to support children who are not his own offspring. The mother has explicitly defrauded him. In other cases, the man is legally required to support his own child, but the woman has implicitly defrauded him. She tricked him into an encounter that he assumed was "safe," meaning safely contracepted.

One shocking fact about paternity frauds is that there is almost no legal penalty for the woman. If a woman tricks a man into fathering a child, the law does not consider this a fraud. If a woman knowingly sues the wrong man for child support, which is an explicit fraud, she faces almost no legal penalty. Only if the man is sophisticated enought to insist on DNA testing will he discover whether he is the father.

Sometimes the man attempts to sue the woman for paternity fraud. But as far as I can tell, winning a paternity fraud case means that the woman and the courts stop inflicting pain on him. Usually, he no longer has to pay. He is no longer at risk for being jailed for non-support. (Although in one case, an Indiana man paid child support for eleven years before he discovered the child was not his. Yet the court did not allow him to stop paying—even in the future [26]) But he is not "made whole," as the law would ordinarily require in fraud cases. I have never heard of a case in which the man recovered what the courts previously required him to pay.[27] The woman is hardly ever charged with any wrongdoing. In short, women can defraud a man, with a very low probability of facing any serious penalty.

The issue of paternity fraud creates a dilemma for the consumer-based view of sexuality. If you believe there should be a presumption that the man ought to be billed for years of child support, you are implicitly accepting the organic view of human sexuality. The argument would run something like this: Having sex always entails the possibility of pregnancy. It does not matter that he didn't fully understand that the woman intended for this particular sexual encounter to be fruitful. It is immaterial whether the man failed to give specific consent to becoming a father, whether through misunderstanding on his part or deliberate deception on her part. Men have to accept the consequences of their actions, and pregnancy is a natural consequence of having sex. By having sex, the man tacitly agreed to assume responsibility for any child that might result, regardless of the woman's explicit denials that she wants child support, or even a child at all.

On the other hand, if you have doubts about whether he should be charged with child support, the paternity fraud cases demonstrate the moral superiority of the organic view of sexuality over the consumer-based view. The man certainly did know that he and the lady had no commitment to one another that would support raising a child together. To him, perhaps, this was just another, morally indifferent sexual encounter. By taking the consumer-based approach to sexuality, this man has bought himself a lifetime of trouble.

The woman also has taken the consumer-based approach, and specifically rejected the holistic, organic view of sexuality. To her, the sexual encounter was an opportunity to get something she wanted, namely, a baby. This woman's behavior is a radical separation of sexual activity from spousal unity and love. Her sexuality results in a child, but not in any kind of deepening of love between herself and the father. Instead of being the focal point of their love and unity, as well as the result of their sexual activity, the child is the source of contention between them. Doesn't a child have a right to something better than this?

And don't the adults have a right to something better than being used? The man used the woman for sexual pleasure. The woman used the man to get a baby. They are mutually using each other, instead of mutually loving each other. They are being irresponsible in the sense that they are imposing costs on each other. The only thing they can say in their own defense is that they are mutually agreeing to be used.

We can also describe these sorts of actions as anti-social, in the sense of forestalling the community that could have been. Instead of creating a trinity of persons, united by love, the woman's actions have created a dyad out of herself and her child. And the wider community will almost surely be called upon to help her with this child. If the father does not willingly pay what she thinks she is due, the family court system will be pressed into service to make him pay. Whether he pays or not, the odds are that this unmarried mother will need additional assistance from those from around her, whether from her blood relations, friends, employers, or the state.[28] Instead of contributing, she is a net drain on the community. This "morally neutral" sexual encounter that separates spousal unity from procreation is profoundly anti-social.

Conclusion

I have tried to show that the consumer based approach to human sexuality is destructive of human relationships and genuine community. Since this is the case, it simply cannot be that people are entitled to do whatever they want. The proviso "as long as it doesn't hurt anyone else" is a proviso so seldom satisfied as to amount to a prohibition.

Next, I want to show that far from promoting morally indifferent sex, the sexual revolution has created a rigorous moral code of its own. This code imposes stringent demands upon us all, whether we willingly accept those demands or not.

Why Morally Neutral Sex Isn't

WHAT IS A MORAL CODE and what does it do for us? People ordinarily think of a moral code is an internal set of guidelines for behavior that may or may not have the binding force of law. A moral code tells us both what we ought to value and how we ought to treat other people. A moral code has both an individual dimension and a social dimension. Knowing what we ought to value is the private or individual aspect of morality. Even if we were alone on a desert island, we would need to know what we ought to consider a cost worth avoiding and a benefit worth pursuing. Once we are off the desert island and in the company of others, we need to have an idea of how to relate to those people. The social dimension of a moral code helps us by establishing what attitudes we ought to cultivate and what actions we ought to take, even if it means inconveniencing ourselves. In the previous chapter, I showed how sexual actions have an impact on others and therefore are rightly the subject of moral deliberation. In this chapter, I talk about what it means to value something.

We can interpret the idea of what we ought to value in cost-benefit terms, but probably not the kind of cost-benefit terms a utilitarian has in mind. If morality tells us what we ought to value, then part of its job is to tell us what we ought to count as a cost and and a benefit.

Defining Costs and Benefits

A utilitarian theory says simply that we ought to avoid pain and seek pleasure. This theory is incomplete because it doesn't give us any guidance in situations where pain and pleasure are ambiguous in some way. Should we avoid the pain of studying for an exam, for instance, or the pain of getting a vaccination? The utilitarian theory isn't really usable until it has something to say about what kinds of pain are worth bearing, and for what reasons.

Some people are willing to bear the cost of studying because they judge that the future benefits outweigh the immediate pain. But a calculation of this kind is by no means a sure thing. A person who has made that judgment has decided that finishing school will bring a string of desirable consequences: a better job, a better choice of mate, a better choice of places to live. Before this argument can persuade anyone to bear costs, the person already has to accept the claim that jobs, mates, and houses are good things and that having more such choices will contribute to making a person happier. A person with a terminal illness and six months to live might not stress himself to study for an exam.

Likewise, a person who decides to get a vaccination has made the judgment that the pin prick of immediate pain is worth bearing, because the long term benefits of good health outweigh the immediate pain. But it is not obvious that these conclusions are true. The person must accept the objective of prolonging life as a good thing. A clinically depressed person who didn't want to live might not bother to get a vaccination.

Making these calculations also requires some skills which are not universal. For instance, the ability to delay gratification is by no means a omnipresent skill. Likewise, the ability to look into the future and project the likely consequences of one's actions requires sophisticated cause-and-effect thinking. Impulse control, planning ahead, and delayed gratification all have to be taught and learned. Some people appear to have a greater aptitude for them than others.

These examples are not meant to be examples of explicitly moral reasoning, because there are certainly contexts in which getting a vaccination or studying for an exam could be either morally praiseworthy or morally blameworthy. These examples are meant to show only that "avoid pain and pursue pleasure" is not a fully defined guide for action, much less a fully defined moral theory. Only a genuine moral theory can fill in the blanks and tell us which pains are worth bearing in which contexts and which pleasures are worthy of pursuing.

Everyone recognizes the statement "sex outside of marriage is wrong" as a moral claim. Using the idea that a moral code tells us what to count as a cost or a benefit, we can see that the statement "sex is or ought to be morally indifferent" is also a moral claim. Both "sex is for marriage" and "sex is for fun" tell us that we should ignore certain kinds of costs and define certain kinds of things as benefits.

The Costs of Consumer Sex[1]

For instance, the students who drug themselves in order to participate in semi-anonymous, uncommitted sex are making a kind of moral statement. They are implicitly celebrating the freedom that the "hook-up" represents. They are enjoying the bodily pleasures of sex without imbuing it with any particular social significance. Their moral code tells them that these are benefits worth pursuing.

But their moral code also tells them that certain costs are worth bearing. The self-anesthetized students believe they are required to stifle the discomfort they evidently feel about their hook-ups. The embarrassment of the Walk of Shame is not supposed to count as a cost that persuades a person to change his behavior. Neither should the fear of being hurt or used dissuade a modern college student.

Feeling ignored while the other person works on his own orgasm: that's just a cost of doing sexual business. The quid pro quo is that we get to take a turn working on our own orgasm, maybe ignoring the other person in the process. That opportunity for using the other person is supposed to be good enough to cancel the bad feeling any normal person has from being used himself.

Campus sexual morality requires the students to suppress any desire to assign meaning to their sexual encounters. Having a sexual encounter with another person doesn't necessarily mean anything. "We're just friends," is the socially acceptable default posture to assume with respect to a sex partner. If I want it to mean something, if I want to really matter to the other person, then I am the problem person. There is something wrong with me and my desires. That secret feeling that I've been taken for a ride, because the whole thing mattered more to me than the other person, well, I am required to keep that a secret. The vulnerability that I feel, that is a cost I am required to bear.[2]

The morally neutral sexual morality also requires people to suppress a desire for sexual exclusivity or permanence. The person who wants exclusivity is being possessive and demanding. Jealousy, however natural it might be, is considered an almost unforgivable infraction of the modern moral code. A demand for exclusivity is an open-and-shut case of one person trying to control another, trying to limit the other's freedom. The person expressing a desire for exclusivity is the person with the problem. The unsatisfied longing to be the other person's one-and-only, to be the undisputed star of the show, is painful, but it is a pain we are required to bear. It is not socially acceptable to complain about that particular unsatisfied longing.

There is some social space for ending a relationship because you want exclusivity and the other person doesn't. But there really isn't much social space to stay in the relationship and insist on monogamy. If it really bothers you that much, you can break up. The implicit or even explicit moral statement is that the person who insists too much is the person with the problem.

The moral code of morally indifferent sex places particularly stringent demands upon young women. A modern woman is required to assign a higher place to her desire for autonomy than to her desire for connection. She is supposed to be tough enough to stand on her own two feet, without worrying about whether her partner in a one-night stand will ever call her again.

Of course, college students are hardly the only ones who have to bear these kinds of costs in the name of sexual freedom. Young adults venturing out into the business world, looking for a social life, have to play by similar rules. And if a person re-enters the dating scene after a divorce, he is likely to find the whole thing revolting, something he doesn't care to participate in.

This is not really morally indifferent sex. The students have a moral code, given to them by the authorities around them. Their universities enlist them in the sexual revolution by placing them in co-ed dorms. The students are taught about birth control and sexual harrassment. They are taught that date rape is wrong, but casual consensual sex is not. They are not taught anything about building long-lasting, loving relationships. In fact, it appears that any possible connection between sexual activity and life-long love is carefully concealed from them.[3]

The Costs of Abortion

This priority of autonomy over connectedness shows up in the rhetoric of abortion as well as around the attitudes towards sex itself. A modern woman is supposed to place a higher value on completing her education and launching her career than on giving birth to a baby and caring for it. Even adoption, ostensibly one of a woman's choices, is considered suspect. An ambitious college student or emerging career woman is almost required to abort her baby rather than bring it to term and place it for adoption.[4]

She must suppress any negative feelings she might have about having an abortion, not only before she has it, but forever afterward.

Women who regret their abortions have virtually no place to go in the modern, secularized world. No one in that world will listen to them talk about their doubts or their depression. The pro-choice morality has no place for regrets; bad feelings are not supposed to exist. A woman is required to affirm the socially accepted norm that negative feelings about her particular abortion are a price worth bearing for the sake of the more general "right to choose." If she voices her regrets, she might give aid and comfort to the pro-life enemy. So, as a practical matter, she is morally required to suppress any such feelings.[5]

If abortion were truly a matter of moral indifference, the demand for a "no regrets" posture would make no sense. People have regrets about all sorts of choices that might not have turned out the way they hoped or planned. People lament their choice of doctor, or house, or school, or car. People have disappointments about all sorts of perfectly legal, medical procedures that are truly morally indifferent. People wish they hadn't gotten a tooth pulled if they learn there might have been a way to save the tooth. People rue their choices about medications, doctors, health care plans, hospitals, x-rays and just about anything else you could name. So why isn't a woman allowed to express any misgivings about having an abortion?

Some might reply that this problem would disappear if only the pro-lifers and their rhetoric would disappear. If the whole society finally accepted that the choice to have an abortion is no more a moral decision than the choice of ice cream flavors, voicing regrets would have no potential fallout. The lifetime blackout on any grief from any woman is necessary only because the right to choose abortion is so politically precarious.

This argument doesn't hold up under examination. People don't ordinarily suppress all complaints about an issue just because there is an element of political contentiousness about it. People gripe about unexpected side effects of medications. Nobody assumes that these complaints are a cover for a ban on anything but all-natural remedies, even though there are ideologues who are committed to exactly that outcome. People complain about their doctors and HMOs all the time. But no one assumes that every grievance is a surreptitious attempt to socialize the health care system. The health care establishment does not try to censor all criticism of its work.

There is something uniquely powerful about the rhetoric of abortion that indicates that there really is a pro-abortion morality at work. Women are supposed to be so grateful for their right to choose, and so grateful to the people who made that choice possible, that they will suffer in silence and never complain.

One therapist has recounted the power of pro-abortion morality in *The Forbidden Grief*.[6] Theresa Burke did not begin her career intending to do abortion recovery counseling. But she kept stumbling over issues of post-abortion trauma.

Her eyes were opened when she was facilitating a group of women with eating disorders. One of the women mentioned that she had had an abortion. Other women in the group had visceral, negative reactions. One of them yelled at her. One of them ran out of the room crying. Another tried to change the subject to a non-threatening topic: "Do you like my new sweater?"

Over the next few sessions, the therapist discovered that six out of the eight women in this group had had abortions. The group had been assembled around eating disorders, not around abortion or anything to do with sex. Yet six of the eight had this experience in common. Burke thought the issue was worth exploring. However, when she brought it up with her supervisor in the professional group with which she was affiliated at the time, he did more than dismiss the idea. He positively forbade her to bring it up with the group. He asserted, without proof, that the two were purely coincidental and had no causal relation.[7]

This is not a morally neutral position. Post-abortive women have a moral code, given to them by their elders, their doctors, their therapists, the media, and perhaps even their spiritual advisers. Women are taught to suppress any negative feelings about abortion. Therapists are required to deny any evidence of a connection between the experience of having an abortion, and eating disorders, depression, drug abuse, or suicide.[8] When such evidence emerges, it must be squelched or explained away. The government requires the medical profession to give warnings about virtually every medication or procedure. But there are no comparable warnings about the possible side effects and complications associated with abortion.

Waiting Periods for Abortion

The tacit moral code of the sexual revolution sometimes shows up in very specific policy controversies. For instance, some states have attempted to legislate mandatory waiting periods between the time a woman first presents herself at a clinic for an abortion and the time the abortion takes place. Waiting periods do not prohibit any abortions. If the woman still wants an abortion after the three-day waiting period, she can obtain it. The courts have frequently held these requirements to be unconstitutional infringements on a woman's right to choose.[9]

By contrast, many states impinge on people's "right to choose" major appliances by mandating "cooling off" periods after signing a purchase agreement. Consumers in these situations have the right to terminate the contract during, for example, the first three days after signing the agreement. These requirements do not prohibit any contracts: they simply define the limits within which contracts may be made. Any experienced adult can imagine a situation in which a consumer might feel bullied into buying a refrigerator or other consumer durable good. Allowing people to step back from a high-pressure salesman might be inconvenient for the salesman, but it creates an environment in which consumers can make more reasonable assessments of the costs and benefits of the purchase they propose to make.

The judicially-imposed prohibition on waiting periods for abortion are tacit statements that these common-sense consumer protections are unnecessary for the purchasers of abortion services. Is it really inconceivable that providers of abortion services might overstate the benefits and understate the harms associated with their product, that a woman might feel bullied by the clinic, or by her boyfriend? But the law allows no provision for this possibility. If it is reasonable to suppose that someone might change her mind about buying a car, surely it is equally reasonable to suppose that the same person might have second thoughts about an abortion.

One might respond that cooling-off periods differ from mandatory waiting periods because they are optional, not mandatory. The law does not require a buyer to wait three days after her encounter with the salesman before buying the product. She can take possession of the car or refrigerator immediately if she chooses. The law simply allows her a period within which she can change her mind, subject, of course, to the proviso that she not damage the product while it is in her possession.

It is true that the waiting period laws provide for a mandatory, not optional, delay before procuring an abortion. But they serve a similar function for a service that is ultimately irrevocable. If a woman changes her mind three days after an abortion, she can't go back to the clinic and demand her baby back. She cannot take the clinic or doctor to court and receive restitution that would make her "whole," that is, restore her to the condition she was in before she purchased the service. The waiting period offers a woman some time to rethink her decision and perhaps obtain further information. A mandatory waiting period is a reasonable adaptation of existing consumer product protections to the unique characteristics of the abortion service.

And make no mistake: some women do experience regrets about their abortions—sometimes, instant regrets: "When it was over, I was led into the 'recovery room.' I ended up sitting next to the same women I had been with when we were all still pregnant. Nobody was happy. A great heaviness hung over all of us. As we talked, between the tears, I made the remark that I was about 12 weeks pregnant. The woman next to me looked at me and said, 'You were. . . .' That's when it really hit me. My baby was gone . . . forever.[10]

Waiting periods for abortion would appear to be a minor inconvenience for both the pregnant woman and the abortion provider. But the abortion lobby has worked hard to have these provisions ruled unconstitutional. The activists argue that women who live in rural areas might have to make more than one long, expensive trip to a distant abortion provider. But that objection hardly applies to the vast majority of the population who live in metropolitan areas.

The fact that waiting periods could easily be construed as something that enhances the woman's decision-making process suggests that "choice" is not really the abortion lobby's ultimate objective. The courts that hand down these rulings and the activists who agitate for them are making a tacit set of moral judgments, quite apart from any judgment about when life begins, and about what legal protections ought to apply to the life in the womb. These are judgments about the likelihood of having to bear certain costs, judgments about the likely extent of those costs, judgments about whether those costs should be thought worth bearing by members of the society as a whole.

The consumer of abortion services must bear all the risk of a mistaken decision, because the cost of mistakenly having an abortion is judged to be so low that it can be safely neglected. The law tacitly judges that the inconvenience of waiting three days is a greater cost than reducing the number of abortions that women later regret. The implication is that any sensible woman would want an abortion with as little delay as possible.

Society is willing to inconvenience car dealers in order to prevent people from bearing the costs of buying a car they couldn't really afford or didn't really want. But the costs associated with a poor choice of car are all reversible. The person can resell the car to someone else or sue the car dealer if it is defective. If worse comes to worst, the disgruntled consumer still has the use of a perfectly functional car he just didn't really want as much as he thought he did. The cooling-off period is a social statement that we are willing to help people avoid those kinds of costs and that if necessary car salesmen can take a few lumps.

We are constantly told by pro-abortion radicals that women seek abortion out of desperation. Any and all abortions should be permitted because of the extreme vulnerability of the woman with an unwanted pregnancy. If this is true, women considering abortions are far more vulnerable than the average purchaser of a car.

Our unwillingness to provide both groups with comparable safeguards is not a morally neutral position. It is not a pro-woman policy. It is a statement that abortion is a positive good, with negligible negative consequences. It is a pro-abortion policy. There is a vigorous, if tacit, pro-abortion morality in the background of this policy. The "pro-choice" fundamentalists insist on imposing their moral code on everyone, without even acknowledging that an ethical code is at work.

The Cost of Careerism

In addition to the costs associated with consumer sex, there is also a set of costs associated with the careerism that is often allied with it. In other words, part of the whole lifestyle revolution is the entry of women into more intensely demanding careers. Virtually everyone applauds the entry of women into jobs with higher status and income. Most people also realize that there are costs attached to these career advancements. Some of the costs, education, hard work, discipline and focus, are common to men and to women. But some of the costs fall with particular force upon women. There is a whole set of costs associated with delayed childbearing. These costs include a smaller number of children, the possibility of missing out on marriage, and the possibility of infertility. Women are supposed to bear those costs without complaining.

Sex without Guilt

There is another kind of cost that might be associated with sexual activity: the cost of a guilty conscience. The idea that sex can be morally indifferent or morally neutral offers the prospect of engaging in any kind of sex, in any amount, in any context, without guilt. Not having enough fun is the only thing I should be troubled about. My desire for commitment from my partner is the feeling I ought to purge from my psyche. But all of my sexual arousal, all of my sexual actions, all forms of sexual desire, are intrinsically worthy and no cause for shame. The sexual revolution promises a life without guilt. I believe this is the single most appealing feature of the sexual revolution.

Seeing that sex without guilt is the ultimate objective of the revolution in sexual attitudes helps us see why the purely libertarian objective of being left alone by the state has been both elusive and politically unstable. Libertarians want to be left alone, but they don't expect any special treatment from the state; in fact, they abhor the very idea of state privilege. This combination of views has allowed libertarians to make alliances with people whose overall political philosophies are quite hostile to their own. Libertarians differ from the genuine sexual radicals, who have never been satisfied by a policy of simply being legally permitted to do whatever they want.

The libertarian is happy to give up politics after the victimless crime of his choice has been legalized. When legal prohibitions against sodomy, or abortion, or cohabitation are repealed, libertarians are satisfied. They go home to enjoy their private pleasures, knowing full well that many of their neighbors disapprove of certain aspects of their conduct. The libertarian does not demand acceptance or approbation from others. Nor does the libertarian insist upon being protected from discrimination, disagreement, or even rude comments. Live and let live, we always say. I have a right to be a slut; you have a right to be a jerk. I'm a grown-up. I'll get over it. Or, if you're really a jerk, I won't even have to get over it, because I can easily dismiss you and your obnoxious behavior.

Not so for the genuine sexual revolutionary. "Live and let live" has never been good enough. If the goal is guilt-free sex, then mere legality of an activity is not and never will be sufficient. Anyone who voices moral objections has to be silenced.[11] For that person's ideas and arguments might influence others and cause them distress about their actions. That distress might cause them to feel guilty about what they are doing. They might decide that, on balance, they don't want to do this anymore. They might have to reform their behavior.[12]

Hostility to the Opposition

The desire for sex without guilt can help to account for the intense hostility in many quarters to the Catholic Church.[13] Although this is an aside to the main issue, it is an interesting political observation. If a person takes a completely objective perspective, the attacks on the credibility and reputation of the Catholic Church seem to be out of proportion to any actual threat it poses to anyone's freedom. The Catholic Church is not the only religious option in the United States. There are literally hundreds of churches and sources of spirituality. Some of them teach odd things. But very few generate the hostility that the Catholic Church does. Why should this be?

There is no established church in America, and if there were it would not be, and would never have been, the Catholic Church. The Catholic church in America has no political authority. There is no Catholic political party. The Catholic Church's opinion is not legally binding on anyone; it is only morally binding on those who voluntarily associate themselves with the Catholic Church: its own members. All the Church can do is voice moral objections to certain kinds of behavior. Anyone who disagrees with Catholic moral teaching is free to cover his ears, or walk down the street to another church he finds more congenial. The Catholic Church can not "impose its morality" on anyone in America.

But for some radicals, the very existence of the Catholic Church is an affront. This voice must be silenced if possible, or discredited at least. One group of homosexual activists essentially demanded to receive Communion at the National Shrine of the Immaculate Conception. When they were refused, they went to a nearby hotel, where the Conference of Catholic bishops were holding their annual meeting. They stood with their hands out, waiting for someone to give them Communion. When they refused repeated requests to leave, both from the hotel and from police, they were arrested for trespassing.[14]

When they went to court, the judge might have thrown them out, saying something like this, "Grown up people do not go around the world demanding unlimited approbation from every person they meet. The Catholic Church did not seek you out in order to harrass you. You went looking for trouble and you found it. You are free to join any church you find congenial. You are not entitled to harass other people's worship. Grow up."

But the judge didn't say that. She gave them a handslap, and took the opportunity, from the bench, to deride the Catholic Church for its teachings on homosexuality. "Tremendous violence was done to you . . . when the Body of Christ was denied to you," the judge said.

Their claim to be "emotionally shattered by the refusal of Communion," rings hollow. As does their claim that they went to the hotel to "find healing among the people who caused me so much suffering," considering that a gay activist group had informed the Church in advance that protesters would be attempting to receive Communion. "Prosecutors said the three, members of the gay activist group Soulforce, carefully choreographed a protest in the hotel, where they knew a crowd of reporters was there to cover the bishops conference." No serious person can believe that the self-esteem of these men was harmed by a bit of guerilla theater that they themselves staged.

The hysterical assaults on the Catholic Church do not make sense unless we understand that the objective is guilt-free sex. The Church will never agree to the proposition that every person is entitled to sex without guilt or consequence at all times. Even when high-ranking members of the Church heirarchy violate the Church's standards of morality, the Church does not change its teaching in order to protect their egos.

Most of the rest of the world is busily redefining virtually every sexual act as non-sinful. There is even a move afoot to normalize pedophilia.[15] There is a movement to celebrate polyamory, those who object to any social privileging of monogamy, even serial monogamy, much less lifetime monogamy.[16] Even other religious bodies are rewriting the ancient moral law of Christianity in order to prevent their members and potential members from feeling guilt.

For anyone who needs a world in which there is no sin, the voice of the Catholic Church is a voice that must be silenced or discredited.

Cohabitation without Cost

The libertarian view of cohabitation is that I am entitled to live with a man to whom I am not married. The state has no right to prohibit my lifestyle of consensual cohabitation. The sexual revolutionary goes a step further: I am entitled to be treated as if I were married, simply because that's how I want to be treated.

There is a movement to remove all remaining social and even legal stigma from cohabitation. In 1997, the Canadian parliament commissioned a group to study the institution of marriage. The commission's report, *Beyond Conjugality*, presented to parliament in 2000, recommends that judges concentrate on whether the individuals before them are "functionally interdependent," regardless of their actual marital status. That same year, in the United States, the influential American Law Institute published a report, *Principles of the Law of Family Dissolution*, which likewise suggested that judges disregard the distinction between married couples and long-time cohabiting couples.[17]

If one considers only the facts of the law, these recommendations don't make sense. If a couple would like to have the legal advantages of marriage, they should get married and accept the legal responsibilities associated with marriage. This suggests that something other than law is really the point of the more radical moves to blur the lines between marriage and non-marriage.

The point is to allow people flexibility in their living arrangements without any penalty. The flexible living arrangment amounts to this: I wish to see myself as subversive and avant garde, so I refuse to get married as a matter of moral principle. However, when things go sour and the relationship fails, I insist that the law protect my interests, interests that I knowingly and willingly sacrificed on the altar of my image of myself as being ever-so-beyond the need of such a retro institution as marriage.[18] The point of these proposed legal changes is to allow people a bit of bravado and self-deception without penalty. Sex without commitment; sex without responsibility; sex without guilt.

The subtext of the radical agenda is that American, capitalist, bougeois society is a foul thing against which any self-respecting person would want to rebel. The law stigmatizes and penalizes deviant behavior but is not really providing rules that offer reasonable protection of society against socially disruptive behavior. The law is a power grab, pure and simple: the deviants are the true heroes of society. Being deviant is a moral adventure that the law ought to protect. Sexual deviance has the twin advantages of being both socially subversive and a whole lot of fun.[19]

Whatever one might think of this set of propositions, we can safely say this: these are not recognizable as libertarian positions. There is no necessary connection at all between the posture of "deviant" and the building of a society of free and responsible individuals. Permitting and celebrating every kind of "different" behavior does not necessarily result in smaller, less instrusive government. Some social norms allow a smaller government to emerge, while other social norms will hasten the demand for an ever larger political and government sector. Deviance in the defense of liberty is no virtue.

I've just described the posture of the genuine revolutionary who savors his or her self-image as Cultural Rebel. For the average cohabitant, however, the point of cohabitation is probably quite a bit more mundane. Most reasonably normal people who cohabit have more or less glided into living together. They have been told repeatedly that marriage is "just a piece of paper." As Barbara Dafoe Whitehead reports, though, many cohabiting women go on faintly clinging to the hope that they will one day acquire that little document that is supposed to be so insubstantial. These women see moving in together as a step toward marriage. And the men view living together as an alternative to an actual decision to commit themselves.[20]

Radicals might reply that these poor innocent souls are the object of the proposed redefinition of law. These accidental cohabitants aren't really subversive; they didn't take a principled stand against the hegemony of matrimony. When their relationships break up, they are entitled to protection and assistance from the state.

These people may very well be victims, but they are not victims of the state or of an irrational prejudice in favor of matrimony. They are victims of the continually repeated claim that marriage is nothing but a piece of paper that truly committed, loving couples don't need. They are victims of the concerted cover-up of the costs of cohabitation. Offering them the protection of law, a protection they could readily have obtained by getting married, simply continues the radical strategy of deliberately blurring the boundary between lifelong monogamy and other sexual relationships. It is not fair for the radicals to blame the state, or social norms, for a confusion that they themselves willfully created.

Even before we reached this radical redefinition of law, the anti-discrimination laws had been pressed into service to protect cohabiting couples from some kinds of disapprobation. For instance, cohabiting couples are entitled to rent any property they wish and can afford. No landlord may discriminate on the basis on my marital status. I am protected from having to answer any questions, or to listen to anything negative they might have to say about my living arrangements. The fact that the landlord owns the property does not give him the right to exercise his own ethical principles in deciding who can live there. In effect, I am protected from having to offer an account of myself to my potential landlord.[21]

Needless to say, libertarians would not endorse this application of anti-discrimination laws. Libertarians are happy with a situation in which no one arrests them for their living arrangements. Libertarians don't demand that every landlord grit his teeth and smile at them as he gives them the keys. Private property, according to libertarians, is a powerful tool for enforcing widely held social norms. If you can't find a property owner willing to rent you an apartment, that's your problem, not the problem of the law, or of society at large.

Abortion without Guilt

Likewise, the abortion issue reveals the cleavage between political libertarians and sexual revolutionaries. Libertarians differ among themselves about the morality of abortion. For libertarians, as for the vast majority of Americans, the dispute hinges on their views of when life begins and when the law should protect a new life. But mere legal permissibility was never sufficient for the radical abortion rights advocates.

The radical position is more than being legally entitled to procure an abortion. The activists have worked to make abortion free, not only of financial costs, but also of psychic costs. I am entitled not to listen to any possible moral reservations about abortion. Here are some examples of outrageous regulations that would be defeated if proposed for virtually any other area of public life.

Many doctors don't like performing abortions; so a relatively small number of doctors perform a relatively large proportion of the abortions in this country. The activists find this alarming. So they have worked to improve "access" to a service that few doctors voluntarily provide. For instance, some states now legally require all ob-gyns to take training in abortion, even if they have no intention of ever performing any.[22]

Many rural communities are served only by religious hospitals. Their religious convictions against performing abortions are now seen as socially suspect, and possibly illegal. Catholic non-profit hospitals provide a significant percentage of health care in some areas, and these hospitals bind themselves to operate in accordance with Catholic teaching. They do not offer abortion, sterilization, or contraceptive services. A California law passed in 2003 significantly curtails the ability of these hospitals to sell their own property. The law prohibits the state attorney general, who approves the sale of Church-owned and non-profit health care facilities, from consenting to an agreement if the seller restricts the type or level of medical services the buyer can provide. It thus prevents Catholic hospitals from requiring their buyers to follow directives that forbid procedures counter to Catholic teaching.[23]

The radical pro-abortion advocates have attempted to curtail the free speech rights of sidewalk abortion counselors, claiming that all such people are necessarily threatening and potentially violent. In all these areas, the libertarian position of abortion without legal penalty was politically overridden by the social revolutionary position of abortion without guilt.

For some workers at abortion clinics, helping their clients avoid guilt is a higher priority than helping them deal with any negative feelings that can sometimes result from an abortion. Theresa Burke reports that she was once approached by an abortion clinic counselor who recognized that some of her clients needed help coping with the aftermath of their abortions. The counselor had heard that Burke ran groups for abortion recovery. But the clinic counselor demanded to know whether Burke was pro-life or pro-choice. Burke replied that she was a therapist who helped women deal with their feelings. "Well, we have some women who may need some help . . . but we can't send them to you if you're going to make them feel guilty." Burke reiterated that the only women who came to her were those who sought her help because of their own conflicted feelings. This answer was almost incomprehensible to the woman on the other end of the phone. She never did refer the women to Burke's practice.[24]

Some abortion clinic workers have unresolved issues from their own abortions. One such worker later admitted as much in the process of working through her own abortion: "I was completely driven to help other women obtain abortions. I was totally invested in keeping abortion safe and legal. I never recognized how pushy and one-sided my counseling was until I became pregnant and wanted a child. Everyone around me was so critical of my own pregnancy. I realized then that I had been the same way toward every pregnant woman who entered our clinic. It's almost like we needed them to abort so that we could feel better about our own abortions. I was too busy justifying what I had done to be aware that I carried any grief about it."[25] The desire to protect the self from feeling shame and guilt it is a powerful a part of the human psyche. Guilt-induced pressure from abortion clinic workers may be more prevalent than is commonly known.

Parental Notification for Abortion

One of the most dramatic illustrations of the distinction between the libertarian and libertine positions is in their attitudes toward a legal requirement that parents be notified before their minor daughters procure an abortion. Several states have crafted laws that require parents to be notified of, without requiring their consent for, their daughter's abortion.[26]

The only libertarian who could object to such a requirement would be a radical advocate of children's rights. This position holds that children should be completely emancipated from their parents, except for a requirement that the parents provide for their physical necessities. In all my adult lifetime as a libertarian, I have only encountered a handful of people who actually hold such views.[27] Yet the mainstream of the abortion lobby completely rejects parental notification requirements. I need not add that pro-choice advocates are typically not ideologically pure libertarians.

There are only two coherent explanations for the abortion lobby's absolutist position against parental notification laws. One possibility is an economic explanation. A set of legal rules that allows secret abortions for any girl, no matter how young, increases the number of abortions performed. It is easy to understand why a chain of abortion clinics might want such rules. Planned Parenthood sells abortion services, and they want the demand for their services to be as high as possible. They want the costs associated with getting an abortion (other than their fees) to be as low as possible.

It is the second possibility that interests me here: the desire for sex without guilt that is at the heart of so much of the sexual revolution. Abortion rights activists oppose parental notification laws because such laws will expose young, sexually active girls to the disapproval of their parents. The prospect of this disapproval, in turn, might induce young girls to avoid abortion, or to avoid sexual activity altogether.

It is easy to imagine a pregnant teen being embarrassed about her parents finding out. She probably wants the whole situation to just go away. She wants everything to be the way it was before she got pregnant. In her immaturity and fear, she imagines that an abortion will restore her life to normal. A secret abortion helps her preserve the illusion that nothing ever happened.

The last line of pro-abortion argument is that she might be afraid of abuse by her parents. She might fear that her parents would beat her up if they knew she was pregnant. But the child abuse argument is a red herring, a strategic changing of the subject. If a clinic worker or guidance counselor or teacher has serious reason to believe that a pregnant girl's parents would assault her, that girl needs more than a confidential abortion. Those adults should call Child Protective Services as part of their responsibility as mandatory reporters of suspected child abuse. This particular pregnant minor should be in protective custody.[28]

The truth is that there are probably very few pregnant girls in imminent danger of assault by their parents. Surely the most common reaction of parents is to scream and cry and yell and be really upset. That's unpleasant for any teenager. The thought of avoiding that confrontation might make a secret abortion seem appealing. But not every unpleasantness is an act of child abuse. The constitutional right to choose does not require the states to protect an underaged girl from anything potentially disagreeable that might be associated with that choice.

The abortion lobby seems to think it is desirable for even a very young girl to abort without any adult influence. But honestly, if a four-teen-year-old girl babysits for your family, you walk her home. If your thirteen-year-old has to go to the orthodontist, you take her and wait for her in the waiting room. We wouldn't send a sixteen-year-old to buy a car or a seventeen-year-old to choose a college without any adult guidance. Yet, under the guise of protecting her autonomy, the abortion lobby wants to let her go through the decision to abort, the abortion itself, and all its aftermath, completely on her own, with no support from the people who love her. This is not respectful; this is abandoning a young girl at one of the most vulnerable moments of her life.

This is not a morally neutral position. It is a statement that in-dividual autonomy is a value so great that it overrides the value of parental involvement and family solidarity in a crisis. It is a statement that the value of terminating a young girl's pregnancy is so great that it outweighs any benefit she might potentially receive from parental involvement.

The absolutist position against parental notification also has em-bedded within it a set of empirical claims that are potentially refutable or verifiable. This position says that the potential harms from having a secret abortion are so minimal that they can safely be disregarded. The harms might include a sense of social isolation, a reluctance of the girl to seek help after the abortion if she experiences complications, or an erosion of whatever trust existed in the family.

The extreme pro-privacy position says that the law can safely assume that the average parents are more likely to be abusive than helpful to their underaged pregnant daughter. The absolutist position tacitly assumes that the only girls who would have a secret abortion are those in imminent danger of child abuse. No teenage girl with a good relationship with her parents would be tempted to have a secret abortion. It is an empirical matter whether the law provides a significant temptation to a pregnant teen to avoid an encounter with her parents that might, in fact, be in her ultimate interest. The opponents of parental notification evidently cannot imagine that a girl would avoid telling her parents, not out of fear of abuse, but out of fear of embarrassment.

Statutory Rape and Rape with Adjectives

This absolutist position against parental notification may have even more serious negative consequences. The over-zealous concern for a minor's privacy may result in preventing police notification of child sexual abuse. Health care personnel are ordinarily mandatory reporters of child abuse, but a recent survey has prompted the question of whether abortion clinics take this responsibility seriously. A woman called Planned Parenthood Clinics across the country and told them she was thirteen and pregnant by her twenty-two-year-old boyfriend. The overwhelming majority of the clinics told her she could come in for an abortion with complete confidentiality; they would not report her boyfriend for statuatory rape.[29]

Abortion rights advocates attacked every feature of the survey. It was dishonest. The caller was an actress, not truly a thirteen-year-old in distress. The survey was sponsored by a pro-life organization they considered sleazy and disreputable. No one in their right mind would expect the person answering the telephone to do the kind of crisis intervention necessary to handle the case suggested by the caller.

But even if every one of these objections is well-grounded, they miss the question: Do abortion clinics have the same responsibility to report possible child abuse as other health care workers, therapists, and teachers? In part because of the publicity given this nationwide survey, officials in Los Angeles County asked California's attorney general to clarify the state's policy regarding the reporting of suspected statuatory rape.[30]

The abortion lobby contends that a "woman's right to choose" requires complete confidentiality. But the issue here isn't what an underaged girl is going to do about this pregnancy. The issue is whether the State of California should, as a matter of public policy, assume she has "chosen" this particular sexual relationship in any meaningful sense.

If a fourteen-year-old comes to a clinic, maybe the father of child is the boy next door, a nice kid her own age. But then again, maybe not. According to the Alan Guttmacher Institute, the research arm of Planned Parenthood, seven in ten of girls who had sex before age thirteen reported that their first sexual experience was unwanted or non-voluntary. Further, among fifteen- to seventeen-year-old sexually active "women," 29 percent have partners who are three to five years older and 7 percent have partners over six years older. Surely there is some age at which the duty to protect the young outweighs the "woman's" right to privacy.[31]

The abortion lobby fears that the child abuse reporting requirement would become a de facto parental notification requirement. According to the same Alan Guttmacher report cited earlier, almost 40 percent of minors who have abortions do so without their parents' knowledge. A requirement to report suspected child abuse would almost certainly lead to parents' knowledge of the pregnancy. Abortion proponents contend that a requirement for parental notification, even without a requirement for parental consent, is an unacceptable and unconstitutional infringement on "a woman's right to choose." But surely there is some girl young enough that abortion providers should at least ask her about the age of her partner.

The desire for everyone to have sex without guilt, shame, or embarrassment is the only logical explanation for an absolutist position of this kind. Each and every objection to parental notification can be addressed if we are serious about protecting young girls from sexual predators. Unwanted pregnancy may be the result of unwanted sexual activity. Those who perpetrate rape, including statutory rape, should be prosecuted to the fullest extent of the law. Yet, in the name of protecting a "woman's" right to choose an abortion, the abortion lobby has lobbied to change the interpretation of the laws to protect a young girl from having to inform her parents or guardians. These are the people most likely to protect her. This combination of policies doesn't protect the girl; it protects the rapist.

The policy of abortion without parental notification is part of a policy of abortion with no questions asked. Ironically, this general "no questions" policy doesn't protect young girls who actually are being sexually abused by family members. A victim of incest is shrouded in a family system of secrecy. When a girl becomes pregnant through incest, that can be an opportunity for her to escape a destructive family situation. Her pregnancy is a visible sign that she is sexually active and may propel her to seek some sort of medical attention outside the family.

But a health care policy of not asking any questions of any girl, no matter how young, thwarts her opportunity to get help. The perpetrator or enabling family members are frequently the ones who pressure the girl into having an abortion. They may make all the arrangements, without even telling the girl what the "operation" is all about. They may be the ones who take her to the clinic. Sometimes, women who were incest victims as girls testify long after the fact that none of the health care personnel even asked them who the father of the child was.[32]

A moral code tells us what kinds of costs are worth bearing for the sake of a higher end. In this case, the abortion lobby is telling us very plainly what costs we should be willing to bear for the sake of a "woman's right to choose." We should be willing to accept the costs of young girls being sexually victimized, rather than ask her any questions or require any adult input.

Conclusion

Admitting that sex in some contexts is better and more praiseworthy than others opens us up to the possibility of feeling guilty. If we embrace the idea that the question of when and how to have sex is intrinsically a moral question, we will have to be accountable to ourselves for how we live up to that standard. If we fall short, we're going to feel guilty. Feeling guilty certainly counts as a cost. How can we be sure that a cost of that magnitude is really worth bearing? How in fact do we bear it, especially if we have a history of doing things we have secretly known all along were wrong?

The sexual revolutionaries seemed to believe that it is possible to create a world in which there are no costs, only benefits. I don't believe such a thing is possible. Nor do I think it would be desirable. No one is, or can be, perfect. Everyone will, from time to time, do things that are wrong, and which he knows in his heart of hearts are wrong. Feeling bad about doing wrong is a good thing: it helps steer us away from behavior that we really ought to steer clear of. Guilty feelings connect us to the universal human experience of imperfection. Shame has the potential to help us connect with others in their imperfection, as well as the potential to help us improve our behavior.

The alternative to feeling shame some of the time is not to feel unalloyed self-esteem at all times. The alternative is to be shameless, and to behave shamelessly, at least some of the time. The alternative to acknowledging that you have done wrong is not that you will never in fact be wrong. The alternative is to be wrong some of the time, yet be absolutely committed to never admitting it. This is not a recipe for happiness inside a family or within a society. Life without guilt or shame is neither possible nor desirable.

That shame and embarrassment you feel about casual sexual encounters? Go ahead and count it as a cost. Your body is trying to tell you something. Allow that embarrassment to be enough of a cost to deter you from casual sex.

That desire for permanence? Don't count that as a cost; you needn't be ashamed of it. The desire for life-long love is a good thing.

The desire to have a child and take care of it? That is a wholesome desire, not a bad thing, not a cost a woman should suppress for the sake of her career. The longing to nurture a child is one of the primary sources of social glue that hold society together.

So give up the idea of life without guilt. In the last part of this book, I will propose an alternative set of things to consider costs and benefits. The alternative to consumer sex is self-giving love.

PART III

SELF-GIVING,
RIGHTLY UNDERSTOOD

Self-Giving, Rightly Understood

NOW THAT I HAVE TAKEN APART the whole modern sexual edifice, what's the alternative? The alternative to consumer based sex is natural, organic sex. But behind each of these two different approaches to sex there lie entire theories of the human condition. These competing theories all have something to say about what will make us happy, what we ought to do and not do, and, as I showed in the previous chapter, what we ought to count as a cost and pursue as a benefit. I maintain that the organic, natural approach to human sexuality works better than consumer sex because it is based more deeply on the reality of the human condition. You and your spouse are going to be in a much stronger position in your efforts to build and sustain lifelong love if you work with the natural, organic concept of sexuality and the whole theory of the human condition that goes along with it.

In a way, I am sorry to have to put you through this exercise. You might not have any particular interest in political philosophy or in economic theory. (I've lost track of the number of people who have told me how much they hated economics.) Perhaps you would have prefered a plain-vanilla self-help book with a list of bullet points explaining how to keep your marriage alive. But in order to construct any useful list of specific things to do and not do, I think it is necessary to dissect the bad ideas we've been working with and replace them with some better ideas. Here is the logic of what I am going to do in Part III, and how it leads up to you and your spouse.

What is a more reliable way to pursue happiness? Self-giving, rightly understood. What do I mean by "self-giving?" I mean the sincere donation of self to another person. It can be a complete giving, as in married love, or a partial gift, as in friendship or parenthood. What do I mean by "rightly understood?" Self-giving has to be placed in its proper context. There is a time and place for giving the self, and a time and place for protecting or withholding the self.

Why is this a more reliable way to pursue happiness than self-interest? Self-giving is more in tune with deeper truths about the human condition than is the pure self-interest approach. Human beings need love, to give and receive love. People need and want to contribute to others and to ideals larger than themselves. These particular preferences deserve special attention, rather than being treated as a special case of generic preferences that people satisfy in the process of pursuing self-interest.

Isn't it risky to give myself to others? It sounds as if I might be consumed or used up. It sounds as if my autonomy and individuality could be threatened. Even the very foundations of a free society could be at risk if too many people allow their autonomy to be consumed by self-giving. I believe, on the contrary, that self-giving provides a more secure foundation for defending a free society than the self-interested approach more commonly used.

Why should the ordinary reader care about the difference between self-giving and self-interest? Because each theory directs us to cultivate some attitudes and actions, and avoid other kinds of attitudes and actions. Self-interest tells us to ask, "what's in it for me?" Self-giving tells us to ask, "how can I help?" One theory has a far higher likelihood of producing a happy marriage than the other.

And that is why you should care.

⁊ 7 ⁋

The Law of the Gift

THE RADICAL ALTERNATIVE TO CONSUMER SEX is natural, organic sex. Behind that pair of alternatives is a pair of competing views about how to pursue happiness. One approach says that we can, and should, pursue our self-interest. The alternative says that we most successfully pursue happiness by being in relationship with others. We find our true happiness by giving ourselves to others, and being able to receive others as gifts to us.

This is the Law of the Gift: we find our greatest happiness not in isolation, but in seeing ourselves, and others, as gifts. Our best opportunity for human flourishing is not in looking out for Number One, but in the generous gift of self to others. A genuinely human existence is always coexistence, a meeting with others wisely.[1]

The Law of the Gift has two parts. First, our lives are gifts to us. This has implications both for how I see myself and for how I see other people. My own life is a gift to me. Other people's lives are gifts to themselves and ultimately to me as well. An immediate corollary to this is that it is always a serious wrong to use another person. Second, we find our deepest happiness when we give ourselves to others and when we are receptive to the gifts of others. In other words, a life without self-giving love would not be a truly happy or satisfying life, no matter how many other accomplishments, achievements, or possessions the person might accumulate.

The gift approach begins with the person in quite a different situation from the autonomous, choosing self. Instead of an initial presumption that each individual is a rational agent endowed with rights and a presumption of freedom, start with the idea that each human life is a gift. Our capacities, including our capacity for rational thought and choice, are also gifts.

I am fully aware that the "self-interest" perspective can be expanded to accommodate love, charity, and many other aspects of the human experience that are not narrowly self-interested. As a matter of fact, this is one of the things the "rightly understood" qualifier is supposed to encompass for the concept of self-interest. Allowing self-interest to include these other-regarding considerations is one of the ways rational-choice theorists rescue their theory from the charge that they are assuming and encouraging ordinary selfishness. Any reasonably sophisticated account of self-interest has to have some scope for relationships and altruism.

Nonetheless, I believe for questions concerning sexuality, marriage, and the family, the Law of the Gift is a more fruitful starting point than the so-called *homo economicus*. Human sexuality is fundamentally about the mutual gift of self of the partners. In the area of human sexuality, the best and most reliable way to pursue our happiness is to give ourselves completely to our sexual partners. If we start from self-interest, concern for the other person is added after the fact. We have to redefine our desire to please another person as a variety of self-regard.

But this is taking the long way around. Why start from self-interest and redefine self-interest to accomodate love, when we could just start with love? When the content of the preferences is doing as much work as "the preference for self-giving" or "the preference for love" or "the preference for altruism," those preferences deserve attention on their own merits.

The Law of the Gift is True

Our lives are gifts. When I say that our lives are gifts to us, I mean to include more than the mere fact that we exist. I also include all the contingent facts, those features of our lives and situations that might have been other than they are. Each of us was born in a particular time and place, to particular parents, in a particular social class. We are all embedded within a society, the small society of the family, as well as the larger social, cultural, and political society that surrounds the family.

I was born in the twentieth century, in the United States of America, to Catholic working-class parents, the third of six children. I could have been the only child of fabuously wealthy parents. I could have been born to homeless drug addicts, or placed in an orphanage immediately after birth. I could have been born in the nineteenth century, in England or in Poland. I could have been a princess or a serf. I could have been born a little boy, instead of a little girl. I did not "deserve" or "earn" these most basic facts of my birth.

In addition to these social facts, each of us was born with a particular endowment of talents, strengths, weaknesses and idiosyncracies that are embedded within our own bodies. I am healthy, intelligent, and optimistic. I could have been born with any of a number of serious ailments or chronic illnesses. I could have been born with a visual processing disorder that makes it difficult to read, or an auditory processing disorder that makes it difficult to listen to other people. I could have been born autistic or retarded. I could have been born with a latent mental illness that would express itself only later in life.

I could have been born with a hot temper, or with a tendency to depression or lethargy. I could have been born with a proclivity to alcoholism or obesity. I could have been born self-concious and shy.

I had nothing to do with any of the things that seem to be the most basic facts about who I am. I didn't earn or deserve any of my talents. I cannot claim to be entitled to any of the details about my historical, social, or physical situation. These facts simply are what they are, quite apart from anything I say, think, feel, or do about them.

This is the most basic reason why we should start with the Law of the Gift: It is true. It allows us to face up to more aspects of human life than the alternatives. Here are some of the advantages of seeing our lives, and the lives of others, as gifts.

Personal advantages. The first advantage of viewing the human person as a gift is that this perspective inspires gratitude. It is harder to go through life feeling cheated if one continually reminds oneself that one's entire life is a gift that need not have been given. The modern obsession with "fairness" quite often takes the form of self-pity: "I could have acheived as much as so and so, if only I had had his advantages in life"; "I could really make something of myself, if only the world were more fair, so I could have had an equal chance." If we remember that our lives, our talents, our relatives, are not of our own making, we are less apt to feel sorry for ourselves. The proper attitude toward any gift is not to feel cheated that somebody else got a bigger present.

And why should we feel grateful, rather than cheated? Isn't this just another trick, designed to oppress the lowly and keep them satisfied with submission? If somebody cheats us, then of course we should seek justice. But the basic facts of our birth are not issues of justice.[2]

Here is something you can try for yourself. When you feel cheated, or sorry for yourself, check and see whether you objectively have been cheated by some identifiable person from whom you could seek restitution. If not, you can rule out the possibility that you have genuinely been defrauded in some way. In that case, try listing things for which you are grateful.

Try talking yourself into feeling even more gratitude for the good things in your life, especially things you had nothing to do with creating. Remind yourself of acts of kindness that other people have done for you. Ask yourself whether the person who taught you to read ever could be compensated for that great gift. Bring to mind sights or sounds of great beauty and cultivate an appreciation for those things, some of which, surely, you did nothing to bring about. Many beautiful things simply exist in the world as pure gifts from somebody or other, to you. I think you will find, beyond any shadow of a doubt, that the attitude of gratitude feels much better than the posture of being picked on. And even if I am completely mistaken, and the experiment fails, you have done yourself no harm in the attempt.

The gift perspective also puts a new spin on the modern understanding of equality. An older, more modest understanding of equality confined it to very broad general categories of treatment: equality before the law, for instance. The same laws should apply equally to everyone similarly situated.

The modern, more expansive view of equality, on the other hand, sees equality as something that is essential to human dignity. Therefore, society should strive to bring about equality in as many areas of life as possible. A truly good society should try to do more than ensure equality before the law: it should strive to bring about equality of opportunity, which may include equality of education and incomes. The insistence on this kind of equality has gradually morphed into a demand for equality of outcomes: a society should be judged by how equally income is distributed. Such demands may also include statistical equality across a broad range of demographic categories, such as race, sex, age, national origin, sexual orientation, and religion. And the equality may include not only incomes and educations, but also equality of representation in occupational groups, in athletic participation, and even in choice of academic major.[3]

But seeing that the most important facts about us are not in any way earned or deserved moves this whole project of equality out of the realm of justice. There is no injustice under the older understanding, if men and women prove to have different patterns of strengths and weaknesses, likes and dislikes, even if some of those skills and preferences are differently rewarded or penalized by the marketplace. If, on the other hand, we embrace the modern idea of justice as equal incomes, someone will have to do something about either our different strengths and weaknesses or about the patterns of rewards and penalties.

That is how this expansive view of equality has led so many people to be highly resistant to any evidence that suggests men and women differ in important ways.[4] It appears easier to attribute different patterns of earnings to some injustice that can be rectified than to admit that some differences in underlying patterns of skills and interests are hardwired. But maintaining the fiction that men and women are identical in every socially significant way requires a staggering amount of self-deception.[5]

Likewise, rigging the entire social system to ensure equal outcomes, when the starting points are so different requires an enormous amount of aggressive intervention into people's private lives. The evidence that the overall population of men and women has a different distributions of strengths, weaknesses, interests makes the demand for equality seem impossible and even implausible. But once we see that this kind of equality is not a necessary component of human dignity, then these demands become not only less plausible, but far less urgent.

For instance, men tend to perform better than women in areas requiring mathematical ability and spatial reasoning.[6] This is not an injustice, only a fact. This general fact has nothing to do with anyone's particular combination of strengths and weaknesses. I, for instance, am quite good at math. But I am so hopeless at spatial relationships that I still can not reliably tie a square knot, even after years of coaching from my husband, and more recently, from my teenage son. I've learned to live with the embarrassment of hearing, "Mom, that's a granny knot." I accept these facts about myself, and so do those who know me. If anything important hinges on the tying of knots (like the canoe on the roof rack), someone else does it.

There is no injustice in this little disability. It actually isn't a disability in any absolute sense, only in comparison with others. Admitting to any weakness gives me the opportunity to accept help from others and to be appreciative of their distinctive gifts. When I face up to my own deficiencies, I am in a better position to be realistic about what I can and cannot do. I can accept the fact that I cannot do everything myself, that I sometimes require help from others. I can be grateful for what I can do and appreciative of what others can do for me.

This leads to another distinct advantage of the gift perspective: it provides an antidote to the extreme forms of competitiveness that sometimes mar human relationships. Competition can be constructive as an accountability mechanism in economics, but it can be destructive in human relationships. We can spend our time and psychic energy comparing ourselves with others, even in situations that are not really commensurable. If I regard myself as better than the other person, I walk around feeling superior and smug. If I regard myself as worse than the other person, I walk around feeling inadequate and bad about myself. Neither smug superiority nor dejected inferiority is generally a reasonable attitude.

But if I see my life as a gift to me, the question of who is better than whom becomes much less troubling. After all, I didn't earn my life. Neither did the other person earn his. Our relative talents and abilities are a reflection of what we were given more than of our intrinsic merits. We can focus more upon what we choose to do with what we have been given than on worrying about who has more or less. What we choose to do or not do is the essence of our moral blameworthiness or praiseworthiness in any case. Some part of what we have and who we are was simply given to us, and has nothing to do with our deserts. Reminding myself that my whole life is a gift has a way of short-circuiting that entire destructive process of personal comparisons.

Happiness in relationships. In addition to these advantages, the gift perspective changes how we see other people. I can see other people, not only as gifts to themselves, but also as gifts to me. It requires no great stretch of the imagination to see how the economic world of exchange can easily accommodate the idea that other people are in some way gifts to me. Economics has always appreciated the fact that the differences among people are a source of opportunity for everyone. The free market, with its gains from trade, depends upon people having differing talents, tastes, and endowments. I am grateful that some people are fascinated by medicine and the human body, since I am squeamish at the sight of blood or injury. I am happy to pay these people, both because they know things I don't know and because they feel things that I don't feel. In this way, even a stranger in an arm's-length business transaction becomes a gift.[7]

But this is a fairly abstract and distant way of appreciating other people. The real power of the gift perspective lies in how we view our intimates in personal relationships. I've already pointed out that feeling grateful is more pleasant than feeling picked on. It is also true that our spouses feel better when we thank them than when we nag them.

Many marriages have been strained over seemingly trivial issues surrounding the division of household chores. The modern rhetoric of equality in marriage has not been helpful. That rhetoric has given women a high-powered, socially acceptable excuse for good old-fashioned nagging. We feel justified in demanding that our spouses do their fair share. What we mean is that we want him to do half of everything on our list of things that we regard as important. It requires an effort for me to think about changing the oil in the car or cleaning the gutters or fertilizing the lawn. He surely thinks it is fair for me to do half of everything on his list. Arguing over what really belongs on The One True List of household maintenance does not really improve the quality of married life.

Gratitude, however, does. We have a much better chance of eliciting help from other people when we make a habit of thanking them than when we continually measure whether their contributions are "equal" to ours. Like many things, I had to learn this the hard way. I thought

I was entitled to demand that my husband do half of what I thought was important. He was not very receptive to my demands; he didn't appreciate my various forms of proof that I had done more and that he owed it to me to do what I wanted.

I finally gave up trying to control him and decided to take responsibility for doing what I thought was important to do. I reasoned that even if somebody thought taking care of household chores was demeaning to women, I still have to live in my house. I want it to be comfortable for me.

He had his own set of things that mattered to him. I made a decision to stop criticising him and start thanking him. That meant I had to make the effort to notice when he did contribute something. I made a point of thanking him, even for small things: "Thank you. I really appreciate you doing that for me."

At first, he looked at me like I had lost my mind. He was suspicious. He figured I was angling for something. I had to tell myself that I had earned his suspicion, since I had been fussing at him for a long time. He'd look at me sideways, take a deep breath, purse his lips and say, "You're welcome."

I kept thanking him, as often as I could. I had to remind myself to do it, because I didn't really feel it. I still sometimes smoldered over what I considered his shirking. But I told myself that equality in the relationship was not as important as the relationship itself. Eventually, I even came actually to feel grateful to him. And eventually he was able to say to me, "You don't need to thank me. You do so much for us."

This was the crucial moment. I had to suppress the urge to cheer or say something like, "It's about time you noticed." Instead, it was my turn to bite my tongue. I just said, "That's true. I do a lot. I still appreciate your doing that for me."

It took quite a while to get to that point. But it was worth it, because it gave him an opening to feel grateful to me and to feel that it was safe to volunteer to help. No one feels like contributing if he feels he will never satisfy the other person; no one wants to help if he feels the other person is taking his contributions for granted. I really do think husbands often feel this way.

Gratitude can cut through all of this. My husband is a gift. I have to have soft eyes that will allow me to see all that he gives, not only by what he does, but also by being who he is. Sometimes I want him to help with clean-up, and I look outdoors and see him playing catch with the boys. I didn't think of doing that at that particular time. There will be time enough for clean-up later. And they will all contribute, the boys most of all, because their dad has taught them to help their mother. He insists that they respect me, help me, and show gratitude to me. I doubt very seriously that he would be doing that today if I were still nagging him the way I was earlier in our marriage.

Our children are gifts to us that we didn't earn, deserve, or create, in spite of our obvious contributions to their lives and what they ultimately become. My husband and I participated in bringing our daughter into being. We gave her life and all her genetic material. We also gave her braces, school, dance lessons, and a home with lots of books. But we didn't "make" her; she is a gift to us, far beyond anything we did or failed to do. And certainly, we didn't deserve or earn this child.

Our adopted son is a gift to us of a different kind. Adoptive parents sometimes tell their kids, "You are so special, we chose you out of all the children in the world." But that isn't really true in our case. We chose to be open to accepting whatever we received from the adoption agency. We truly didn't know whom we were getting. As a matter of fact, if we had known what we were getting into, we would have been too scared to choose him.

But that is exactly what makes him a gift beyond all choosing. All the problems we adopted along with him would have scared us away if we had been solving an optimization problem, carefully comparing the expected stream of costs with the expected stream of benefits. Those problems upended our lives in ways we never could have anticipated. He didn't just surprise us and thereby frustrate all our pretense at calculation of costs and benefits; he changed what we consider a cost and a benefit in the first place, in ways we never could have known.

At the most mundane level, he rescued me from my careerism: I had planned to have my baby the first summer after I got tenure. I would put the baby in day care and get right back on the career ladder, without allowing my human capital to "depreciate." My first surprise, of course, was that I didn't have the baby on schedule. Four infertile years later, our little two-year-old boy arrived from Romania, unable to speak a word in any language. It would have been cruel to put him in day care, even "high quality day care." He had had enough institutional care. He needed a mommy: me.

That was his first and greatest gift to me; he forced me to discover my own maternity, far more so than our birth daughter, who was born from my own womb six months after my son arrived on a jet plane. She was so easy, so cooperative, so by-the-book, that I could have gotten away with putting her in day care. But as it became obvious that our son needed more mom-time, I stayed home more and worked less. In that indirect way, our daughter benefited from our son's neediness.

Because he had been alone in a room full of babies in an orphanage for two and a half years, we learned how important human contact is in the lives of infants. We came to see that love really is at the center of any human life, because without it, no one can possibly thrive. Nothing in my economics training prepared me, and nothing in my husband's engineering experience prepared him, for what we learned from our son. It is no exaggeration to say that I could not have written this book, or my previous book, without him. I never would have thought of asking the right questions. He is, without question, a gift. He was the start, and at the heart, of a whole new life for us.

Not the least of the gifts of our son is that he forced us to grow up, really quite against our wills. We had to come out of our self-centeredness, slowly, stubbornly, but surely. The day care decision was only the first of many kicking-and-screaming steps. I kept him home, but I still did what any self-respecting career woman would do: I hired a nanny. It took a long time to get it through my head that there were things more important than me and my career. Because my husband and I cared about him and loved him and wanted him to be well, we had to open ourselves up to changing what we cared about, and learning to value different things. We like our new values better. They are a gift from our son, the very son we would have been too frightened to choose.

And our foster children are gifts to us too. We did nothing to bring these children into being. We got them essentially by answering the telephone. But they now have our imprint on them: love and lots of teaching of many kinds. And we have their imprints on our hearts: gifts, pure and simple.

Each one of them has brought new things and people into our lives that have positively graced us. We meet people we wouldn't normally meet in our professional offices. Not the least of the benefits is that we get the pleasure of knowing that we have contributed something to someone's life. This kid is a pain in the neck; that kid is a pleasure and a comfort. This child has educational needs; that one has psychological needs; this one has medical problems. Each child brings his own delights and satisfactions, even if it is just the satisfaction of knowing that we were absolutely the best family to try and help this particular kid at this particular time. We know we can't meet all his needs perfectly; but we do know we have contributed.

The Risks of the Law of the Gift

I realize that arguing for the Law of the Gift is risky in at least two ways. If I say that self-giving makes people happy, there is always the possibility that someone can say, "I tried that and it didn't make me happy. I don't do anything the way you suggest, and I am perfectly content as I am." Of course, at one level, there is no possible reply to an argument of that sort. This objection reveals both the weakness and the strength of arguing from subjective preferences. The strength is that the individual always wins. Our preferences are whatever they are. Every individual is his own private expert on his personal preferences. Case closed.

The weakness of this subjectivist argument is that the individual is always alone. If we literally have nothing to say beyond "I want it, therefore it is good," there is no possibility for dialogue between persons. People cannot meet one another on the ground of moral argument. Using personal preferences as the trump card in every argument is a way of ending the discussion. You are on your private island with your private preferences, and I am on my private island with mine. Our autonomy is intact, but we are both alone.

I am offering a suggestion about how people might change their preferences in constructive ways that will increase their probability of happiness. At that level of analysis, any reader can take it or leave it. All theories of human nature implicitly or explicitly make predictions about what will make people happy. My confidence that my approach is potentially helpful is based on my confidence in the theory of human nature that underlies my suggestions.

Moreover, my theory is relatively harmless in the following sense: even if I turn out to be completely wrong, you won't be harmed by trying the things I propose. This contrasts with the major competitor with the Law of the Gift. The theory that unlimited sexual activity will make a person happy is risky in exactly this sense. A person may certainly discover by trial and error that it is false. But he may destroy his life in the process.

The second potential risk associated with my line of argument is more political. "Well, Dr. Morse, this is all very well," someone might say, "but if you really believe you have an accurate account of human nature, and a realistic picture of what will make people happy, you can join a long line of well-meaning tyrants who have littered the twentieth century with corpses. Totalitarians, left and right, have promised they would ring in a new era of human happiness, if only they had enough power to implement their programs. Why should I embrace your philosophy of what makes people happy? Why shouldn't I, and everyone else, pursue my own individual version of happiness? How can 'society' have anything to say about such a personal issue as human happiness, especially in matters of sex, marriage, and the family, without becoming totalitarian?"

Totalitarianism is a legitmate thing to fear. I maintain, however, that the self-giving perspective retains all the advantages of Western individualism and curbs some of its excesses. And as a matter of historical fact, these excesses of individualism are among the things most likely to radicalize critics of the free society and the Western tradition in which it is embeddedd. For this reason, I believe that embracing the Law of the Gift is distinctly superior to the defense of the free society based primarily on self-interest. Everything good and true about the self-interest paradigm can be retained or even enhanced by the self-giving approach.

The Self-Giving Defense the Free Society

The self-interest paradigm lies behind the free society, or at least behind one of its most common defenses. One argument in favor of the free society is that the consumer-based, market economic system gives people what they want at lower cost than the alternative systems. But why do we think that is a good thing? We value giving people what they want because we trust people to have reasonable wants and we want people to be happy.

Another argument in favor of the Western liberal tradition is that democratic, participatory governments reflect the preferences of larger numbers of ordinary people more effectively than alternative forms of government. The rule of law preserves the rights and dignity of ordinary people more effectively than alternative legal systems. These political institutions of participatory government and the rule of law protect individuals from the arbitrary encroachments of the state.

Why do we care about that? After all, in the grand, historical scheme of things, the protection of the weak against the powerful is rather an unusual idea. Americans value the rule of law because we believe that each individual has an intrinsic dignity, worthy of such protection. In both the economic and political spheres, the fundamental reason for valuing the free society is that we believe each human being has an intrinsic value that no one has the right to ignore.

But the main business of society is more than business and the politics that supports it. The main business is the human business, the dignity and value of each and every person, no matter how lowly. That is and always has been the distinctive mark of the modern Western liberal society. We have abolished hereditary classes. We don't allow ourselves to believe that some classes of people are intrinsically more valuable than others. Every person, no matter how poor, has a right to participate in the political system, a right to the protection of the laws, and a right to make a living without the burden of unreasonable restrictions. This underlying value of the individual is one of the modern Western world's most appealing features.[8] Indeed, a great many of the criticisms leveled at the free society have to do with failures to live up to a standard far higher than anything attempted by the despostisms, tyrannies, monarchies, and aristocracies of the world.

The Law of the Gift takes nothing away from this appreciation of the individual. On the contrary, viewing each person as a unique and irreplaceable gift actively enhances the value of each individual. Likewise, the insight that I can find my greatest happiness in the sincere gift of self to others does not in any way demean me as an individual. It would not be sensible to think of myself as worthless trash and simultaneously believe I have done anyone a favor by self-giving. A doormat is not much of a gift.

Believing myself a gift, and seeing others as gifts, provides a balanced perspective on my place in the world and my relationship to others. I can value myself, without literally seeing myself as "God's gift," an expression that usually means that the person is insufferable. The fact that other people are every bit as important and valuable as I am provides an effective counterpoint to this all-too-human tendency to excessive self-valuation. At the same time, seeing myself as a gift has the potential to protect me from being used by the unscrupulous. If I am supposed to value other people, and find my greatest happiness in giving myself to others, I am vulnerable to being exploited. Remembering that I too am valuable and worthy of care helps to shield me from this form of exploitation.

This is how I can say that it follows as a collorary that using other people is always a serious wrong. Even if the other person agrees to be used, I ought not to do it. Mutually using one another is not the same as mutually valuing one another. Even if the particular way of using another person is a wrong that isn't and shouldn't be legally prohibited, it is nonetheless wrong. Getting away with it legally is not the ultimate standard in ethical behavior.

Some defenders of the free society express this high status of the individual as individual self-ownership. Each individual owns himself, and no one has the right to commandeer his life, time, talents, or treasure. No one is entitled to take the person or the fruits of his labor. Neither the state nor some amorphous "society" has a claim to take possession of the individual.

In the self-giving perspective, our lives, talents, and capacities still belong to the individual and can be understood in the property-rights sense so familiar to economists and lawyers. No one else has the right to take our lives or exploit our talents. Each person owns himself and his endowments in much the same way as in the private property image of the self. I have no more right to help myself to other people's gifts than I would to help myself to their real or moveable property.

Self-giving takes nothing away from this moral conviction that people may not be used by others. In some respects, the self-giving approach actually provides the individual with more protection than the property-rights approach to self-ownership. Rather than treating the dignity of the person as a category of property law or contract law, the self-giving approach emphasizes our distinctly human characteristics. It claims that using other people is always a serious wrong, even if the other person consents to being used. Allowing ourselves to be used is something we have an obligation to avoid. In this way, the self-giving perspective magnifies the most appealing features of the self-ownership perspective.[9]

The emphasis on the gift of self also highlights the fundamental incoherence of compelling people to give their resources. A compulsory gift is a contradiction in terms. The gift perspective helps us to see that something of value is lost in the very fact of compulsion, even if large quantities of resources are successfully transferred from rich to poor. Tax-supported relief for the poor transforms the donor into an impersonal taxpayer rather than a person responding to the needs of another. The recipient becomes a client of a state agency, rather than a neighbor in need.[10]

The gift perspective also preserves the universality principle that is so important to the Western philosophical and legal tradition. Not only am I a gift to myself, so is every other person a gift to himself. There is a powerful egalitarian ethos in the gift approach. Although we may differ in our gifts and talents, each one of us is still a gift as much as any other. We cannot sensibly view one person as a solution and another as a problem. On this level, no one really has reasonable bragging rights. I didn't create my intellect, my health, or my family background, any more than I created my own life. The gift perspective helps us to see that each of these talents and endowments was entrusted to us and is not fundamentally of our own making.

Thus, the gift perspective maintains crucial features of our Western system of legal rights and obligations. We do not lose the conviction that each individual is valuable and worthy of respect. We do not lose our autonomy, in the sense of our self-ownership, nor do we lose the elements of universality and reciprocity.

Restraining Excesses

The gift perspective also offers us a way of curbing some of the excesses of the Western tradition. Even very good things can be overdone or misapplied. It is easy to take a good and noble idea and treat it as if it were the ultimate good to which everything else should be sacrificed. The Western tradition has done just that in at least three areas—or, perhaps I should say, some defenders of the Western tradition and some of its legal and cultural institutions have taken noble ideas to ignoble extremes. These three areas are utilitarianism, legalism, and scientism. The gift perspective provides a corrective to these immoderations, without losing the essential truth of the underlying point.

A too narrowly utilitarian view limits us to thinking that only someone who contributes economically has a place in society. This particular excess presents the problem that the "usefulness" of the person may be in conflict with the basic dignity of each individual that is the really core value of our society. If we see each person as a gift, we will be less tempted to discard those who are not currently economically useful.

The second problem flows from our emphasis on the rule of law applied equally to each individual. We have developed a tendency to over-emphasize legal rights and obligations to the exclusion of claims and duties that are culturally demanded, but not legally enforceable. The gift perspective provides a counter to this form of legalism. A gift is not a legal entitlement; giving is not a legal requirement. Yet a society without gifts and giving would be a grim society indeed. Seeing each person as a gift helps to overcome some of the excesses of legalism without denigrating in the slightest the importance of the rule of law or equality before the law.

Finally, we can easily slide from genuine and legitimate science into a sterile scientism. If we do that, we may come to believe that all our thinking must fit into antiseptic, morally neutral categories, without ever broaching the questions of value, justice, truth, or goodness.[11] Value comes to mean exclusively economic value. Justice means procedural justice and exact reciprocity. Goodness and truth are only goodness and truth for me, with no necessary implication for anyone other than myself. If we limit the discussion to these value-neutral categories, using semi-scientific language, we will blind ourselves to some of our most promising options for interacting with one another in a humane way.

Utilitarianism and Economic Value. In the Anglo-American tradition of liberty, utilitarian arguments play a prominent role. But utilitarianism cannot tell people what to value or why. It only tells us something about how people will respond to incentives, given the values they actually do hold.

Some have taken this value-neutrality as a great point in utilitarianism's favor. We do not and need not impose our value judgments on others: we simply take their values as given, respectful of their autonomy. Some have concluded, therefore, that the ultimate value really is money. Since we can use money to purchase anything, more money is always better than less, no matter what particular things we happen to value.

Not all economists, certainly, would subscribe to this monetary interpretation of utilitarianism. Some valuable things do not have explicit price tags on them. Economists infer the values of goods based on people's willingness to pay. An economist might say that productivity in the market is too narrow a definition of an object's or a person's economic worth. Economists would point to many situations in which people willingly give up profitable market opportunities for the sake of some objective that they value more highly. A mother, for instance, may very well (and very rationally) value time spent taking care of her children more highly than time spent working in the market for wages. She demonstrates, by her decision to stay home, that time with children is valuable, even though no money changes hands.[12]

So utilitarianism doesn't really have anything specifically to say about how we treat our families. What it does say is that our values really are at the core of everything. This is an important point, because it tells us that our attempts at value-neutrality are self-defeating. Utilitarianism takes values as given. "Self-interest rightly understood" leaves the "rightly understood" qualifier to do all the work. But if we really take value-neutrality seriously, we won't be able to offer a co-herent account of why some forms of self-interest are more rightly understood than others.

Self-giving offers an answer both to the question of what to value and of what "properly understood" interests might be. In this respect, self-giving is superior to self-interest as an organizing principle for one's values. It tells us that we may not use other people. It also provides a corrective for the kind of self-centeredness that can sometimes flow from an excessive focus on oneself that the self-interest paradigm seems to encourage.

The other problem with an excessive utilitarianism is that it can not answer the question, "Useful for what purpose?" If we become too focused on utility, or our own self-interest, we are going to have difficulty dealing with our family members who are legitimately dependent on us. Most everyone at sometime or another will have some relative who is either temporarily or permanently dependent. If we look at these people through the lens of utility, understood as self-interest, we will have a hard time figuring out what to do with them.

On the other hand, the self-giving paradigm has no trouble with dependency, either permanent or temporary. In fact, self-giving implicitly recognizes that dependency is a fact of the human condition. If I ask myself, "What does love require in this situation?" I get a very different answer than if I ask myself, "What is in it for me to continue to be in a relationship with this person?" Self-giving invites us to see this other person as a gift, even if he is not economically productive or is completely dependent at this particular time.

The self-giving paradigm permits a better response to changes in our own situation. I may be perfectly healthy and independent today and able to help my more needy relatives. But I could experience an accident or illness that would render me economically unproductive or physically dependent on others. The reciprocity that is at the heart of self-giving allows me to see that my current state of dependence or independence is not the source of my ultimate value.

Legal and Cultural Obligations. The Anglo-American tradition of liberty is strongly framed in terms of legal rights and obligations. The most basic of the American rights are negative rights, that is, rights that require other people to refrain from doing something. No one has the right to kill, steal, or commit fraud. But these negative rights confer no positive obligation on anyone to do anything for any particular person, including relatives or the radically dependent person.

But there is more to our relationships than legal rights. Entitlement is not the proper way to look at family relationships: love is not a legal category. If we frame all of our relationships in terms of contractual obligations or legal rights, we are going to have an impoverished personal life. Marriage is far more than a contract, an exchange of value for value. The contractual mentality can actively impede self-giving. The contractual mentality encourages us to ask whether we have gotten our due from the other person, or whether we have done what we are required to do.[13]

The self-giving approach suggests that we ask "What does love require in this situation?" We ask our partners, "How can I help?" rather than ask ourselves, "What's in it for me?" The self-giving approach tells us to look at our children and other dependents and ask, "What is in their interest for me to do right now?" Sometimes, it is not in their interest for me to do as they ask. Sometimes people are only feigning dependency, and it is not in their interest for me to encourage them. The self-giving paradigm does not create an infinite obligation to do whatever the other person wants. Rather, it creates an open-ended obligation to remain in a loving relationship with him, even when he is being difficult or unreasonable.

The condition of the legitimately dependent is the Achilles' Heel of the free society. It is fair to say the impression that the free society is indifferent to the needy has been one of the most long-standing complaints against it. The numerous other acheivements of the free market and the free society are counted as nothing in comparison with this objection. So it is well to take a closer look at the legitimately dependent, using the paradigm of self-giving.

The care of the needy combines both legal and cultural elements. Part of the cultural element is the decision about what constitutes a person's "usefulness" to the rest of society. Large segments of American culture presume that a person's ability to contribute economically is the primary measure of his social usefulness. Large numbers of us also presume that a person's ability to think, make decisions, and choose rationally are at the heart of his humanity. If we have already decided that the person is not useful, that usefulness is the measure of a person's legal rights, and that legal rights are the only rights, we will be reluctant to insist that the dependent be cared for. The reluctance to create a legal right stems in part from the cultural assessment that a person without economic productivity is unworthy of such an entitlement. Likewise, once we decide that a person who cannot think is not completely human, we will be reluctant to assign legally binding obligations to others to take of him.

But the gift paradigm turns these cultural assessments on their heads. Even the weakest, most frail person is a gift. His presence in our lives allows us to be grateful for what we have and to realize the ultimate fragility of our own existence. Economic productivity is not the ultimate source of a person's value, nor is his ability to think, reason, and choose for himself. If we really believe in the value of each individual, what better way to demonstrate it, than by taking care of those who are legitimately dependent upon us?

Besides, we have more decisions to make, than merely adopting a set of legal requirements. The legal structures we enact reflect the value we place on the dependent. But the private decisions we make, the institutions we establish, the kinds of schooling we implement also reflect our values. Legal responsibilities and entitlements are not the end of the question of how we ought to relate to the legitimately dependent people in our midst. It is almost as if we think that a question is not worth raising unless we are willing to create a set of legal rights and categories based on the answer to that question. But no libertarian, certainly, should allow that assumption to go by unchallenged.

We might support a set of cultural norms that endorse and celebrate the decision to care for the weak. We might create institutional arrangements, outside of the government, that make it easier for people to do so. We might make movies and write plays and books that sneer at people who abandon the weak. We might even inconvenience ourselves to do this work when it presents itself to us in the form of a relative or friend who becomes incapacitated.

All of this suggests, however, that taking good care of the dependent requires that we reassess our understanding of the dependent. If we define "usefulness" too narrowly, we will not be able to convince ourselves that the dependent have enough value for us to extend ourselves to them. If we believe that our legal obligations exhaust our social obligations, we will be unwilling to take any personal responsibility. Libertarian political theory has always emphasized that society is more than a collection of legally binding duties and responsibilities. I would add that a person is more than the sum total of his legal rights and obligations.

Scientism, Truth, and Goodness. Economist Robert Nelson has argued that economic analysis, and the public policy analysis based upon it, usually has deep philosophic and even theological presuppositions embedded within it. He argues that we would have more constructive policy conversations if we were willing to acknowledge these assumptions, rather than cover them with scientific-sounding jargon.[14]

I agree with his general proposition that the discussion and defense of actual values are more productive than a pretense of value-neutrality. In particular, I believe the free society needs a more robust defense of our personal obligations to our families and to the dependent. I am willing to label my presuppositions and defend them as reasonable. I am willing to defend the conclusions based on these assumptions as outcomes that would be desirable.

I have argued earlier in this chapter that the Law of the Gift is true, not just true for me, but true in general. The Law of the Gift is true because it is grounded in observable and undeniable realities. My aim the next chapter is to show that the Law of the Gift is appealing and good. The Law of the Gift is good in the sense that it helps us to grow in happiness, maturity, and, ultimately, in our humanity.

I am going to do this in a way that might surprise you. I am going to deal with the difficult people in our lives. Everyone can think of situations in which the people closest to him are not gifts at all, but problems: the human equivalent of the hideous tie for Father's Day. We don't feel like giving ourselves to them: we just wish they'd go away and leave us alone.

Even if the vision I have presented seems appealing, surely, one might argue, there are cases that are too big, too difficult, too over-whelming to be handled adequately by the Law of the Gift, cases that require some retrenchment from the ideal of self-giving.

On the contrary, I believe the most difficult people are precisely the situations in which the Law of the Gift operates most powerfully to the benefit of the person brave enough, strong-hearted enough, to embrace it consistently. These are the cases which demonstrate, beyond any shadow of a doubt, that the Law of the Gift is not only realistic and true, but also appealing and good.

Some difficult people present us with the question "Why do the innocent suffer?" Other problem people force us to ask, "Why do people knowingly choose to do wrong?" The gift perspective has something to say about these universal and enduring questions of the human condition. These questions also open up areas in which science has really nothing to say. Authentic science recognizes the limits of its competence and gives way in these arenas. Scientism, the insistence that only science provides legitimate answers to all important questions, must be left behind here.

8

People with Problems
and Problem People

W E COULD DIVIDE OUR PROBLEMS with other people into
two categories. Sometimes people present a problem that
they are not truly responsible for. Serious illnesses, disabilities, and other unavoidable misfortunes sometimes end up being my
problems because they are somebody else's problem, and I happen
to love that particular somebody. These are People with Problems,
unavoidable problems.

The other kind of person, the Problem Person, is tougher precisely
because he brought his problem on himself and in the process created a problem for me. Drug addictions, criminal activity, meanness,
manipulation, or just plain cussedness: most of us would cross the
street to avoid people with those kinds of problems and behaviors.
But sometimes I discover them right under my own roof. What kind
of "gift" is this supposed to be?

A certain amount of either kind of trouble is inherent in being in
relationships with other people. The more we care about someone, the
more vulnerable we are to the pain associated with both unavoidable
and self-inflicted problems. As long as we are in relationships with

others, a certain amount of trouble is going to land in our laps, in spite of our best efforts to arrange our lives to prevent it.

Realizing this helps us avoid feeling we have been cheated when problems arrive. Intimate relationships bring us into direct contact with the truths of human imperfection and limitations. The vulnerability that comes from really allowing another person to matter is part of the price we pay for allowing love in our lives. The alternative, life without love, is worse.

How the Law of the Gift Helps

What sorts of gifts do the difficult people in my life present to me? The person who so vexes me may very well be pointing me to something I need to deal with. Maybe this person is presenting me with an opportunity to develop a particular virtue. It might even be a virtue that I would not be inclined to work on without some provocation. Maybe I have the same annoying trait myself and need to work on it. Only after I get into a real snit about his behavior can I see that I am guilty of it myself.

The spouse or sibling who doesn't do things my way can teach me that my way isn't always the best way. I can learn that the world will go on even if things don't go exactly the way I want them to. I can learn to give way to others, discovering that my self-esteem does not depend on getting what I want. When others irritate me, I can practice keeping my mouth shut. It can be a great growth in maturity to learn how to suppress the urge to blurt out every thought that pops into my mind. I can learn not only charity toward others, but humility. Humility does not mean groveling in the dirt. It means having a realistic perspective on my own importance and the importance of my opinion.

The child who needs correction might teach me to be more responsible and less lazy. Perhaps it is not in this particular child's interest for me to overlook his misbehavior. Love demands that I not simply take the path of least resistance or least cost to myself. But rather, I need to evaluate the situation honestly and make the effort required to give periodic course corrections on this particular child.

These are fairly tame problems, but all of us might know someone who has broken up a marriage over problems of this magnitude, and we perhaps can see in retrospect that divorce was unnecessary. Despite this, one might argue, there are surely some problems so big and overwhelming that seeing the person as a gift is impossible. The drug addict, the philanderer, the violent spouse: these are Serious Problem People. The autistic child, the brain damaged spouse, the parent with Alzheimer's: these are People with Serious Problems. How can I possibly see any of these people as gifts? And if I can, by some miracle, manage to see them as gifts, how will it help me cope with the situation more effectively?

Gifts from Whom?

One way to approach these issues is to ask from whom these people and situations are gifts. For what purpose were these gifts given to me? Suppose it is true, as people of faith believe, that each person is an unrepeatable gift from a loving God. Then one possible explanation for the difficult person is that God put him into my life for my sanctification. To put it in a way that might be more palatable to nonbelievers: God put these particular people in my life so that I can grow up and mature.

I don't claim to be able to prove this; I put it forth as a potentially useful hypothesis. One way to judge the usefulness of the God hypothesis is to compare it with its chief competitors. (A disclaimer at the outset: I make no attempt to defend the God hypothesis with respect to other topics. I am not interested in competing theories of the origins of life or the universe, for instance.) For the purposes of my limited discussion here, the God hypothesis states that God put these problem people into my life for my sanctification, my personal growth, or in some form or fashion my benefit.

Neither the God hypothesis nor its competitors can be proved or disproved. All these alternative theories are on equal footing as far as decisive proof is concerned. The choice before us is not which of these hypotheses has been demonstrated or falsified. We must choose, knowing we cannot be sure which is true. In fact, we can't avoid choosing. When confronting a difficult relative, we will, as a matter of fact, behave as if we believe one of these hypotheses.

The relevant questions are these: Which one will give us the most reliable guidance? Which one will steer us in directions most likely to make us happy and steer us away from directions that are likely to land us in irrevocable trouble? And must we embrace one of these hypotheses at all? Many people, perhaps even most people, most of the time, just muddle through, acting as if they believe one thing on one occasion and another thing on another. Is there a problem with the muddling-through strategy, or would we be better off committing ourselves to one of these hypotheses?

I maintain that the God hypothesis is the most useful of the alternatives. The hypothesis that even my difficult relatives are gifts from a loving God offers the most useful account of why the innocent suffer, why people choose to do wrong, and how we ought to react to our more challenging relatives. If a person is willing to accept that this is a more reasonable belief than the alternatives, it will open up a realm of possibilities for sustaining loving relationships.

The God Hypothesis and Its Competitors

What are the alternatives to the God Hypothesis?

A. There is no God, but the Universe is benevolent enough that I can still act as if these people are in my life for my good. We might call this the moral equivalent of the God hypothesis. For all practical purposes, this belief is indistinguishable from the belief that a personal God intends that I have an opportunity for growth from my relationship with my difficult relatives. A person with this view can believe that Good will prevail in the end, and he can perservere in doing what goodness requires. This might be the view of Tolkien's hobbits, for instance, who perservere in their quest without any explicit theological belief in the goodness of a personal God.[1]

B. God put these difficult relatives in my life out of pure malevolence. There is no natural or supernatural benefit from putting up with the pain of these difficult people. Therefore, I am permitted to avoid the pain of my association with them, if I deem it desirable for any reason to do so.

C. There is no God, but the Universe is malevolent. These people are in my life as a torment to me. I can legitimately avoid these people whenever I deem the pain to be too great. These two hypotheses, B and C, are functionally equivalent. In a malevolent universe, whether driven by God or nature, pain is meaningless, and I am entitled to avoid it if I deem it too great, all things considered. This means in turn, that I can avoid the Problem Person, which means, in turn, I have no right to object if other people choose to avoid me when they deem me to be a Problem Person.

D. There is no God, and these people are in my life for no reason. I have no particular obligation to them; I have only the general obligation of reciprocity, to refrain from initiating force or fraud against them. In other words, Problem People exist for no reason whatsoever.

E. God (or the Universe) put these people in my life as a punishment for something I did wrong. I actually deserved or earned these people in some sense. Job's friends think this about his otherwise inexplicable afflictions. "Job, you lost your whole family, all your property and you are sitting there covered with boils. You must have done something wrong to deserve all these calamities."[2]

As a behavioral matter, these six possibilities can be reduced to three. First, the God hypothesis and its functional equivalent: God or an impersonal Universe put these people into my life for my benefit. Second, the Universe or God is malevolent and placed these people in my life as a torment to me.

The "no reason whatsoever" position appears to be a distinct position. But it comes down to the "malevolent Universe" view in the following sense. The belief that difficult people are in my life for no reason implies that I have no obligations to them and can expect neither subtle supernatural nor long-term natural benefits from my association with them. This view will sooner or later (and probably sooner) amount to the view that I am entitled to avoid them when I choose. As a practical matter, believing that there is no particular reason for difficult people to be in my life amounts to the malevolent Universe view.

That leaves the position of Job's friends. The problem people are in my life because I somehow deserve them or caused them to be there. The Universe is not necessarily benevolent, and it is not necessarily malevolent, but it is just. This position, if embraced consistently, has behavioral implications of its own. I might as well put up with whatever pain lands in my life, since I can't really escape a just Universe.

There is one further point to mention. Any reasonable hypothesis about the overall goodness of the Universe must offer some account for the opposite tendency. In other words, if a person concludes that the Universe is basically malevolent, he must have some explanation for the existence of things and people that appear to be good, since, after all, there are things and people in the world that appear to be good. Likewise, if a person concludes that there is love at the center of the Universe, he must offer some account of the presence of evil in a Universe otherwise ordered toward love. So what appears at the outset to be a simple hypothesis about the goodness of the Universe turns out to be a compound hypothesis, one that requires a supplement.

Notice that none of these hypotheses can be proved or disproved. I cannot prove that God put these particular people into my life for my moral development. But we cannot, in the nature of the case, demonstrate that God, or the Universe, is malevolent. Neither can we demonstrate that either a personal God or an impersonal Universe conspired to place difficult people in my life merely as a torment. Nor can we show that the whole universe is based upon Justice, so that we actually deserve everything that happens to us. We can't even prove that people are in my life for no reason whatsoever and that it doesn't matter what I do or don't do.

If we cannot prove which hypothesis is correct, we must choose on some other basis.

The Malevolent or Indifferent Universe

The materialist or scientific worldview, so common in the modern world, is a variation of the malevolent Universe hypothesis. The Universe is utterly indifferent to me and my problems. In fact, the Universe will wipe me out if I am sufficiently inattentive or unrealistic, just as a part of the struggle for survival.

Take the example of unavoidable pain: Why does my child have a life-threatening illness? A purely scientific approach cannot offer satisfying answers to this question. Science might be able to tell us how things are what they are, or perhaps something about how things came to be as they are. A doctor might be able to explain the medical causes of the child's illness. An evolutionary anthropologist might tell us that illnesses of this very sort are inevitable by-products of some trait that once had survival value. A biologist might observe that this particular illness is nature's way of eliminating unfit elements from the gene pool.

But when distraught parents ask, "Why?" this is not the sort of answer they are seeking. Parents will not and should not be satisfied with a scientific answer to what is, in the end, an existential question.

The child with the life-threatening illness poses the question of why the innocent suffer, a non-scientific question if ever there was one. People ask themselves that sort of question because they think it will help them answer the very practical question: How should I deal with it? Knowing the exact origins and causes of your child's illness doesn't tell you whether to treat the illness medically, or simply resign yourself to losing him. It doesn't tell you whether to stay and comfort him in his last moments, or whether to desert him to spare yourself the pain of watching him die. Science can't tell you whether you ought to kill him immediately to spare him the pain of treatment, or whether you should spare no effort to prolong his life. Neither science nor any other form of the malevolent Universe view can tell you how you ought to balance your pain against his pain, or even the loss of his life against the loss of a few minutes of your own time sitting in his hospital room. Something else, something other than science, has to answer those questions.

In the grand scheme of things, it is relatively easy to convince yourself that you have some duty to stay by the bedside of a sick child. It is the other set of problems that send people over the edge: the relative who is difficult, and not because of some unavoidable problem that randomly dropped in his lap. The Problem People really are tougher than People with Problems. My relatives are being deliberate, willful pains-in-the-neck. They could choose to do otherwise, but there they are, displaying their addiction, or their temper, or their narcissism, or their irresponsibility right in my face. How am I supposed to behave toward them?

Like the question of why the innocent suffer, the question of why people choose to do wrong is not the kind of question science can address. Why has my spouse become addicted to gambling or cocaine? A psychologist could, perhaps, explain the psychic or even chemical causes of your spouse's addiction. But that doesn't help you figure out why you in particular are afflicted with this specific problem. Nor does it tell you why your spouse succumbed to whatever temptations he faced, when he had every reason to know he was about to do something wrong. And it certainly does not tell you whether you ought to stay married, or for how long, or how you ought to deal with the situation in the meantime.

It is not satisfactory for materialists to tell people that they really ought to grow up and stop asking stupid, pointless questions about why things happen and what they mean. We are still going to ask these questions. It is, in the end, cruel to tell people that questions of ultimate meaning are meaningless. Materialists and scientists quite literally have no right to tell people that they cannot ask "Why?" when confronted with unavoidable pain.[3]

Likewise, it is not fair to say that common decency requires us to stay at the sickbed of a dying child unless we have some reason to believe that common decency is grounded in something. It is not fair to say that common sense requires us to give a swift kick in the pants to an adult child who is addicted to drugs and wants to live at home with us. Without some grounding for common sense, that sense can easily become uncommon. The claims of common sense or common decency cannot sustain themselves. We need something else to provide us with our sense or decency. I suggest that the something else is none other than the God hypothesis, still held in an inchoate way by many people, even in our post-modern, post-Christian world.

The scientific version of the indifferent or malevolent Universe hypothesis might answer our question this way: My difficult relatives are gifts from the primal soup, bequeathed to me through some evolutionary process for no particular purpose at all. To invert a common bumper-sticker: My relatives are random acts of unkindness and senseless bits of ugliness. If a scientific answer were the sole acceptable basis for how we should behave, the only honest behavioral corollary would be that it doesn't much matter how I treat my relatives.

But this answer is worse than useless. We all know perfectly well from experience that how we treat our relatives and friends matters greatly. How we deal with the inevitable, periodic crises of life has everything to do with how we shape ourselves and our characters. Our response to our family members, either in the best of times or the worst of times, largely determines what kinds of relationships we have with them. This in turn has a major impact on how happy we are, how our lives unfold, and what kind self-respect we have.

So there isn't much help in the purely materialist account, even if it turns out to be, in some other context, true. If a theory, such as the malevolent or indifferent Universe theory, doesn't help answer the question at hand, or if it gives an answer that experience demonstrates is false, then that is sufficient grounds to reject the theory. There are other truths that are more relevant to the problem of how we deal with difficult relatives. It is these truths that we need to discover.

When Napoleon asked the mathematician Pierre Simon de Laplace about the place of God in his *Traite de la mechanique celeste*, his account of the origins of the universe, Laplace supposedly replied, "Sire, I have no need of that hypothesis."[4] There is no record of what Laplace said a few years later when his only daughter died in childbirth. At that point, he might well have admitted that he had need of the God hypothesis.

Many consider David Hume a hero for the equanimity with which he faced his death. This very tranquility in the face of his demise scandalized his contemporaries. He did not believe in an afterlife and had been very public in his skepticism about revealed religion generally. In his own account of his impending death, he displayed no sign of any fear, no sign of recanting his opinions. As he put it, "It is difficult to be more detached from life than I am at present."[5] He is even said to have played cards on his death bed.[6]

But Hume never married and never had children. He never had to face the death of a child. The question of why the innocent suffer was not a particularly pressing one in his philosophy, or perhaps in his life. We would presumably think differently of him had he played cards not at his own death bed, but at his child's.

So the malevolent or indifferent Universe hypothesis offers no particular insight into how we ought to respond to our difficult relatives or the difficult situations of innocent suffering. It doesn't explicitly rule out any particular answers either. One might decide, on balance, that viewing one's relatives as if they were gifts from a loving God or benevolent Universe might be the best course after all, based on observation and experience. But that view, like any honest scientific position, is always subject to re-evaluation on the basis of new data.

It might be difficult to sustain that view in the face of a real personal tragedy: it is all too easy to revert to the view that the Universe is out to get me. Unfortunately, this is precisely the time when we most need to be sustained by our faith in the fundamental goodness of the Universe, for this is when we are most likely to give up and run from the difficulties we face.

Under the indifferent or malevolent Universe hypothesis, we have no independent standard by which to judge our behavior. This is how it becomes acceptable to make my own judgments about when I have had enough of this or that person. I have no duty to anyone; I owe nothing to anyone. The person has no particular purpose in my life. When I decide I have had enough, for any reason or no reason, that is good enough to justify my walking away. Nothing in the malevolent Universe view can tell us that we can't—or when we should.

Job's Friends

We turn to the next hypothesis, the view that I somehow or other have deserved my difficult relatives. If that is true, then I ought, as a matter of justice, to endure them to the end. Whatever pain they cause me I have somehow brought upon myself. It also makes no sense to attempt to avoid the pain. If I really deserve it and the Universe is really just, I will get caught in the end anyhow. So I might as well face the music now rather than later.[7]

This hypothesis basically says that the question of why the innocent suffer is poorly posed. If we looked carefully enough, we would discover that the suffering soul is not so innocent after all. He, or perhaps his parents, somehow caused this misfortune. Maybe the person has a disability because of something his mother did during pregnancy. Maybe my current, seemingly inexplicable, illness really does have its origins in something I did. If only I had exercised more or eaten better or avoided unnatural food additives, I wouldn't be facing this particular illness at this particular time.

Sometimes people become almost frantic in their quest for an explanation for their misfortune. We are strangely comforted by the thought that we have an answer to the question "Why?" even if the answer involves some guilt or responsibility on our own part. The thought that we are responsible empowers us: it allows us to believe that we are not the playthings of malevolent gods or of mere caprice. If we did something to bring this trouble upon ourselves, then we are still in the driver's seat, even if it is the seat of a slightly damaged car.

I must say, in defense of Job's friends, that the appeal of their position is that it is, often enough, true. People sometimes do suffer because they did something stupid or short-sighted or immoral. In those cases, it is certain that the better part of wisdom is to face up to one's own culpability, tell the truth, accept the consequences, and move on. In fact, it isn't even possible to "move on" without some measure of realistic self-assessment, contrition, and restitution.

In a sense, you could say that this is what divorcing couples have to deal with. I picked this person to marry, and he, for whatever reason, has turned out to be enough of a problem for me that I don't want to be married to him anymore. However, we have a thousand and one intimate connections, so that severing all attachments with him is not as easy as it seems. We have children, and perhaps will eventually have grandchildren, in common. We must endure a certain amount of pain involved with our association with each other, simply as a matter of natural justice. There are natural consequences to our earlier choices, consequences that would be unjust and even irrational to try to avoid.

In spite of the obvious fact that sometimes Job's friends are correct, however, their view is incomplete. For there really are situations in which we face trouble that we didn't bring on ourselves.[8] In fact, the Voice from the Whirlwind tells Job's friends to get lost. The Voice tells them it wasn't Job's fault; he really didn't bring his pain on himself. The Justice view, if rigidly adhered to, doesn't help us discern what we ought to do when we contract an illness or get hit by a truck or caught in a wildfire. How should we face unavoidable pain or grief?

Nor does the Justice view help us discern what we ought to do when our loved ones become addicted to drugs or get arrested for shoplifting. Once we acknowledge that they are going to face some very unpleasant natural consequences of their actions, and resolve to let "nature take its course," it is not so obvious what else we ought to do. We might completely sever our ties with the Problem Person. We might become very involved with their rehabilitation. Nothing in the Justice hypothesis guides us toward one of these courses or the other, or toward any of the many others. We need some other insight into the human condition to discern how best to proceed toward a desirable outcome. In fact, we need some guidance to even know what a desirable outcome would be.

God is to Blame: Theodicy for Children

In my experience as a foster mother and an adoptive mother, I have seen children struggle with the question of why the innocent suffer. This question is urgent for these particular children. It is anything but academic for them, and they are not very well equipped to deal with it. These kids have objective reason to believe that the Universe is indifferent or malevolent. For a child, parents take the place of God. The parents are supposedly All-Powerful, All-Knowing, All-Present and All-Loving. When parents fail catastrophically on any of these counts, the child's perception of the Universe is bound to suffer. If the parents neglect the child, the child can easily conclude that the Universe is indifferent to him and that he is on his own. If the parents are actively abusive, the child may conclude that there is evil at the heart of the universe.

The child is also genuinely innocent in that he is not to blame that his parents are drug addicted or mentally unbalanced or pathologically preoccupied with themselves. Not only is the child innocent in the sense of being blameless, he also has no capacity for self-protection. The child is completely at the mercy of his parents. So if the parents fail, the child could easily conclude that the Universe is malevolent or indifferent. Even if the child matures to the point of being able to distinguish between his parents and God, that doesn't necessarily help. After all, God picked out these parents, so God is to blame for the parents' neglect. One way or the other, God is guilty.

What is striking to me is how seldom children adopt the view that the Universe is either malevolent or indifferent, even though they are surrounded by evidence that seems to support that view. Instead, many children implicitly adopt the view of Job's friends: if there is trouble around here, I must deserve it, I must have caused it. They find it easier to believe that they are the cause of their own pain than to believe that the Universe is chaotic or evil.

Of course, when I say that the kids "adopt" or "reject" a view, I am speaking metaphorically. They do not sit down and say to themselves, "Look what happened to me. That proves theory X." Rather, they act as if they adopt or reject a view of the Universe. Their actions give testimony to an underlying vision of How Things Really Are that animates and motivates their behavior.

Here's how these kids might display the view of Job's friends. They think it is their fault that their parents abandoned them. I once asked a child, "Whose fault do you think it is that you are in foster care?" He answered without hesitation, "Mine." Objectively, it was not his fault at all: that's why I asked him the question. I wanted that unexpressed thought to be on the table, so we could look at it together. His parents were for a variety of reasons unable to take care of him. But it was easier for him to believe that it was his fault than to think ill of the parents who are, after all, small gods in his little world.[9]

These kids often do not have what we would normally regard as a wholesome sense of self-esteem. On one hand, they believe they are worthless, bad kids, who cause every manner of trouble. On the other hand, they are so self-centered they are oblivious to other people. They interpret every event solely in terms of the impact it has on them.

In fact, these two seemingly contradictory views of the self are contradictory only if we view the child through the lens of pop psychology. Increases in self-esteem are supposed to be unambiguously good: only when we feel good about ourselves can we behave ourselves and be happy. So this theory suggests that if we build up the child's self-esteem, he will behave well.

But this turns out not to be true. Adults can shower these children with affirmation without improving their behavior at all. In fact, their behavior might well deteriorate, as they feel empowered without feeling empathy. They feel affirmed in their view of themselves as being at the center of the universe, which in turn can provoke an even more calloused disregard for others.

The way to resolve the apparent confusion is to reject the theory that self-esteem is an unvarnished good and see that these kids are trying to make sense of a world that seems hostile to their very existence. They have concluded that they are bad, because in their minds there is no other reasonable explanation for what happened to them. They don't really want to relinquish the negative self-image, because that view of themselves empowers them. It allows them to believe that they are living in a sane universe that they can influence and control in predictable ways.

This is why it is so often counterproductive to give these kids unconditional positive regard. Self-esteem cheerleading usually backfires. "You are such a good boy. I love you so much." The adult who utters these words does not build up a child's self-image. The message "you are such a good boy" simply makes no impression on him. He has no way of making sense of it.

In fact, it isn't unusual for the child to decide that the adult is a clueless idiot who needs to be set straight. The child will therefore embark on a course of really bad behavior: "You think I'm a good girl, do you? Well, let me show you who is in charge here. I know for a fact that I am bad, so here is dose of badness to prove it." One therapeutic foster mom (with far more experience than I) reports that a single comment of effusive praise from a well-meaning stranger in the grocery store can provoke days of nasty behavior.[10]

Building up a reasonable sense of self-esteem requires a more subtle strategy that disrupts the child's established habits of thought and behavior. Rather than dishing out affirmations, adults can praise the child for specific actions that the child can verify: "You did a really fine job sweeping the steps." The child can see for himself that the steps look cleaner than they did before. He knows full well that he was the one who swept them because foster mom made sure he did it himself. "I really like the way you folded that laundry. You did an A+ job." He can see the stacks of neatly folded laundry for himself.

In addition to fundamentally disbelieving that they are good kids, they do not want to accept anything from another person. Accepting a compliment means empowering the person who gave the compliment. The implicit thought process goes like this: "If I let myself feel good because of something you said, then you have the power to dispense or withhold my good feelings about myself. That is too risky for me and too much power for you. I don't need your stinking compliments."

Specific praise, focused on a readily observable accomplishments addresses both of his problems. A child can accept the concrete compliment because it doesn't rely on the good will of the other person. He can see it for himself. He can feel good about himself because he can see the empty dishwasher and the dishes stacked in their proper places.

As he allows the praise to feel good, he can allow himself to value the person who gave it to him. Valuing another person is actually a bigger issue for this kind of child than his own self-esteem. It is not in his interest to hold an inflated opinion of his own power. It is much more in his interest to trust in the basic goodness of another person so that he can accept praise from him. And this is a much more complicated challenge for him. His healing requires thousands of these little encounters. The stack of folded laundry, the spelling test with all the words spelled correctly, the timed math test hanging on the refrigerator, the freshly weeded garden, these are all tangible and necessary parts of helping this child have a realistic perspective on himself and his place in the world.

So, the view that the Universe is malevolent or indifferent is rejected by people who have every reason to believe it. The abandoned or abused child finds it easier to believe that he is to blame for what happened to him, than to believe that his parents, or the Universe as a whole, are malevolent. It is easier, and in some sense almost more natural, for this child to embrace the view that the Universe is just than the view that the Universe is malevolent. He will embrace this view at the cost of believing the worst about himself. He cannot live with the position that the Universe is malevolent.

But the view that the Universe is just is also, in its own way, intolerable to him. The huge responsibility of being the cause of everything, good or mostly bad, that takes place is overwhelming. To really embrace this view of the self is to embark upon self-destruction; it ends in suicide. We cannot live with the idea that we are somehow fundamentally wrong.

So these children have a strategy to help manage the thought that they have caused every manner of evil. Whenever they actually do something wrong, they absolutely deny it. Specific evidence that they did something wrong is freighted with so much meaning, so much power, that they can't handle it and have to run from it. They will deny even trivial offenses ("Who spilled the milk?"), even when five other people saw them do it.

When somebody gets hurt, they are never the one who did it. When somebody confronts them with the evidence that they did do it, they change the subject. They tell you all about how they didn't really do it at all, but the other kid deserved it because he did it first, and so forth, for as long as they are allowed to speak. With this posture, they never have to be accountable for anything, even while they allow themselves to believe that they are powerful enough to have driven their birth parents away.

This combination of generalized power and specific innocence allows them to manage their pain, but at the cost of a lack of realism and a lack of connection with other people. The idea that they are responsible for the worst things that happened to them gives them protection from the view that the Universe is too dangerously irrational to live in. The idea that they are completely innocent of any specific, observable wrong protects them from the pain of believing that they really are so bad that their mommy would leave them.

The Battle for the Child's Soul

So, how does this help us resolve the questions surrounding the God hypothesis? Let me pose this hypothetical situation. Suppose you have some connection with one of these children. Maybe you adopted a child who turned out to have this view of the world. Maybe a friend of yours has such a child. Maybe you are in the helping professions and you have encountered kids like these. For whatever reason, imagine that you have a relationship with one of these kids or some responsibility for him. You care about him and want him to be well.

Do you want him to cling to the view that the Universe is just and that he deserves whatever happened to him? Of course not. My earlier discussion about helping the child to develop a balanced sense of self was predicated on the assumption that no one would want to leave a child he cared about in this condition. That discussion only makes sense for an adult who wants to preserve the child's sense of cause and effect, while helping him adopt a more balanced view of the world and his place in it.

Does it matter to you what worldview you move him toward? Are you indifferent to the possibility that the child believes that the Universe is indifferent or hostile to him? No sensible adult would want a child he cared about to adopt this point of view, if for no other than a self-interested reason. If the child does take the position that the Universe is hostile or indifferent, he won't be able to accept that you are trying to help him.

The only reasonable position toward which to move this child is the position that the Universe is benevolent, that he belongs here, that he can in some very deep sense trust the Universe. All therapeutic efforts with these kids are designed to encourge them to trust their primary caregiver, who is now their attachment figure. The child has to believe that this person is not indifferent or hostile to him. Healing requires that the child come to believe that this primary attachment figure is trustworthy, has his interests at heart, and is in loving control of the situation. It is almost impossible to be in any kind of relationship with a child who really and truly thinks otherwise.

Maybe he will eventually come to trust you, but even that won't be good enough. You don't really want a child you care about to believe that you are the one and only decent human being in an otherwise inhospitable world. If he comes to that view, you want to move him toward the position that there is genuine goodness in the world. If the child settles for the view that his adoptive parent, therapist, or friend is the only trustworthy soul, his connection with the human race will always be fragile. His trust in the world can easily be disrupted by his caregiver doing something he doesn't like. For the child really to be ready to participate in a social order of any complexity, he must generalize from the safety of the particular attachment figure to the Universe as a whole, or at least to a fairly wide scope of people. The child cannot function in society if he truly believes that no one but his therapist or adoptive mother is trustworthy and the rest of the human race is out to get him.

The Reasonable Choice

Here is what this has to do with our choice between the God hypothesis and its alternatives. The people who have most reason to embrace the malevolent or indifferent Universe alternative reject that view. They choose the view that the Universe is just and they caused or deserved what happened to them. But they cannot really live with that view either. In fact, the hold of that view on their hearts makes it almost impossible for them to accept responsibility for the small problems that they truly do cause. Something is not quite right with these alternatives to the God hypothesis, something that makes it difficult or impossible to really embrace them consistently.

Nor are you, an adult who cares about these kids, willing to allow them to settle for these alternatives to the God hypothesis. The only position that is both reasonable and stable is the view that my life is a gift from a loving God, who really is, in some deep way, in loving control of the situation.

Once these kids surrender the idea that they are in control of every significant event in their lives, they come face to face with the reality of evil. The question "Why do the innocent suffer?" takes on a new and poignant meaning for these kids who wonder why their parents hurt them. It is the question of how evil can exist in a loving world. Why does a loving God allow this to happen? I have to be ready for this question, even if they don't ask it directly. They ask it indirectly, all the time.

Quite often, we find that the kids are very angry at their birth parents—and ultimately at God. Since neither the birth parents nor God seems immediately available, guess who is the target of their anger. You guessed it: me, the substitute mom. But the issue isn't really me. This child is angry at God.

Sometimes, I try to encourage the child to say to God whatever he needs to say. I can recall taking a child to our parish church, and telling him to tell it to God. "If you are mad at the condition of the world, don't take it out on me. I'm just a flunky. Tell it to the Boss. He is right there in the gold box [the tabernacle]. Tell him whatever you need to say."

The child finds that his anger, large and overwhelming as it is, won't destroy the Universe. Nor will God destroy him as punishment for being angry. The child can begin to face reality on reality's terms, finding some acceptance of and peace with the situation as it really is.

And if he looks beyond the tabernacle, at the crucifix, he will see that he is not alone in his suffering. God takes the suffering of the innocent very seriously, and in fact aligns himself with them in the most radical possible display of solidarity. The God-man, the completely innocent, suffered and died and rose again. And so, the child may come to think, can I.

The child might learn to say, in effect, "In my life are many people who choose poorly. I may have to protect myself from them. There are other people in my life who can help protect me. I am not obliged to remain in close contact with the people who hurt me. But I have many choices in how I view them and how I deal with them. I can remain in a posture of love toward them. I can take the position that their lives, too, were gifts from God, gifts that they perhaps squandered. Or perhaps they used their gifts from God as best as the limited resources of their situation would allow. And God put them in my life so that I can learn something particular about love. For some reason that is not yet clear to me, God wants someone in the world to know this particular thing that this particular person has to teach me."

He can learn to accept people and situations that seem to be evil, and perhaps are evil. He learns that they can be reconciled with the possibility that God is good. The loving God at the heart of the Universe allows us, all of us, to choose love. For love without choice is a self-contradiction.

Unavoidable Tension

These two positions, that my life is a gift from a loving God and that people sometimes choose wrongly, must be held in tension with one another. If we believe only one or the other, we will go off the deep end into both unrealism and inhumanity. If we believe only that there is a deep love at the heart of the universe, without acknowledging the possibility of human wrong-doing, we will certainly be unrealistic. Our kids really would be justified in thinking us idiots. We would be unable to account for the evils that present themselves regularly.

In our need to deny the evil, we will be tempted to make excuses for it. We also need to be able to confront our own evil, our own wrong-doing. For surely the most appealing part of believing that all is well with the world is believing that all is well with me. If we allow our belief in the ultimate goodness of the universe to blind us to our own capacity for sin, we will end up absolving ourselves, in advance, for our own wrong-doing. We may become perpetrators of evil ourselves, unwilling to hold ourselves accountable.

Likewise, if we believe only that people sometimes choose wrongly, without acknowledging the possibility of deep, redemptive love, we will be tempted to despair. We will not recognize goodness, even when we encounter it. We will be like the attachment disordered child, who cannot see that the people around him are trying to help and are worthy of trust.

So for all these reasons, I believe it is most reasonable to embrace the God hypothesis. My life is a gift from a loving God. My difficult relatives and my seemingly intractable problems were placed in my life by God for my sanctification. The evil that I see is not caused by God, but is permitted by God, who can redeem even the worst evil and transform it into something constructive. People sometimes choose to do wrong. The people around me cause me trouble by their wrong choices; I cause my own trouble by my choices. But these elements of justice are not the final word. For the God hypothesis holds out the possibility of those very wrongs being transformed into something good. Not the least of the possible transformations is my own. I may repent of the wrong I have done and tell the truth to myself, to that same loving God, and to other people. And in that process of repentance lies the key to far greater growth than I could have imagined.

None of this can be proved from first principles, but all of it is reasonable to believe. I really don't care what you believe about evolution or cosmology. The God hypothesis is superior to the alternative beliefs about the meaning of suffering, evil, and the possibility of redemptive love. And anyone can verify for himself by experience the usefulness of this hypothesis.

9

The God of the Gift

So let us suppose that each person is a gift, not from the primal soup, but from a loving God. This hypothesis gives us useful guidance about how to deal with our difficult relatives. But it is not "useful" in the sense of always giving us the correct answer easily. Rather, the guidance we get from this insight alone has a higher probability of making us happy than does any of the plausible alternatives.

Under the God hypothesis, God is the one responsible for putting me into my particular time and place. Evidently, God wanted me to be born into the twentieth century, to working-class American parents. Part of a life well-lived is to figure out why he wanted me in this time and place, so I can both benefit from and contribute to this particular situation. Rather than rail against the unfairness of it all, I can see that I belong here, in some deep way that often eludes me.

True enough, it is an act of faith to believe that I belong here, in this particular time and place. But the alternatives, seemingly simpler, have problems of their own. It is hardly credible that it makes no difference to me or to the world in general that I happen to occupy this particular time-slot of history. Since it obviously does matter to me, to the whole course of my life, to the whole course of my relations with others, why not assign meaning to it? There is certainly nothing "value-neutral" in the argument that I may not assign any meaning to my particular existence in this time and place. It doesn't make any sense to claim that I don't belong in this time or place, that I should have been born in the eighteenth century or in Europe or in a pastoral commune somewhere in the dawn of history.

So, my existence is a gift from God. My location in a particular time and place in history is a gift from God and has meaning and importance. But what about those with whom we started this discussion? What about the Problem Person and the Person with Problems? How does the God hypothesis help me deal with them?

The God of the Difficult

Why me? Why do I have to put up with this particular Problem Person? There is one thing the God hypothesis tells us for sure about any of our blood relations: God put this person in our lives for a reason. We don't necessarily know this about the people we pick out for ourselves. If I am trying to figure out why I am having problems with a bunch of drug-addict buddies, the God hypothesis doesn't have much to say. I picked that particular group of friends myself.

Once God is admitted as a hypothesis, it is fairly easy to see that he is the one responsible for my blood relatives. So I can say with some confidence: God put this person in my life for my sanctification. The problem I have to deal with will, in the end, be good for me to have dealt with. There is no point in trying to run away from the difficulties presented by my parents, siblings, or children. If God is trying to get me to see something, or learn something, or change in some way, he will keep putting the same issue in front of me until I get it.

So far, I have spoken only of blood relatives. This, by itself, says nothing about our spouses. Since this book is mainly about marriage,

I need to say something more specific about spouses. And this cannot be a generic statement about marriage and religion, since religions have so many different things to say about spousal love. Rather than try to say something bland that doesn't offend anybody, I will say something about my particular religion and how it deals with the question of whether your spouse is a gift or a problem, or something in between.

The Catholic religion takes seriously the passage in Matthew's gospel that forbids divorce and remarriage.[1] The indissolubility of marriage moves the conjugal relationship to the same level of permanence as the blood relationship. We simply can't divorce our parents or our children. We can avoid seeing them. We can get angry at them and make their lives miserable. But their role in our life is in a certain sense non-negotiable. Even if we never see them again, they are still our parents, for good or for ill. They are a central and unavoidable fact of our lives.

Likewise, the truth is that our spouses are a permanent feature of our lives, whether we admit it or not. When we have children together, we've created a permanent relationship, a blood relationship with our mutual child. Both for the sake of that child and for our own sakes as individuals, indissoluable marriage keeps the relationship at the same level as a blood relationship: a non-negotiable fact. Whether or not we ever see the spouse again is not entirely relevant. By moving the relationship to the level of permanence, we acknowledge that we have to deal with the other person. So we might as well get on with the business of dealing with him, rather than trying to avoid him.

My spouse, who is being a pain in the neck, was placed in my life by a loving God for my ultimate benefit. It is true that I chose my spouse. Maybe I chose poorly. Maybe he was a complete jerk all along, and I was young and in love and totally deluded. No matter. If I went through a valid sacramental marriage, God has taken our union in hand. He will grace this union, if we have the wisdom to see it. Or maybe even if we don't.

The virtue of this view is that it gives us the stamina we need to hang in there for the long run, dealing with issues and behavior that make us uncomfortable. There is one thing I can know about my spouse. God wants me to love this person, and this fact places responsibility upon me.

And the fact that God wants us to love our spouses can give us very specific insights as to what we ought to do or not do. For instance, the God hypothesis suggests something about how we should manage the conflict that inevitably arises in any marriage. Quite often, people misinterpret the conflict in their marriages. If our comfort level is our gauge, then we assume that discomfort indicates that something is dreadfully wrong with the marriage. Maybe I chose the wrong person; maybe there is something wrong with one of us. I secretly hope that he is the one with the problem but secretly fear that I am.

But a much more straightforward interpretation is that the conflict and discomfort don't indicate any serious problem. It may be that our spouses are holding us accountable for our misbehavior, and we don't like it. We're uncomfortable being confronted with our own foolishness. We'd like it to all go away. If making the discomfort go away is the goal, it can seem easier to make the other person go away than to face up to our own issues and to our own participation in whatever the problem might be between us.

Everyone has some room for improvement. Our spouses usually have quite a bit of insight into our flaws, but we don't want to hear about it. Nobody does. But it is, in the end, in our interest to get this information. Look at it this way, would you rather hear about your faults and character flaws from your spouse who cares about you and is trying to help, or from your boss during an exit interview?

Comfort is not the objective of life: my comfort level is not the issue. One of the challenges of married life is that it moves us out of our comfort zone and into our growth zone on a regular basis. Knowing that God wants me to love my spouse helps me live with the discomfort, which it is ultimately in my interest to do anyway.

Perhaps some readers are wondering about domestic violence. Doesn't the argument for the indissolubility of marriage collapse in the case of domestic violence? The first thing to say about marital violence is how rare it actually is. An entire cottage industry has grown up to exaggerate the dangers of domestic violence, to discourage women from marriage. The facts are these: recent studies of divorce that looked at the causes given by the divorcing couples find, at most, 6 percent of the couples listed violence as a contributing cause of the divorce.[2] Women are by far more likely to be assaulted by their cohabiting partners than by their marriage partners.[3]

In addition, the increase in divorce has almost no relation to the increase in domestic violence. People could always get a divorce for "cause" even under the fault-based divorce systems of the dreaded 1950s. Domestic violence always counted as a legitimate cause for ending a marriage. The increase in divorce over the last forty years has arisen almost entirely due to an increase in divorce among couples in "low-conflict marriages." And these low conflict marriages, with no domestic violence, no alcoholism, nobody in jail, are exactly the ones in which being willing to live with some discomfort can produce the greatest dividends in the long run.[4] The domestic violence argument is almost always a strategic changing of the subject. The subject is ordinary men and women in ordinary marriages with low levels of conflict that could be managed.

Even the most rigorous Catholic defense of the indissolubility of marriage does not require people to remain in the proximity of a violent spouse. The most devout Catholic couple can separate. The prohibition is on remarriage, not on separation from an uncontrollably violent partner.

Even in that most extreme situation, I can still know one thing: God wants me to love my spouse. Maybe I can't live with him. I have an obligation to protect myself and my children. Maybe the most loving thing to do is to throw a drunken, abusive husband out the door and hope and pray that he will eventually shape up. But that is a different matter than giving myself permission to end our union and to attempt to take on another relationship of comparable marital commitment.

This is how our difficult relatives, including our difficult spouses, are gifts from God. They call our attention to areas of needed growth. They draw us into relationship and out of ourselves. Even in the extremely difficult cases, perhaps especially in the extremely difficult cases, they teach us loyalty and love.

The God of the Dependent

In addition to the Problem People in our lives, we also sometimes have to deal with People with Problems. Our spouse or child develops a serious illness, or becomes mentally disabled, or becomes seriously depressed. The person whom I love has become dependent upon me, through, let us suppose, no fault of his own. How can it be that this person is a gift from a loving God? And what does love require of me in this situation?

The first thing to see about this kind of problem is its absolute egalitarian quality. This could happen to anyone. We may be perfectly capable of taking care of ourselves at the moment, but we need not be forever. Any one of us could get a bump on the head that would render him dependent upon others. We who are in the prime of our lives, at the peak of our productive capacities, sometimes lose sight of the fact that everyone is vulnerable in this way.

The gift perspective offers us the deepest possibilities for appreciating and respecting those who are dependent upon others. Like many advocates of the free society, I had always tended to avoid the issues presented by the radically dependent. I came to see that this avoidance is not really a good political strategy, nor is it necessary. Seeing that the other person, especially the deeply dependent person, is a gift from God helps us to look at him with fresh eyes.

I can recall one occasion on which our family was dealing with the possibility of someone having a serious mental illness. We thought we might lose this person, not necessarily that he would die, but that he would become mentally lost to us. I remember feeling that God was pushing me down the stairs of a very dark, foul-smelling basement, filled with spiders and crawly things. I was most upset with Him.

But then I realized that there were probably things down there that he wanted me to see. And I knew then, as I know now, that I would never have gone down there voluntarily.

So what sort of things did I "see"? I saw that sometimes people do lose possession of their mental faculties. This was something I did not particularly want to know, since I was very attached to the idea that people are rational and have choices and control over their behavior and the main features of their lives. This experience with the seriously ill relative helped me to have compassion for other people. It helped me to face up to my own inherent vulnerability. It helped me once again, to learn that I am not in control of all the big pieces of my life.

It also helped me to see that sometimes, some people are legitimately dependent upon others. This particular relative recovered from his condition. But if he had not, the whole family would have had to make decisions on his behalf and take care of him far beyond the kind of care that people normally must offer to one another. And all of that helped me to rethink the place of dependency in human society.

But the main reason advocates of the free society ought not to avoid the issue of dependency is that it is simply a fact. We come into the world as helpless babies. We leave the world as helpless dying people. It doesn't make much sense to ignore the issue of dependency during the entire period of our lives in between.

Facing reality has always been one of the strong suits of the philosophy of freedom. Advocates of the free market have always understood that it is a fool's errand to abolish private property and reorganize the entire economy as if it were one big happy family. When socialists tried to eliminate the instinct for self-interest and self-preservation by destroying economic incentives, free market economists persistently tried to point out that this vision was doomed. Economics has been successful as a science because it is based on something true: people are self-interested and respond to incentives in a systematic and predictable way. This is also the underlying reason that free societies work reasonably well: they are based on reality.

But self-interest is not the only enduring and universal truth about human nature. It is equally true that we are dependent, all of us, some of the time (during infancy), and some of us (the disabled and the elderly) all of the time. The fact of dependency creates an unavoidable need for human solidarity and interdependence.

It is also true that we have a desire to assist others, and to something good that extends beyond ourselves. This desire is as much a part of the human condition as the self-interested impulse that economists spend so much time talking about. Indeed, we might suppose that the desire to contribute is the basis for belief in various socialist projects, however poorly conceived. We will not lose the advantages of individual motivation and effort, a crucial part of the case for the free society, by acknowledging these facts.

Paying attention to the condition of the dependent is realistic in that it is based on these enduring facts about the human condition. We cannot reasonably expect to ever abolish human dependency. We cannot expect that people will stop caring about their infirm or dependent relatives. Nor finally, can we assume that family members will never need some assistance from the wider community.

The Law of the Gift addresses the problems associated with dependency in a more realistic and humane way than the self-interest paradigm can. It is easy to see how someone useful to me could be a gift to me. But people who are useful in the ordinary sense receive some form of compensation in the world of exchange. The person who fixes my car does me a great service that I could never perform for myself. In this, I can (and do) marvel, and no doubt this is very satisfying to my mechanic. He nonetheless expects to be paid.

But the person who can perform no service for me, how can I see that person as a gift? We can get a glimpse of an answer by looking at how people ordinarily respond to a newborn baby. It is always amazing to see a room full of people watching a tiny sleeping baby, as if it were the most fascinating creature in the world. An economist might subsume this question as a category of captial investment: we value the potential for life and productivity that a newborn child represents. A sociobiologist might say that we are hard-wired to feel drawn to the infant's neediness, because the survival of our own genes depends upon it. But these seem more like rationalizations than reasons.

The newborn baby draws out our ability to care for another person in a more intense way that we have perhaps ever experienced before. The fact that the baby is counting on me in a radical way forces me to look inside myself to find the resources to meet his needs. I find out how much I can give, how much sleep deprivation I can stand, how much love I am truly capable of. I do not maximize an existing, known utility function. I discover that my happiness can be enhanced in ways that I had never imagined.

The babies also point us to the deeper realities of human existence: our own vulnerability, fragility, and ultimate demise. We need our parents for our very survival. We can't really do anything for them except be cute, smile, and make them laugh. Infancy is the realm of the pure gift. It is possible that a mother nursing a newborn baby is performing a complicated calculation that her action will result in a secure old age for herself—possible, but not likely. More likely, she is entering into the world of pure love. She nurses the baby because her body cries out to nurse. The baby is certainly not involved with a convoluted series of exchanges with his parents. Our parents make the first move in our game of life. We come to trust that the world is a safe place, fit for our existence, and that we ourselves deserve to live.

In taking care of a baby, I can learn to see my own vulnerability in a different light. I can realize that some of my discomfort at that vulnerability is a fear that the Universe will not respond to my neediness, that no one will take care of me. I do not really trust that anyone will be there for me in my time of need.

How does this help us understand the value of the adult dependent? These people allow me to enter the world of trust, the world of gift. They can be a gift to me, precisely because I have to be the visible giver.[5] The helpless person invites us to enter the realm of unconditional love, a realm that we all need to inhabit at least some of the time.

The God of the Jews and the Christians

The vision that I am proposing is a specifically Judeo-Christian vision, although I hope that it will have some appeal to people outside that tradition as well. Judaism very quickly interpreted the prohibition on killing to include a positive duty to aid the weak. "Love your neighbor as yourself," is a Jewish commandment. Christianity expanded the definition of neighbor to include anyone in need. The Judeo-Christian religion offers people a sense of meaning for taking care of the dependent. It is not simply the promise of everlasting life that motivates people to care for the weak. This religious sensibility also provides assurance that the activity is intrinsically worth doing, one that helps to bring the human person to his or her highest fulfillment.

We can extend that thought to ourselves. We, too, were once completely dependent on others for our very survival. We may, once again, be so dependent. We can come to see our own dependency as something of value to ourselves and to those around us. We can move out of the realm of self-pity and self-indulgence that we so often slip into when our bodies are not working to our satisfaction. We can come to realize that our infirmity gives us the opportunity to learn to trust others. We can give others the opportunity to give to us. We can take the opportunity to learn patience, rather than insisting on getting our own way. We can learn to accept help, rather than insisting that we do everything ourselves, on our own terms. In short, we can enter into relationship with other people.

And in this part of ourselves, we find some peace with the bigger picture of our lives. Our dependency can make just as much social sense, and be just as much a social contribution as our ability to produce. In fact, our ability to produce takes on new meaning when other people are dependent upon us. We work harder when our work is motivated by love. Perhaps that is why married men with children have always earned more money than single men.[6] It is not just that employers show favoritism to fathers: the fathers themselves are more intensely motivated.

The Judeo-Christian religion and the culture it has created helps people to discover the part of themselves that can respond to the neediness of others. Although religion is not essential to this transformative process, it is certainly helpful. We do not usually enter this realm of the gift automatically or untutored. We need to have it brought to our attention.

Those who have been steeped in the Christian tradition are surely familiar with the injunction to see the face of Jesus in the face of the poor and suffering. And even those not steeped in Christianity can realize that this Western culture of ours has been profoundly influenced by this concern for and attention to the weak.[7]

Mother Teresa used to say that she and the sisters should see Jesus in the distressing disguise of the dying people on the streets of Calcutta. Some of her houses have a chalk board in the entryway, showing the number of people who had come into the home on a given day and the number who had died. And at the bottom, the phrase, "This we do for Jesus."

Jean Vanier is a priest who has founded a series of homes for the mentally disabled. People come to live among the disabled and care for them. The most severely disabled have a full-time assistant who lives with them, taking care of their bodily needs. Young people come from all over the world to staff this network of 120 communities in twenty-nine different countries. Father Vanier explains why they do it:

> I can witness that many young volunteers who come to our communities live an experience of transformation. Jesus is waiting for them in the poor and the weak. They discover something

fundamental about being human and being a follower of Jesus. First of all, they gradually discover their own hearts, their own deepest selves. People with learning disabilities are crying out for affection, faithful friendship and for understanding. They have a mysterious way of breaking down barriers around people's hearts. They awaken what is deepest within us, our hearts and our desire for relationship. . . . Many young volunteers come to our communities wanting to do good to the poor, but what they discover is that it is the weak and the poor who are healing and transforming them, leading them into compassion. . . . [8]

Christianity has made attentiveness to the weak a hallmark of its civilization. But this is based on universal truths. The weak really do call out to our hearts, if we let them. We can know this by looking at the babies. We civilize them, and they civilize us. We humanize them, and they humanize us. That experience is universal and can be generalized to other people dependent upon us.

Conclusion

This is why I believe that the Law of the Gift is appealing and good. It allows us to face more aspects of the human condition than the alternatives. It also allows us a more sophisticated defense of the free society. It retains all the advantages of the self-interested defense of the free society, while addressing some of it excesses and oversights. And in the end, seeing each human life as a gift from a loving God allows us to live with one another in a posture of mutual love and respect, far more readily than do the alternatives.

This allows us greater possibilities for sustaining our marriages for a lifetime. It helps us to have realistic expectations about other people, so that we don't expect our spouses to be infinitely patient and supportive. And it helps us to have higher expectations for ourselves, so that we will ask more of ourselves in our relationships with others. It does not claim that we will never have difficulties in our married lives. It only claims that the costs are worth bearing.

The Law of the Gift can help us move beyond consumer sex into the more natural and organic approach to sexuality. By seeing ourselves and others as gifts, we are in a better position to appreciate the fact that sexuality builds up the community of the family. We will be less likely to use other people if we understand that using people is always a serious wrong, even if we can in some sense get away with it. By seeing the value in self-giving love, we will be less likely to settle for being used ourselves. In short, we will be less afraid to give ourselves to others.

The Adventure of Life-Long Love

LIFE-LONG LOVE IS AN ADVENTURE not for the faint-hearted. We enter into our married lives without knowing for certain how it will turn out. We may have every prospect of living happily with our mate for a lifetime, and something could happen entirely beyond our control. Someone could become seriously ill or injured. One of us could choose to do serious wrong. We might have major disappointments with our careers, communities, or children. Sustaining our love for each other under these circumstances will require every ounce of our strength, all of our talents, and all of our stamina. And yet it is worth doing.

How you and your spouse weather these storms is your contribution to building up the community of life and love. What you do matters to those around you: your children, your parents, the kids your kids go to school with, the kids in your neighborhood, the taxpayers at large. Your spousal love has the potential to sustain and maintain your own family, as well as others around you. Not only will you contribute in the material sense, but you can inspire those around you. It is demoralizing to others to see marriages fall apart around them. Likewise, it can be inspiring to see other couples not only make it,

231

but thrive. You have a decision to make about which kind of couple you will be.

Our free society depends on individual choice and responsibility. Our economic and legal system rests on the assumption that people have the capacity, and indeed the right, to make independent choices for themselves. Around this legal and economic system we have created a culture that celebrates the individual, glorifies autonomy, and reveres personal choice. Our system of free enterprise, constitutionally limited government, and culturally sanctioned individualism works reasonably well for most people most of the time. We have a society with higher standards of living and greater amounts of personal freedom than any system that has ever existed.

Part of the reason for the success of the free society is that it harnesses the energies, talents, and motivations of more people than most any other kind of society. People use more of their talents and knowledge when they are rewarded for their efforts. People contribute more when they are treated with respect and are recognized for their contributions. People work harder when they are working for their own goals and for the well-being of those they love.

But it is simply not adequate to leave the defense of the free society to economists and political scientists. If ordinary people are too frightened to give themselves in lifelong love, there will not be mothers and fathers and husbands and wives who can support each other and those who are legitimately dependent upon them. And if family members do not serve each other in these ways, the demands for the state to take up the slack will be almost irresitible.

A society that too readily accommodates a widespread fear of commitment will not be a genuine society. It will be an agglomeration of individuals, held together by commercial transactions, government bureaucracy, and legal sanctions. Marriage will be replaced by a series of short-term contracts made in an environment of mutual suspicion. Parenthood will be replaced by a series of government programs, without even the potential for building up human connections. The primary motivation for good behavior will be fear of legal sanction, rather than the satisfaction of doing the right thing.

The vision of the free society must be humanized. We can do this in part by facing the reality of human dependence, along with the reality of human autonomy. We can build up a free society by embracing those who are legitimately dependent on us. We can take personal care of our own children, so they know they are loved and that the world is worth being part of and contributing to. We can take care of the disabled so that we have the opportunity to take a vacation from the world of exchange and live in the world of the gift at least some of the time. We can take care of the elderly and help them to know that they are loved, and that their lives have meaning and value.

And we can love our spouses, even when they are difficult. Maybe, especially when they are difficult. If I don't love my husband, who will? If he doesn't love me, who will? Our egalitarian impulse can be humanized in this way. We can stop worrying about whether people are getting equal amounts of money; we can relax about gender equality. Instead, we can respect the fact that there is someone for everyone. The other person's husband is not interesting or important to me. It is my husband who is at the center of my life, and I am at the center of his life. Everyone deserves to matter to someone.

The contribution of women is particularly important. Women have the potential to build up the society of life and love. For over thirty years, women have been taught to value their work in the market, to see themselves as competitors with men. The most highly educated and privileged women have been taught to establish themselves in careers, and only then to add marriage and family as an afterthought.

Many people across the generations are beginning to see how problematic this is for women themselves. Far too many women are entering middle age alone, unmarried, and with no prospects of marriage or children. That afterthought of family life then becomes the foremost thought, sometimes an obsession, sometimes a rolling series of losses.

But as long as we women hold these priorities, we are going to have these kinds of consequences. We have the power to turn the situation around, for ourselves and those around us. We can decide that love is a higher priority than status. We can decide to place our intellects, our talents, and our energies at the service of our immediate and extended families, rather than at the service of our employers and our egos. We can re-evaluate our situation and choose to value ourselves for how we handle the distinct, particular problems that life hands us, rather than whining and complaining that someone else got a better deal. Satisfaction in a job well done can mean more than successfully completing a business deal or getting tenure at a major university. The job well done can include remaining in a posture of love, even when our spouses are difficult and our children disappointing.

Perhaps you saw the great swashbuckling movie *Master and Commander: The Far Side of the World*. I can see in my mind the men on the *Surprise* rounding Cape Horn, the southern tip of South America, battling gale force winds. A mast breaks off the ship. A man overboard must be abandoned for the safety of the entire ship. The outcome is never certain. Success requires every ounce of every man's ability.

The captain calls out, "Every man to his post." There is no other way around Cape Horn. Each man must do his assigned part. There is no pretence of equality, no shame in hierarchy. In the end, each man receives the reward of having contributed to the success of the mission.

Marriage is like that. There is nothing fair about it. Each marriage weathers different storms; each person makes different contributions and bears distinct responsibilities. The outcome is frequently in doubt. And great things, noble and important things, hinge on the successful completion of each couple's mission.

Every man to his post, indeed. And every woman to hers.

Notes

Prologue

1   Most famously Alexis de Tocqueville argued that the doctrine of "self-interest, rightly understood," was the means by which Americans counteract the ill effects of excessive individualism. "American moralists do not claim that one must sacrifice oneself for one's fellows because it is a fine thing to do, but they are bold enough to say that such sacrifices are as necessary to the man who makes them as to those gaining from them." *Democracy in America*, translated by Gerald E. Bevan, (New York: Penguin, 2003), pg. 610. You might say that my self-appointed task in this book is apply de Tocqueville's observation to our sexual and family behavior. It is in our interest to accept certain limitations on our sexual and familial behavior, because of the kinds of creatures human beings are. Self-giving is in our self-interest.

2   Rodney Stark, *For the Glory of God: How Monotheism Led to Reformations, Science, Witch-Hunts, and the End of Slavery*, (Princeton, NJ: Princeton University Press, 2003).

1 The Gift of Marriage

1   This syndrome is known as the Kaspar Hauser syndrome, or psychosocial dwarfism. See *Comprehensive Textbook of Psychiatry/VI*, Vol.2, Sixth Edition, Harold I Kaplan, M.D. and Benjamin J. Sadock, M.D., Editors, (Baltimore: Williams and Wilkins.) See Chapter 40, and sections 43.3, 47.3. Shelley E. Taylor cites a compelling example from a pair of orphanages in post-WWII Germany. One of the

orphanages was supervised by a forbidding figure named Fraulein Schwarz. Even when the children in her care were given special food rations of extra bread, orange juice and jam, these children gained less weight than the children in the other orphanage, which was overseen by a much kinder woman. *The Tending Instinct: How Nurturing is Essential to Who We are and How we Live*, Shelley E. Taylor, (New York: Times Books, 2002), pp.7-9.

2   See Ibid, Section 43.3, "Reactive Attachment Disorder of Infancy or Early Childhood." The locus classicus is the work of John Bowlby, *Attachment and Loss, Vol. 1: Attachment*, (New York: Basic Books, 1969). Also, Mary Ainsworth, Mary Blehar, Everett Waters and Sally Wall, *Patterns of Attachment: A Psychological Study of the Strange Situation* (New Jersey: Lawrence Erlbaum Associates, 1978).

3   Deborah Blum, *Love at Goon Park: Harry Harlow and the Science of Affection*, (Cambridge: Perseus Publishing, 2002), especially p. 214, where John Bowlby tells Harry Harlow, "Harry, I don't know what your problem is. I have seen more psychopathy in those single cages than I've seen anywhere on the face of the earth." The monkeys were sucking themselves, rocking back and forth, cuddling their own bodies. "You've got some crazy animals."

4   Foster Cline, *Understanding and Treating the Severely Disturbed Child*, (Evergreen Colorado: Evergreen Consultants, 1979). For the risks of attachment disorder from orphanage children, see *Science News*, 157: 343, (May 27, 2000) "Attachment disorder draws closer look." For a very human look at the daily life of an attachment disordered child, see "Disturbed, Detached, Unreachable," by Margaret Talbot, *New York Times Magazine*, May 24, 1998, pp. 24-54.

5   The terminology of "trust bandit" is due to Ken Magid and Carole McKelvey, *High Risk: Children without a Conscience*, (New York: Bantam Books, 1987). For some harrowing case histories by a therapeutic foster mother who specializes in treating attachment disorder, see *Dandelion on my Pillow, Butcher Knife Beneath*, by Nancy Thomas, (Glenwood CO: Families by Design, 2002).

6   The attachment cycle is described by Foster Cline in Hope for *High Risk and Rage Filled Children: Reactive Attachment Disorder*, (Evergreen, CO: EC Publications, 1992) pp. 17-49. On the physiology of attachment, see generally, *Hardwired to Connect: The New Scientific Case for Authoritative Communities*, (New York: Institute for American Values, 2003), pp. 16-18. For the relaxation response to maternal contact, see Stephen J. Suomi, "Attachment in Rhesus Monkeys," in *Handbook of Attachment: Theory, Research and Clinical Applications*, ed. Jude Cassidy and Phillip R. Shaver, (New York: Guilford Press, 1999), pp. 181-197, especially pg. 183: "Several studies have documented that initiation of ventral contact with the mother promotes rapid decreases in HPA activity... and in sympathetic nervous system arousal... along with other physiological changes commonly associated with soothing."

7   For an accessible discussion of the physiology of attachment, see generally, *Hardwired to Connect*, pp. 16-21, and *A General Theory of Love*, by Thomas Lewis, Fari Amini, and Richard Lannon, (New York: Random House, Vintage Books, 2001), pp. 16-34.

8   Lewis, *A General Theory of Love*, pp. 39-40.

9 Ibid., pp. 152.

10 Ibid., pp. 77-78; Blum, *Love at Goon Park*, Chapter 8, "The Baby in the Box."

11 There is now evidence from the experience of Romanian orphans that the ability to cope with stress is impaired by early deprivation. "Social Ecology and the Development of Stress Regulation," Mary Carlson and Felton Earls, in *Developmental Science and the Holistic Approach*, ed. Lars R. Bergman, Robert B. Cairns, Lars-Goran Nilsson and Lars Nystedt, (Mahwah, N.J.: Lawrence Erlbaum, 2000), pp. 229-248.

12 Lewis, *A General Theory of Love*, pp. 79-80.

13 For a blistering critique of the Baby Genius fad, see Kay Hymowitz, *Ready or Not: Why Treating Children as Small Adults endangers Their Future and Ours*, (New York: Free Press, 1999), pp. 47-74.

14 According to Allan Schore of the UCLA School of Medicine, "we are born to form attachments, our brains are physically wired to develop in tandem with another's, through emotional communication, beginning before words are spoken." Quoted in *Hardwired to Connect*, pg. 16.

15 Hymowitz, *Ready or Not*, pp. 47-74.

16 Ronald S. Federici, *Help for the Hopeless Child: A Guide For Families, with special discussion for Assessing and Treating the Post-Institutionalized Child*, (Alexandria, VA: Ronald Federici and Associates, 1998, pp. 73-75.

17 John Paul II, *Redemptor Hominis*, 25.

18 For one libertarian who applies a variant of individualism to child rearing, see Sarah Fitz-Claridge, "Taking Children Seriously," http://www.takingchildrenseriously.com/node/87.

19 "The Ethics of Emergencies," in *The Virtue of Selfishness*, Ayn Rand, (New York: Signet, 1964), pp. 49-56.

20 Francis Fukyama, *The End of History and the Last Man*, (New York: Avon Books, 1992).

21 Warren Farrell, *Father and Child Reunion. How to Bring the Dads We Need to the Kids We Love*, (New York: Putnam, 2001). For a poignant look at father loss from the perspective of a Donor Conceived Person, see the postings at The Family Scholars Blog, for instance: http://familyscholars.org/index.php?p=4147.

22 For useful summaries of the voluminous literature on this topic, see generally, William J. Doherty et.al.,*Why Marriage Matters: Twenty-One Conclusions from the Social Sciences*, (Washington D.C.:Institute for American Values, 2002); Linda J. Waite and Maggie Gallagher, *The Case for Marriage: Why Married People are Happier, Healthier and Better Off Financially*, (New York: Doubleday, 2000), pp. 124-149; Paul R. Amato and Alan Booth, *A Generation at Risk: Growing Up in an Era of Family Upheaval*, (Cambridge MA: Harvard University Press, 1997); Judith S. Wallerstein, Julia M. Lewis and Sandra Blakeslee, *The Unexpected Legacy of Divorce: A 25 Year Landmark Study*, (New York: Hyperion, 2000); David Blankenhorn, *Fatherless America: Confronting our Most Urgent Social Problem*, (New York: HarperCollins, 1995), and Patrick F. Fagan and Robert Rector, "The Effects of Divorce on America," The Heritage Foundation Backgrounder, No. 1373, Washington, D.C. June 5, 2000.

23 Gunilla Ringback Weitoft, Anders Hjern, Bengt Haglund, and Mans Rosen, "Mortality, severe morbidity, and injury in children living with single parents in Sweden: a population-based study," *Lancet*, vol. 361, No. 9354 (25 January 2003).

24 McLanahan, Sara and Karen Booth, "Mother-Only Families: Problems, Prospects and Politics," *Journal of Marriage and the Family*, 51, no. 3 (August 1989): 557-80 reviews the relevant literature. Irwin Garfinkel and Sara S. McLanahan, *Single Mothers and Their Children*, (Washington, D.C.: Urban Institute Press, 1986) pp. 30-31 cites research showing that daughters of single parents are 53% more likely to marry as teenagers, 111% more likely to have children as teenagers, 164% more likely to have a premarital birth, and 92% more likely to dissolve their own marriages. Their Chapter 2, "Problems of Mother-Only Families," offers a succinct summary of the problems. See also David Blankenhorn, op.cit. Chapter 2, "Fatherless Society."

25 The impact of losing a parent through death is insignificant, while the impact of losing a parent through divorce is substantial and enduring. Adult children of divorced parents have lower levels of education, income and lower levels of marital trust and support than children of intact families. These effects are stronger for women than for men. Jane D. McLeod, "Childhood Parental Loss and Adult Depression," *Journal of Health and Social Behavior*, (32) No. 3, (Sept. 1991), 205-220.

26 Norvall D. Glenn and Kathryn B. Kramer, "The Marriages and Divorces of Children of Divorce," *Journal of Marriage and the Family* (49) 4. (Nov. 1987) 811-825 seeks to explain the the higher propensity of children of divorce to divorce themselves. The basic fact that enduring divorce as a child increases the propensity to divorce is taken as a given of the study. The divorce of the wife's parents is found to be a particularly strong predictor of divorce in Paul R. Amato and Stacy J. Rogers, "A Longitudinal Study of Marital Problems and Subsequent Divorce," *Journal of Marriage and the Family* (59), No. 3, (Aug 1997), 612-624.

27 See my analysis of the connection between youth violence and parental absence in "Parents or Prisons," *Policy Review*, August 2003: 49-60, available on-line at: http://www.policyreview.org/aug03/morse.html. See also, Harper, Cynthia C, and Sara S. McLanahan. "Father Absence and Youth Incarceration," Working Paper #99-03, Center for Research on Child Well-being, Princeton University, October, 1999. Couglin, Chris and Samuel Vuchinich. "Family experience in Preadolescence and the Development of Male Delinquency," *Journal of Marriage and the Family*, 58 (May 1996): 491-501. Step or single parent families have double the risk of delinquency that begins by age 14. M. Anne Hill and June O'Neill, "Underclass Behaviors in the United States: Measurement and Analysis of Determinants." New York: City University of New York, 1993 Conseur, Amy, et.al., "Maternal and Perinatal Risk Factors for Later Delinquincy," *Pediatrics*, 99 (1997): 785-790; Cornell, Dewey, et.al. "Characteristics of Adolescents Charged with Homicide," Behavioral Sciences and the Law 5 (1987):11-23. See also, Osgood, D. Wayne, and Jeff M.Chambers, "Social Disorganization Outside the Metropolis: An Analysis of Rural Youth Violence," *Criminology* 38 (2000): 81-115, shows that family disruption is highly correlated with youth violence in nonmetropolitan areas.

28 The income differences are substantial and well-documented. See the general references noted above. To choose just one specific example, "When poor single mothers are married to single men of similar age, race and education, their marriage lifts the family out of poverty in about 80% of cases. Overall, child poverty would be nearly a third lower today if the traditional family had not deteriorated between 1960 and 2000." Robert Rector, Kirk A. Johnson and Patrick F. Fagan, "The Effect of Marriage on Child Poverty," Heritage Foundation, Center for Data Analysis, CDA02-04, April 15, 2002.

29 McLanahan, Sara and Karen Booth, "Mother-Only Families: Problems, Prospects and Politics," *Journal of Marriage and the Family*, 51, no. 3 (August 1989) pg. 565.

30 Dawson, Deborah, A. "Family Structure and Children's Health and Well-Being: Data from the 1988 National Heath Interview Survey on Child Health", *Journal of Marriage and the Family*, Vol. 53, (Aug. 1991), 573-584. Similar results were found by Wallerstein, Judith S., Shauna B. Corbin and Julia M. Lewis, "Children of Divorce: A 10 Year Study," in Hetherington, E. Mavis, and Josephine D. Arasteh, *Impact of Divorce, Single Parenting and Stepparenting on Children*, (Hillsdale: N.J.: Lawrence Erlbaum Associates, 1988), pp. 197-214. This is a follow-up study of 52 couples and their children who had been divorced 10 years previously. Among those who had been latent and adolescent at the time of divorce (now 19-29), only two-thirds were in college or had graduated from college or were seeking advance degrees. (the national norm is 85% of high school grads go directly to college.) The authors note that this may be due to abrupt end to child support payments at age 18.

31 Dawson, "Family Structure and Children's Health and Well-Being." Some research also indicates that children of single parents are more likely to drop out of school, largely because children of single mothers are more likely to be poor. Suet-Ling Pong and Dong-Beom Ju, "The Effects of Change in Family Structure and Income on Dropping Out of Middle and High School," *Journal of Family Issues*, Vol. 21, No. 2, March 2000, 147-169.

32 Pong, Suet-Ling, "Family Structure, School Context, and Eighth Grade Math and Reading Achievment," *Journal of Marriage and the Family*, 59 (August 1997): 734-746.

33 For an overview, see Dawson, "Family Structure and Children's Health and Well-Being." Boys in single-mother families are more likely to be aggressive than boys with fathers in the home. "Household Family Structure and Children's Aggressive Behavior: A Longitudinal Study of Urban Elementary School Children," Nancy Vaden-Kiernan, Nicholas S. Ialongo, Jane Pearson and Sheppard Kellam, *Journal of Abnormal Child Psychology*, 23 No. 5 (1995), 553-568. Similar results were found for a sample of rural youth in "Depression, Suicide Ideation and Aggression among High School Students whose Parents are Divorced and Use Alcohol at Home," Michael Workman and John Beer, *Psychological Reports*, 70 (1992) 503-511. Teens in single mother homes and in step families were at greater risk for conduct disorder, anxiety disorder, separation anxiety disorder and oppositional defiant disorder, and major depressive disorder as compared with similar teens in intact families. This study showed significant differences between the responses of girls and boys to biological father absence and step father presence. Stephanie Kasen,

Patricia Cohen, Judith Brook and Claudia Hartmark, "A Multiple-Risk Interaction Model: Effects of Temperament and Divorce on Psychiatric Disorders in Children," *Journal of Abnormal Child Psychology* 24, No.2 (1996) 121-150. Parental divorce during childhood or adolescence continues to have negative effect on adult mental health, even when a person is in their twenties or thirties. "Effects of Parental Divorce on Mental Health Throughout the Life Course," Andrew Cherlin, P. Lindsay Chase-Lansdale, and Christine McRae, *American Sociological Review*, 63 (April 1998) 239-249.

34 Ronald L Simons, Kuei-Hsiu Lin, Leslie C. Gordon, Rand D Conger, and Federick O. Lorenz, "Explaining the Higher Incidence of Adjustment Problems Among Children of Divorce Compared with Those in Two-Parent Families," *Journal of Marriage and the Family*, 61 (November 1999): 1020-1033. Other studies find that parental divorce increases the probability of adult divorce, as well. Jane D. McLeod, "Childhood Parental Loss and Adult Depression," *Journal of Health and Social Behavior*, (32) No. 3, (Sept. 1991), 205-220, finds that adult women are more likely to be depressed than adult men, while Catherine E. Ross and John Mirowsky find no significant differences between men and women, and that the increase in depression can be explained by the loss of income and education associated with divorce. "Parent Divorce, Life-course Disruption and Adult Depression," *Journal of Marriage and the Family* (61) no. 4. (Nov. 1999) 1034-1045.

35 Zill, Nicholas, "Behavior, Achievement and Health Problems Among Children in Stepfamilies: Findings from a National Survey of Child Health," in Hetherington, and Arasteh, op.cit. pp. 325-68.

36 Dawson, "Family Structure and Children's Health and Well-Being."

37 Mott, Frank L., Lori Kowalski-Jones, and Elizabeth Menaghen, "Paternal Absence and Child behavior: Does a Child's Gender Make a Difference?" *Journal of Marriage and the Family*, 59 (February 1997): 103-118.

38 Paul R. Amato and Fernando Rivera, "Paternal Involvement and Children's Behavior Problems," *Journal of Marriage and the Family*, 61 (May 1999): 375-384.

39 Dawson, "Family Structure and Children's Health and Well-Being"; McLanahan and Booth, "Mother-Only Families: Problems, Prospects and Politics," find that remarriage does not fully repair the loss to the children of divorced mothers. Frank Furstenberg also summarizes the evidence in History and Current Status of Divorce in the United States," *The Future of Children*, 4, no.1, (spring 1994) pp. 37.

40 This is the solution actually advocated by TV psychologist, Dr. Phil, in his book, *Family First*, (New York: Free Press, 2004), pp. 15-29. Dr. Phil has probably observed serious and prolonged conflicts between step parents and these observations led him to abandon his usual hands-on, team-work approach to parenting. I discuss some of these issues in my commentary, "Marriage is hard work, but Divorce is Harder," To the source, January 19, 2005, posted at http://www.tothesource.org/1_19_2005/1_19_2005.htm

41 Elizabeth C. Cooksey, and Michelle M. Fondell, "Spending Time With His Kids: Effects of Family Structure on Fathers' and Children's Lives," *Journal of Marriage and the Family*, 58 (August 1996): 693-707. For pre-teens, there was a statistically

significant negative impact on grades of living in a single father household, or living with a step-father who has biological children living in the same household. For teens, the statistically significant negative impact came from living either in a single father household, or in a household with a step-father who does not have biological children in the household.

42 Johnston, Stacy Glaser and Amanda McCombs Thomas, "Divorce Versus Intact Parental Marriage and Perceived Risk and Dyadic Trust in Present Heterosexual Relationships," *Psychological Reports*, 78 (1996): 387-90. Jane D. McLeod, "Childhood Parental Loss and Adult Depression," also finds that children of divorced parents have less trusting marital relationships.

43 Radin, N. "Primary-Caregiving Fathers in Intact Families," in A.E. Gottfried & A.W. Gottfried (eds.), *Redefining Families: Implications for Children's Development*, (New York: Plenum Press, 1994), 55-97; Koestner, Richard, Carol Franz, and Joel Weinberger, "The Family Origins of Empathic Concern: A Twenty-Six Year Longitudinal Study," *Journal of Personality and Social Psychology*, 58, (1990): 709-717; Bernadett-Shapiro, Susan, Diane Ehrensaft and Jerold Lee Shapiro, "Father Participation in Childcare and the Development of Empathy in Sons: An Empirical Study," *Family Therapy*, 23 (1996): 77-93.

44 This minimalist mentality is on display in some of the critical reviews of Mary Eberstadt's *Home Alone America: The Hidden Toll of Day Care, Behavioral Drugs and other Parent Substitutes*, (New York: Penguin Group, 2004). See for instance, Jonathan Kay, writing in the February 2005 issue of *Commentary* who picks at her sources and minimizes the harms, rather than take seriously the book's central claim that children would be better off spending more time with their parents.

45 I make this case in more detail in "Competing Visions of the Child, the Family and the School," in *Education for the Twenty-first Century*, ed. Edward P. Lazear, (Stanford CA: Hoover Institution Press, 2002), pp. 147-176.

1 *The Gift of Sex*

1 The turn of phrase can be found in *A General Theory of Love*, by Thomas Lewis, Fari Amini, and Richard Lannon, (New York: Random House, Vintage Books, 2001).

2 *The Alchemy of Love and Lust*, by Theresa L. Crenshaw, (New York: Simon and Schuster, Pocket Books, 1997), pg. 90-105. *The Tending Instinct: How Nurturing is Essential to Who We are and How we Live*, Shelley E. Taylor, (New York: Times Books, 2002), pp. 24-28, also emphasizes the role of oxytocin in promoting "befriending" behavior among women during times of stress.

3 Niles Newton, "The Role of the Oxytocin Reflexes in Three Interpersonal Reproductive Acts," *Clinical psychoneuroendocrinology in reproduction*, L. Carenza, P. Pancheri, and L. Zichells,eds. (New York: Academic Press, 1978) pp. 411-18. (Cited in Crenshaw, pg.97.) See also Taylor, *The Tending Instinct*, pp. 121-3; Cindy Hazan and Debra Zeifman, "Pair Bonds as Attachments: Evaluating the Evidence," in *Handbook of Attachment: Theory, Research and Clinical Applications*, ed. Jude

Cassidy and Phillip R. Shaver, (New York: Guilford Press, 1999), pg. 341.

4 Men and women often have strikingly different interpretations of the cohabiting experience. See Barbara Dafoe Whitehead, *Why There are No Good Men Left: The Romantic Plight of the New Single Woman*, (New York: Broadway, 2002).

5 This phrase is Theresa Crenshaw's in *The Alchemy of Love and Lust*. See pp. 92-3.

6 Cohabitation increases the probability of divorce, and parental divorce increases the probability of cohabitation. Paul R. Amato, "Explaining the Intergenerational Transmission of Divorce," *Journal of Marriage and the Family*, (58) No. 3 (Aug 1996), 628-640. Married couples whose marriages are preceded by cohabitation are more likely to get divorced "Premarital Cohabitation and Marital Disruption," Vijaya Krishnan, *Journal of Divorce and Remarriage* 28, No. 3-4, 1998, 157-170, and to report lower quality marriages, "Cohabitation and Marital Stability: Quality or Commitment?" Elizabeth Thomson and Ugo Colella, *Journal of Marriage and the Family* 54 (May 1992): 259-267. The increased probability of divorce cannot be accounted for by systematic differences between those who choose to get married and those who choose to cohabit. "Cohabitation and Divorce in Canada: Testing the Selectivity Hypothesis," David R. Hall and John Z. Zhao, *Journal of Marriage and the Family*, 57 (May 1995) 421-427.

7 See for instance, Deborah Sontag, "Fierce Entanglements," in *New York Times Magazine*, November 17, 2002.

8 Crenshaw, *The Alchemy of Love and Lust*, p. 96.

9 See for instance, Murray S. Straus, "Sexual Inequality, Cultural Norms and Wife-beating," *Victimology*, 1 (1976), 54-76; and R. Stark and J. McEvoy, "Middle Class Violence," *Psychology Today*, 4 (1970) 52-65; Kersti Yllo and Murray A. Strauss, "Interpersonal Violence Among Married and Cohabiting Couples," *Family Relations*, 30 (1981) 339-47. Jan Stets and Murray A. Strauss, "The Marriage License as a Hitting License: A Comparison of Assaults in Dating, Cohabiting and Married Couples," *Journal of Family Violence*, 4, No. 2 (1989) 161-180, show that cohabiting couples are higher rates of assault, and the violence is more severe, than among dating or married couples. Jan Stets, "Cohabiting and Marital Aggression: The role of Social Isolation," *Journal of Marriage and the Family*, 53 (August 1991) 669-680 attributes the increased domestic violence among cohabitors to social isolation.

10 Among Indian immigrants to the U.S., arranged marriages still occur. For a recent account, see "Marriage at First Sight," *The Washington Post*, February 23, 2003, available on-line at: http://www.washingtonpost.com/wp dyn/articles/A32226 2003Feb19.html. While most of the article describes the discomfort the American-born bride felt at her family's arrangements, the end of the article describes the contentment she felt when she returned from her honeymoon.

11 On the differences between men and women, generally, see, *Taking Sex Differences Seriously*, Steven. E. Phoads, (San Francisco: Encounter Books, 2004).

12 Crenshaw, *The Alchemy of Love and Lust*, pp. 94, 102-106. Matt Ridley, *Nature via Nurture: Genes, Experience and What Makes us Human*, (New York: Harper Collins, 2003), pg. 42-46.

13 Davd M. Buss, *The Dangerous Passion: Why Jealousy is as Necessary as Love and Sex*, (New York: Free Press, 2000).

14 Not all evolutionary developments are beneficial to the entire species. Sarah Hrdy, for instance, reports that langur monkey males who drive out the dominant male of a troop will attack and kill the infants. This increases their own access to fertile females, by causing them to ovulate sooner than they otherwise would. This male behavior increases the probability of their own genes surviving into the next generation. But it is harmful to the females, who lose all of their maternal investment in that particular infant, to the male he has driven out, and of course, to the infant victim. This behavior can result in the decline of the size of the group, even possibly to the extinction of that particular group. The point for this chapter is this: the males never attack females with whom they have previously had sex. According to Hrdy, "Males use past relations with the mother as a cue to attack or tolerate her infant." Sarah Blaffer Hrdy, Mother Nature: Maternal Instincts and How They Shape the Human Species, (New York: Ballantine Books, 1999), pp. 32-35.

15 Buss, *The Dangerous Passion*.

16 For an argument that female choice plays an important adaptive role in the species survival of primates, see Sarah Blaffer Hrdy, *Mother Nature: Maternal Instincts and How They Shape the Human Species*, (New York: Ballantine Books, 1999), pp. 35-54.

17 Sanford L. Braver, Ph.D., with Diane O'Connell, *Divorced Dads: Shattering the Myths*, (New York: Putnam, 1998), pp. 33-35.

18 Braver, *Divorced Dads*, pp. 28-34, 168-70. Judith A. Seltzer also finds that compliance with child support awards are higher among men who have regular contact with their children. "Consequences of Marital Dissolution for Children," *Annual Review of Sociology*, 20: 235-266, esp. pp. 245-7; and "Father by Law: Effects of Joint Legal Custody on Nonresident Fathers' Involvement with Children," *Demography*, 35, No. 2, (May 1998), 135-146.

19 K. Alison Clarke-Stewart and Craig Hayward found that children living in the custody of their fathers have more positive feelings toward their non-custodial mothers, than children living with their mothers have toward non-custodial fathers. "Advantages of Father Custody and Contact for the Psychological Well-Being of School-Age Children," *Journal of Applied Developmental Psychology*, 17: 239-270 (1996). Daniel Pollack and Susan Mason report that young adults who had grown up with divorced parents perceived their mothers as discouraging contact with their fathers. These young people wanted more time with their fathers than they actually got. "Mandatory Visitation in the best Interest of the Child," *Family Court Review* 42, No. 1, (Jan 2004), 74-84. Julie Fulton, "Parental Reports of Children's Post-Divorce Adjustment," Journal of Social Issues, 35, no. 4 (1979), 126-139, esp at pg. 133, where 40% of ex-wives admitted they had refused to let their ex-husbands see their children. Braver, *Divorced Dads*, pp. 173-5.

20 Divorced men often experience a great sense of loss over being marginalized in their children's lives. See John W. Jacobs, "The Effect of Divorce on Fathers: An

Overview of the Literature," *American Journal of Psychiatry*, 139, No. 10, (October 1982) 1235-1241.

21 Farrell, *Father and Child Reunion*, pp. 62-3. Shelley Taylor also emphasizes the flexibility of paternal love, both in the particular forms of behavior fathers demonstrate, as well as the potential object paternal protection and care. *The Tending Instinct*, pp. 29-34. See also, W. Bradford Wilcox, *Soft Patriarchs, New Men: How Christianity Shapes Fathers and Husbands*, (Chicago: University of Chicago Press, 2004).

22 On the difference in communication styles between men and women, see generally, Deborah Tannen, *You Just don't Understand: Women and Men in Conversation*, (New York: William Morrow, 1990). Men are also less likely to complain about their partner's behavior than are women. See Paul R. Amato and Stacy J. Rogers, "A Longitudinal Study of Marital Problems and Subsequent Divorce," Journal of Marriage and the Family, 59, No. 3 (August 1997), 612-624.

23 Sylvia Ann Hewlett, *Creating a Life: Professional Women and the Quest for Children*, (New York: Talk Miramax Books, 2002).

Prologue to Part II: *The Problem with Consumer Sex*

1 Richard Posner, *Sex and Reason* (Cambridge: Harvard University Press, 1992). He defines the term "morally indifferent sex," at pp. 181-3.

2 A comparable problem arises in the analysis of law. One school of thought, initiated by Oliver Wendell Holmes, argues that the purpose of law is strictly predictive. We analyze law to offer a prediction of how a judge will treat a given case. Critics of Holmes and the legal realist movement he inspired argue that this predictive feature of law is of no assistance to a judge who must actually decide a case. It is of no help to the judge, trying to make a ruling, to tell him, "predict what the judge will do: that is what the law is." The judge himself must make a decision. The object of jurisprudence is to give him some guidance as to what combination of factors to weigh, and toward what end.

My point here is comparable to this critique of legal realism. It is all well and good for an economist to take a consumer's preferences as given, and attempt to make predictions based on those preferences. It is an entirely different matter for the consumer himself. He needs some reasons for prefering one thing to another. His moral code, which may appear as a parameter to an outsider, is a choice variable for himself. In fact, the decision of what to value is probably the most crucial set of choices a person makes in his life. Robert George makes this argument in *A Clash of Orthodoxies: Law, Religion and Morality in Crisis*, (Wilmington, DE: ISI Books, 2001), Chapter 11, "What is Law? A Century of Arguments."

3 *Why Reproductive Freedom Is an Illusion*

1 Gloria Feldt, Quoted in *National Catholic Register*, April 20, 2003, "Abortion Push Starts in Postwar Iraq," p. 1.

2 Joan Williams, *Unbending Gender: Why Family and Work Conflict and What to*

do *About It*, (New York: Oxford University Press, 2000), pg. 261.

3 Farrell, *Father and Child Reunion*, pp. 127-133.

4 For confirmation of this point, from a somewhat different viewpoint, see Sylvia Ann Hewlett, Creating a Life: Professional Women and the Quest for Children, (New York: Talk Miramax Books, 2002). Her respondents reported that among middle-aged childless couples, women felt a visceral longing for children, while the men felt much less urgency about it.

5 The latest statistics on this point are recounted in Warren Farrell's *Why Men Earn More: The Startling Truth About the Pay Gap–and What Women Can Do About It*, (New York: American Management Association, 2005).

6 Steven Macedo uses the food analogy in a somewhat different context. "Homosexuality and the Conservative Mind," *The Georgetown Law Journal*, 84;2 (Dec.1995), 261-300, at 282.

7 Richard A.Posner, *Sex and Reason*, (Cambridge, MA: Harvard University Press, 1992), pg. 182.

8 *Griswold v. Connecticut*, 381 U.S. 479 (1965).

9 Bradley, Gerard V. "Same-Sex Marriage: Our Final Answer?" *Notre Dame Journal of Law, Ethics and Public Policy*, 14, 2. (2000): 732.

10 *Eisenstadt v. Baird*, 405 U.S. 438, 453 (1972.).

11 This point has been well-documented by Steven Rhoads in *Taking Sex Differences Seriously*, pp. 159-187.

12 California Assembly Bill 2194 was signed into law on September 5, 2002. Proponents of the bill claimed it was necessary in order to allow people to "exercise their reproductive choices." Opponents countered that with over 300,000 performed per year, it strained credulity to think there were insufficient abortion providers. http://www.leginfo.ca.gov/pub/01 02/bill/asm/ab_2151 2200/ab_2194_cfa_ 20020625_115351_sen_floor.html. More recently, the state legislature of Colorado proposed a bill (HB1042) that would require all hospitals, including Catholic hospitals, to provide "emergency contraception" to rape victims. Denver Archbishop Charles J. Chaput responded to this legislation in the *Denver Post*, March 16, 2005. http://www.denverpost.com/Stories/0,1413,36%257E73%257E2697961,00. html?search=filter#top.

13 Likewise, the city of New York requires all Ob-Gyn residents in city hospitals to take training in abortion. "Blombergs' Gift," Kathryn Jean Lopez, *National Review Online*, July 1, 2002 http://www.nationalreview.com/lopez/lopez070102.asp. Similarly, the Supreme Court of California recently held that Catholic Charities is required to provide contraception coverage in its health insurance for all its employees. "Free Reign," David E. Bernstein, *National Review Online*, March 3, 2004; http://www.nationalreview.com/comment/bernstein200403030852.asp

14 Sylvia Ann Hewlett, *Creating a Life*: Professional Women and the Quest for Children, (New York: Talk Miramax Books, 2002) offers one of the most balanced accounts of infertility. She recognizes both the intensity of the desire for children, as well as of the disappointment surrounding failed infertility treatments.

15 Donor Conceived Persons have feelings about their situation, including abandonment by their fathers and the sense of being consumer objects to their mothers.

See the postings at The Family Scholars Blog, for instance: http://familyscholars. org/index.php?p=4147. and at http://familyscholars.org/index.php?p=4146.

16 For an insight into the pressures women face to exercise their "right to choose" only perfect children, see Elizabeth R. Schiltz, "Living in the Shadow of Monchberg: Prenatal Testing and Genetic Abortion," in *The Cost of Choice: Women Evaluate the Impact of Abortion*, ed Erika Bachiochi, (San Francisco: Encounter Books, 2004).

17 "The Roe rule's limitation on state power could not be repudiated without serious inequity to people who, for two decades of economic and social developments, have organized intimate relationships and made choices that define their views of themselves and their places in society, in reliance on the availability of abortion in the event that contraception should fail. The ability of women to participate equally in the economic and social life of the Nation has been facilitated by their ability to control their reproductive lives. The Constitution serves human values, and while the effect of reliance on Roe cannot be exactly measured, neither can the certain costs of overruling Roe for people who have ordered their thinking and living around that case be dismissed." *Planned Parenthood of Southeastern PA v. Casey*, 505 U.S. 833 (1992)

18 I make this argument at more length in Chapter 6, "The Mother of All Myths," from *Love and Economics: Why the Laissez-Faire Family Doesn't Work*, (Dallas: Spence Publishing, 2001).

19 This completely autonomous person corresponds precisely to what Joan Williams describes as the "ideal worker." Her idea is that this completely independent person is ideal from the employers' perspective, and is the only kind of person that employers really want. All other workers are measured against this standard of the autonomous, fully capable person. Joan Williams, *Unbending Gender*.

4 Why Reproductive Freedom Is an Illusion

1 For instance, the University of South Florida Counseling Center for Human Development claims that a recent study (not cited) shows that: 52% of women students have experienced some form of sexual victimization; 1 in 8 college women have been victims of rape;1 in 12 college men admitted to sexually abusing women but did not consider themselves rapists. Of the women raped, almost 75% didn't identify it as such.47% of rapes were by first or casual dates or by romantic acquaintances. Over 1/3 of the women didn't discuss the rape with anyone, and over 90% didn't report it to the police. In spite of all these (uncited) statistics, this same website offers no definition of date rape. http://usfweb2.usf.edu/counsel/self hlp/daterape.htm

2 Christina Hoff Sommers documents the ambiguity of many campus rape charges. She cites one instance of a study claiming to show that "one in four" college women had been raped. Upon closer examination of the study, the figures evaporated: only 27% of the women classified as being raped actually considered themselves to have been raped. *Who Stole Feminism? How Women Have Betrayed Women*, (New York: Touchstone, 1994), pp. 210-219.

3 Sommers, *Who Stole Feminism?*, "A Bureaucracy of One's Own," pp. 118-136.
4 Cohabitors are more likely to be depressed than married couples, and the presence of children exacerbates depression among cohabitors, but not among married couples. Cohabiting couples also perceive their relationships as less stable, and this contributes to their overall depression. "The Effect of Union Type on Psychological Well-Being: Depression Among Cohabitors versus Marrieds," Susan L. Brown, *Journal of Health and Social Behavior*, 41, No. 3, (September 2000), 241-255. Cohabitors in general report poorer relationship quality than married couples, "Cohabitation Versus Marriage: A comparison of Relationship Quality," Susan L. Brown and Alan Booth, *Journal of Marriage and the Family* 58 (August 1996) 668-678; "The Link Between Past and Present Intimate Relationships," Jan E. Stets, *Journal of Family Issues*, 14, No. 2 (June 1993) 236-260. Cohabiting women are more likely to have "secondary sex partners" than are married women: "Sexual Exclusivity Among Dating, Cohabiting and Married Women," Renata Forste and Koray Tanfer, *Journal of Marriage and the Family* 58 (February 1996) 33-47. Cohabitors have lower commitment to the relationship, lower levels of happiness and worse relationships with their parents than married couples, " A Comparison of Marriages and Cohabiting Relationships," Steven L. Nock, *Journal of Family Issues*, 16, No. 1 (January 1995) 53-76.
5 See for instance, Murray S. Straus, "Sexual Inequality, Cultural Norms and Wife-beating," *Victimology*, 1 (1976), 54-76; and R. Stark and J. McEvoy, "Middle Class Violence," *Psychology Today*, 4 (1970) 52-65; Kersti Yllo and Murray A. Strauss, "Interpersonal Violence Among Married and Cohabiting Couples," *Family Relations*, 30 (1981) 339-47. Jan Stets and Murray A. Strauss, "The Marriage License as a Hitting License: A Comparison of Assaults in Dating, Cohabiting and Married Couples," *Journal of Family Violence*, 4, No. 2 (1989) 161-180, show that cohabiting couples are higher rates of assault, and the violence is more severe, than among dating or married couples. Jan Stets, "Cohabiting and Marital Aggression: The role of Social Isolation," *Journal of Marriage and the Family*, 53 (August 1991) 669-680 attributes the increased domestic violence among cohabitors to social isolation. Prior cohabitants had a higher rate of pre-marital aggression than did young couples who did not live together. "Prevalence and Distribution of Premarital Aggression Among Couples Applying for a Marriage License," *Journal of Family Violence*, 7, No. 4 (1992) 309-318. About 50% of the women presenting themselves to a southwestern U.S. battered women's shelter were cohabiting with, not married to, their abusers, "A Comparative Study of Battered Women and Their Children in Italy and the US." Laura Ann McCloskey, Michaela Treviso, Theresa Scionti, and Guiliana Dal Pozzo, *Journal of Family Violence*, 17 No. 1 (March 2002), 53-74.
6 According to a study of British child abuse registries, a cohabiting boyfriend is the most serious risk factor for child abuse. Children are safest living with their natural parents, married to each other, next safest living with their mother and her new husband, next safest living with their natural mother alone, still less safe with two natural parents cohabiting and the least safe with their mother and a cohabiting, but unrelated boyfriend. *Broken Homes and Battered Children: A Study of the relationship between child abuse and family type*, Robert Whelan,

(London: Family Education Trust, 1994), esp pg 29, Table 12. See the discussion and interpretation of this report in my *Love and Economics*, pp. 92-95, and in Patrick Fagan, "The Child Abuse Crisis: The Disintegration of Marriage, Family and the American Community" Heritage Foundation Backgrounder, no. 1115, June 3, 1997.

   See Martin Daly and Margo Wilson, "Discriminative Parental Solicitude: A Biological Perspective," *Journal of Marriage and the Family*, May 1980, pg. 282; Michael Gordon and Susan Creighton, "Natal and Non-natal Fathers as Sexual Abusers in the United Kingdom: A Comparative Analysis," *Journal of Marriage and the Family*, 50 (February 1988): 99-105. Leslie Margolin, "Child Abuse by Mothers' Boyfriends: Why the Overrepresentation?" *Child Abuse and Neglect*, 16, (1992) 541-551. In Ontario, Canada, 41% of abused children came from single-parent families, more than three times the provincial rate of single-parent families. "Child Abuse and Neglect in Ontario: Incidence and Characteristics," Nico Trocme, Debra McPhee and Kwok Kwan Tam, *Child Welfare*, 74, No. 3, (May/June 1995) 563-587.

7   Cohabitation increases the probability of divorce, and parental divorce increases the probability of cohabitation. Paul R. Amato, "Explaining the Intergenerational Transmission of Divorce," Journal of Marriage and the Family, (58) No. 3 (Aug 1996), 628-640. Married couples whose marriages are preceded by cohabitation are more likely to get divorced "Premarital Cohabitation and Marital Disruption," Vijaya Krishnan, Journal of Divorce and Remarriage 28, No. 3-4, 1998, 157-170, and to report lower quality marriages, "Cohabitation and Marital Stability: Quality or Commitment?" Elizabeth Thomson and Ugo Colella, Journal of Marriage and the Family 54 (may 1992): 259-267. The increased probability of divorce cannot be accounted for by systematic differences between those who choose to get married and those who choose to cohabit. "Cohabitation and Divorce in Canada: Testing the Selectivity Hypothesis," David R. Hall and John Z. Zhao, Journal of Marriage and the Family, 57 (May 1995) 421-427.

8   This section is based on my article of the same name on the *Boundless* webzine, October 2001. http://www.boundless.org/2001/departments/beyond_buddies/a0000498.html

9   See Barbara Dafoe Whitehead, Why There are No Good Men Left: The Romantic Plight of the New Single Woman, (New York: Broadway, 2002). For a particularly obnoxious example of a live-in couple in which each had distinctly different expectations, listen to this letter to Dear Abby:

   "I have been living with "Ken" for seven years. On two occasions in the past few months, he has told me he's dating someone else. Each time, Ken allowed me to believe it for more than an hour. Then he admitted he was 'putting me on' that he was only testing me to see if I really loved him." Dear Abby responds that this game is sadistic and she should dump him. My observation is only this: would a married man feel himself entitled to make such a joke? "Dear Abby," May 30, 2003. http://www.uexpress.com/dearabby/?uc_full_date=20030530.

10 *Hooking Up, Hanging Out and Hoping for Mr. Right: College Women on Dating and Mating Today*, An Institute for American Values Report to the Independent Women's Forum, Norvall Glenn and Elizabeth Marquardt, Principal Investigators; (New York: Institute for American Values, 2001).

11 *Hooking Up*, p. 63.

12 *Hooking Up*, p. 14. Forty percent of respondants reported that they had hooked up themselves, and ten percent said they had done so more than six times.

13 *Hooking Up*, p. 20. This coed's description of the hook-up culture is eerily reminiscent of Jean Jacques Rousseau's description of sexual encounters in the pre-political, pre-social state of nature.

   "As males and females united fortuitously according to encounters, opportunities and desires, they required no speech to express the things they had to say to each other, and they separated with the same ease. The mother nursed her children at first to satisfy her own needs, then when habit had made them dear to her, she fed them to satisfy their needs; as soon as they had the strength to find their own food, they did not hesitate to leave their mother herself; and as there was virtually no way of finding one another again once they had lost sight of each other, they were soon at the stage of not even recognizing one another."

   The modern hook-up culture has taken Rousseau at his word, by defining "natural" as acting on impulse, and "freedom" as being unencumbered by law, social convention or even attachment to other people. Rousseau captured the essence of the hook-up mentality, down to and including the reluctance to even talk to one's sex partner. *A Discourse on Inequality*, tranlated by Maurice Cranston, (London: Penguin Books, 1984), pg. 92.

14 *Hooking Up*, p. 20-21.

15 *Hooking Up*, p. 15-6.

16 *Hooking Up*, p. 60-65.

17 See my article, "The Hook-up Culture: When Sex Becomes Sport," *To the source*, September 3, 2003. http://www.tothesource.org/9 3_2003/9_3_2003.htm

18 Carrie L. Lukas shows that many entry level Women's Studies classes are more than supportive of women engaging in casual sex. *Sex (Ms.) Education: What Young Women Need to Know (but Won't Hear in Women's Studies) about Sex, Love and Marriage*, (Washington D.C.: The Independent Women's Forum. 2005).

19 Patrick Lee and Robert P. George, "Dualistic Delusions," *First Things*, February 2005, available on-line at http://www.firstthings.com/ftissues/ft0502/opinion/george.htm.

20 "The Desire Gap," *San Diego Union Tribune*, article profiling therapist and author Michele Weiner-Davis, March 15, 2003.

21 Michele Wiener Davis, *The Sex-Starved Marriage: A Couple's Guide to Boosting Their Marriage Libido*, (New York: Simon and Schuster, 2003).

22 David Schnarch, *Passionate Marriage: Keeping Love and Intimacy Alive in Committed Relationships*, (New York: Henry Holt, 1997).

23 Schnarch, p. 170.

5 *Why Consumer Sex Is Anti-Social*

1 *The Catholic Ethic and the Spirit of Capitalism*, (New York: Free Press, 1993).
2 Peter L. Berger and Richard John Neuhaus, *To Empower People: From State to Civil Society*, (Washington D.C: The AEI Press, 1996).
3 Charles Murray, *In Pursuit of Happiness and Good Government*, (Oakland, CA: Institute for Contemporary Studies, 1994).
4 Robert D. Putnam, *Bowling Alone: The Collapse and Revival of American Community*, (New York: Simon and Schuster, 2000).
5 *The Monochrome Society*, Amatai Etzioni, (Princeton: New Forum Books, Princeton University Press, 2001).
6 This is a classic Prisoners' Dilemma. Each would benefit from mutual cooperation, but they can not enforce an agreement to cooperate. In these situations, tit-for-tat, I'll cooperate if you cooperate, the first defection leads to the complete unraveling of the cooperative relationship. I discuss this in Chapter 2 of my previous book, *Love & Economics*, which lists the standard references.
7 For a useful distinction between norms and laws, see Steven L. Nock, "The Legal Construction of Norms: Time and Gender in Marriage," 86 Va Law Review, 1971-1987 (2000): "A norm is a cluster of expectations about what is appropriate in a given situation. ... Social norms are soft boundaries around some realm of institutional behavior. They are soft because they are enforced informally and sometimes violated. ...That is to say, a norm is always viewed as legitimate by most people. .... while ...laws are sometimes seen as illegitimate. ...The fact that most married people are sexually faithful most of the time is not what makes fidelity a norm. Fidelity is a norm because it is widely regarded as right. A norm is an "ought" or "ought not" that is widely shared and deemed to be legitimate."
8 Barbara Defoe Whitehead, *Why There are No Good Men Left: The Romantic Plight of the New Single Woman*, (New York: Broadway Books, 2003), describes the appeal of "Chick Lit" to so many single career women: it describes the frustration they feel about their situation. See pp. 44-51. She also describes the appeal of cohabitation for men: it allows them to drift, at relatively low cost to themselves. See pp. 130-47.
9 Some career women forget to make time for relationships, and need to "retrain" themselves to do so. There are even seminars to help such women. The leader of one such program, Lifeworks, describes her typical client as, "a business executive who forgot to make time for a personal life....Between you and me, these are very prickly women. They've been wearing the pants too long. Men like powerful women, but they don't want to be eaten alive." Among the skills these clients need is the "art of gracious gift receiving." Evidently, "executive women have no idea of how to accept a gift gracefully." Sylvia Ann Hewlett, *Creating a Life*, pp. 161-5.
10 Whitehead, *Why There are No Good Men Left*, pp. 181-3.
11 David Gutman, "Adulthood and its Discontents," *Working Paper 67* (New York: Institute for American Values, 1998). Available online: www.americanvalues.org/html/k-adulthood_its_discontents.

12 Ibid.

13 Single mothers receive more help from and give less help to their young adult offspring than do married mothers. Paul R. Amato, Sandra J. Rezac and Alan Booth, "Helping between Parents and Yound Adult Offspring: The Role of Parental Marital Quality, Divorce and Remarriage," *Journal of Marriage and the Family*, 57, No. 2 (May 1996) 363-374. It is reasonable to suppose that this pattern of giving less and needing more did not begin the day the child turned 18, but rather was an established pattern, in comparison with married mothers. Divorce lowered helping between fathers and offspring, but not between mothers and offspring. Remarried divorced mothers give as much help as continuously married mothers.

14 According to Margaret F. Brinig and Steven L. Nock, "The most stable marriages are those in which the work inequality was recognized by both spouses (both partners agreed that the division of labor was unfair to the wife). This suggests that husband's appreciation of the gift his wife makes by her disproportionate efforts may be more important than achieving strict equality ." "'I only want trust:' Norms, Trust and Autonomy," *Journal of Socio-Economics*, 2003, citing also their earlier work, Brinig, M.F., "Divorce and division of labor," In: Rowthorn, R., Dnes, A.W. (Eds.), *Marriage and Divorce: An Economic Perspective*, Cambridge University Press, Cambridge, 2003). See also, Steven L. Nock, "The Legal Construction of Norms: Time and Gender in Marriage," 86 *Va Law Review*, 1971-1987; (2000.)

15 Steven Nock argues that this absence of a template or a set of accepted social norms, is part of what creates the instability in cohabiting unions. Nock, S.L., 1995a. "A comparison of marriages and cohabiting relationships," *Journal of Family Issues* 15, 53–76. See also, Nock, S.L., 2000, "Time and gender in marriage." *Virginia Law Review* 86, 1971–1987.

16 *Marriage of Burgess*, (1996) 13 Cal. 4th 25. (Cited in Warren Farrell, pp.51, note 139.)

17 Glynnis Walker, *Solomon's Children*, (New York: Arbor House, 1986). pg 84, quoted by Warren Farrell, op.cit. pg. 187. By contrast, only 16% of children who are living with their fathers reported that their dads tried to prevent their mothers from seeing them.

18 Mothers are far more likely than fathers to play the "child abuse card" in divorce or custody disputes. Of court-referred cases of false accusations occurring during divorce and parent-time battles, 94% of those who made false accusations were women and 96% of those falsely accused were men. The men usually had passive personalities; the children were usually females under 8; the mothers who made false accusations were characterized by their anger when an expert did not find evidence of abuse, and by their resolve to find an expert who would prove the child was abused. Hollinda Wakefield and Ralph Underwager, "Sexual Abuse Allegations iin Divorce and Custody Dispute," *Behavioral Science and the Law*, Vol. 9, 1991, pp. 451-68.

19 For example, "Helping families going through Divorce," by Anthony C. Joseph and Sharon Kalemkiarian, *San Diego Union Tribune*, September 12, 2003. Jo-

seph is a retired san Diego County Family Court Judge. Kelmkiarian chairs Kids Turn San Diego, a nonprofit organization that helps children and parents going through divorce. Mindful of the fact that "all the police officers in the world can not protect" children from violent conflicts resulting from divorce. Among their recommendations, "Make Kid's Turn or a Kid's Turn-like program required for every family in a conflicted custody matter, before that matter ever reaches the court.... Commence a public health campaign about the effects of custody conflict on children.... Support alternatives to adversarial divorce proceedings." Programs to reduced the probability of divorce in the first place are conspicuously absent from their list of suggestions.

20 In 1997, about 50% of women having abortions had already had a previous abortion. Twenty percent of women obtaining abortions had had more than 2 previous abortions. Lisa M. Koonin, et.al., "Abortion Surveillance- United States, 1997," *Monthly Morbidity and W Review*, Vol. 49, no. SS-11, pg. 5. For further information about repeat abortions, see M. Jacoby et. al., "Rapid Repeat Pregnancies and Experiences of Interpersonal Violence Among Low Income Adolescents," *American Journal of Preventive Medicine*, 16(4): 318-21, 1999. "Women whose pregnancies ended in spontaneous or elective abortion were more likely to experience RRP (Rapid Repeat Preganancy) than were their peers who delivered at term." M.D. Crenin, "Conception rates after abortion with methotrexate and misoprostol," *International Journal of Gynacological Obstetrics.* 65:183-88 (1999). He finds about 24% pregnancy within a year of the abortion. He notes that this is a far higher fertility rate than would be expected from a population of women using contraception of 90% reliability. He also notes that of the women who had aborted and who later became pregnant, 91% had an abortion, compared with 27% abortion rate of all pregnancies in the U.S.

21 It might be more accurate to say that she is acting as if she believes she is entitled to sex without a live baby resulting. Her actual motivations may be far less calculating or rational. She may get pregnant after an abortion as a way of replacing the child she aborted. Or, she may be reenacting a traumatic abortion experience in an attempt to finally gain healing and closure. Or she may have repeated abortions as a form of masochism. In these cases, it is hardly accurate to call the woman irresponsible. It would be more accurate to describe her as traumatized by abortion. I confine this possibility to the footnotes, because I am trying to accept the pro-abortion position at its word: women choose abortions for reasonable reasons, that other people should accept without question. See Theresa Burke, *Forbidden Grief: The Unspoken Pain of Abortion*, (Springfield IL: Acorn Books, 2002), pp. 145-55.

22 One abortion counselor explained her own ability to accept a woman having not four, but fourteen, abortions by saying that perhaps the woman had made a decision to not contracept. "Isn't that valid?" Cited in Diane M. Gianelli, "Abortion Providers Share Inner Conflicts," *American Medical News*, 3 (July 12, 1993).

23 Cathy Young, *Cease-Fire: Why Women and Men Must Join Forces to Achieve True Equality*, (New York: Free Press, 1999).

24 "Torrance veteran feels mixed emotions," By Jeffery M. Leving and Glenn Sacks, *Daily Breeze*, (Torrance, CA) November 11, 2003. http://www.dailybreeze.com/content/opinion/810898.html

25 "A married woman had an affair with a single man, Michael Hirschensohn. Blood tests showed that Michael was the father. However, the court ruled that Michael did not even legally "exist" as the father- the woman's husband was declared to be the father." Farrell, *Father and Child Reunion*, p. 130, citing the Michael Hrishenshom case.

26 *Fairrow v. Fairrow*, Indiana Court of Appeals, Second District, Sept. 13, 1989, as cited in Liberator Vol. 15, no. 12, Dec. 1989. Cited by Warren Farrell, pg. 183.

27 Warren Farrell, *Father and Child Reunion*, p.129, citing the Matter of Audrey G. [Robert T.]; New York Family Court, Kings County, New York Law Journal, August 17,1989.

28 I make this case in more detail in "Marriage and the Limits of Contract," *Policy Review*, 130 (April/May 2005).

6 *Why Morally Neutral Sex Isn't*

1 When this book was in galleys, I discovered a French political philosopher who makes a similar argument at a very high level of generality. She argues that the modern moral position that appears to accept everything, and condemn nothing is a pose. In fact, this modern position places a very high value on autonomy and individuality, to the exclusion of commitments and relationships to other people. She shows that far from being a morally neutral position, this position promotes a very specific vision of the human person. Chantal Delsol, *Icarus Fallen: The Search for Meaning in an Uncertain World*, (Wilmington DE: ISI Books, 2003), pp. 83-90.

2 Just to show that I am not making this up, consider this letter to advice columnist Carolyn Hax:

"My ex-boyfriend of almost three years and I still keep in contact. The last few times, we ended up sleeping together. I'm totally fine with it.

"The problem? For our last 'visit' we got a couple of drinks and hooked up. Now, he's suggesting skipping the overpriced drinks and going straight to the goods.

"I'm not expecting a lot from the boy, but at least he could shell out money or one drink—or we could eat Ramen. Do I make it clear that dinner and/or drinks come first, then dessert? I'm all for casual sex, but you've still got to treat the person right. Agree?" "Tell me About it," March 6, 2005. http://www.washingtonpost.com/wp dyn/articles/A5656 2005Mar3.html

3 Entry level Women's Studies textbooks are filled with attacks on marriage and celebrations of casual sex. "Sex (Ms)Education: what Young Women need to know (But won't Hear in Women's Studies) About Sex, Love and Marriage," by Carrie L. Lukas, (Washington, D.C.: Independent Women's Forum, 2005), pp. 6-13. A survey of 20 of the commonly used textbook for high school health classes found less

inaccurate information than in the college texts. But the authors still conclude that "the story of marriage and family life contained in these textbooks is not so much wrong—these students will have to wait until they read their college textbooks for that—as it is empty: intellectually, emotionally, and morally vacuous." *The Course of True Love: Marriage in High School Textbooks*, (New York: Institute for American Values, 1998.

4   Women also sometimes feel more than a generalized societal pressure to abort; they get very direct, specific pressure from their boyfriends, who threaten to leave them or worse, if they carry the baby to term. Numerous such accounts are included in the report, "The Realtiy of Abortion: Reflections on My Journey," by Georgette Forney, September 2004, available on-line at http://www.silentnomoreawareness. org/articles/05 01georeport.pdf. For actress Jennifer O'Neill's testimony, see http://www.womendeservebetter.com/voices/Voices%20from%20Winter02 03.pdf

5   Post-abortive women are beginning to talk to each other about this grief and pain. For their testimonies, see these websites, "Silent No More," http://www.silentnomoreawareness.org/testimonies/index.html, "Women Deserve Better," http://www.womendeservebetter.com/voices/index.htm and "After Abortion," http://afterabortion.blogspot.com/.

6   Theresa Burke, with David C. Reardon, *The Forbidden Grief: The Unspoken Pain of Abortion*, (Springfield, IL: Acorn Books, 2002).

7   Ibid., pp xv-xix.

8   See the evidence cited in the appendices to *The Forbidden Grief*.

9   According to the NARAL Pro-choice America Foundation, 30 states have requiring either mandatory delays for abortion or "biased counseling." In 9 of these 30 state, these laws have been found all or partially unconstitutional. http://www.naral.org/yourstate/whodecides/maps/biased_counseling.cfm

10 Burke, *The Forbidden Grief*, pp. 34-5.

11 How else to account for the hostility toward abstinence? At the global AIDS conference in Bangkok in 2004, a young student from Uganda stood up and spoke in favor of abstinence. He was loudly jeered by the audience. "AIDS in Africa—A Betrayal," Edward C. Green, *Weekly Standard*, January 31, 2005, pp. 27-29.

12 According to French political philosopher, Chantal Delsol, "Dogmatic relativism suits our independence-hungry spirit very well....We know that truth compels and we do not want to be compelled." *Icarus Fallen: The Search for Meaning in an Uncertain World*, (Wilmington DE: ISI Books, 2003), pp. 57-58, in the chapter entitled, "The Good without the True."

13 Philip Jenkins, *The New Anti-Catholicism: The Last Acceptable Prejudice*, (Oxford: Oxford University Press, 2003).

14 "Judge Declines to Sentence 3 Catholic Gay Activists," *Washington Post*, January 31, 2003, B1. http://www.washingtonpost.com/ac2/wp dyn?pagename=article&node=&contentId=A3933 2003Jan30&notFound=true.

15 Judith Levine, *Harmful to Minors: The Peril of Protecting Children from Sex*, (Minneapolis: University of Minnesota Press, 2002).

16 Stanley Kurtz, "Rick Santorum was Right," *National Review Online*, March 23, 2005, http://www.nationalreview.com/kurtz/kurtz200503230746.asp, citing a new

law review article called, "Monogamy's Law: Compulsory Monogamy and Poly-amorous Existence," in *New York University Review of Law and Social Change*, 29, No2. (2004), by Elizabeth Emens.

17 Stanley Kurtz, "Beyond Gay Marriage: The Road to Polyamory," *Weekly Standard*, August 4, 2003, p. 30.

18 Kay Hymowitz makes a version of this argument in *Commentary*, March 2003.

19 Anne Hendershott, *The Politics of Deviance*, (San Francisco: Encounter Books, 2002).

20 Barbara Dafoe Whitehead, *Why There are No Good Men Left: The Romantic Plight of the New Single Woman*, (New York: Broadway, 2002).

21 It is a violation of federal law to discriminate in housing by "family status." Laws against discrimination by marital status vary by state. Some 23 states, including large states such as California and Massachusetts, forbid discrimination by marital status. http://www.unmarriedamerica.org/Voters/federal issues 3.pdf

22 Both the state of California, and the city of New York have these requirements of all doctors doing ob-gyn residencies within their jurisdiction. For the California bill, see http://www.leginfo.ca.gov/pub/01 02/bill/asm/ab_2151 2200/ab_2194_cfa_20020625_115351_sen_floor.html. For information about the City of New York's policy, see "Blombergs' Gift," Kathryn Jean Lopez, *National Review Online*, July 1, 2002. http://www.nationalreview.com/lopez/lopez070102.asp.

23 Kathryn Jean Lopez, "California Says Catholic Hospitals Can't Stipulate How They're Sold," National Catholic Register, August 17, 2003.

24 Burke, *The Forbidden Grief*, pp. 58-60.

25 Ibid., pp. 37-8.

26 Laws requiring parental notification have passed in 24 states and laws requiring parental consent have passed in 20 states. The laws in ten of these states have been held unconstitutional in whole or in part. http://www.naral.org/yourstate/whodecides/maps/young_women.cfm. Most recently, Idaho's parental consent law was stricken down by the Supreme Court. "Supreme Court Rejects 'Parental Consent' Appeal, *USA Today*, March 28, 2005. http://www.usatoday.com/news/washington/2005 03 28 scotus wrap_x.htm

27 One of them is Sara Lawrence. See her website, "Taking Children Seriously." http://www.fitz claridge.com/TCS.html, as well as her paper journal by the same name.

28 In a study of 100 low-income pregnant women aged 13-21, 35% had been sexually abused at some point in their lives. The authors conclude that, "Most post-partum family planning interventions are based on the premise that young women need education and contraceptive supplies, but are otherwise free to control their sexual and family planning choices. However, when adolescents are being physically or sexually abused, they are often unable to prevent unwanted pregnancy without additional assistance in ensuring personal safety." In other words, these girls and women need more than an abortion or contraceptives: they need protec-tion from abuse. M. Jacoby et. al., "Rapid Repeat Pregnancies and Experiences of Interpersonal Violence Among Low Income Adolescents," American Journal of Preventive Medicine, 16(4): 318-21, 1999.

29 "All Out Assault" by Maria Elena Kennedy, *Los Angeles Lay Catholic Mission*, December 2002, http://www.losangelesmission.com//ed/articles/2002/1202mk. htm.

30 More recently, Attorneys General in Kansas and Indiana have launched investigations of possible statutory rape. "Group Decries Abortion Record Searches," *Newsday*, March 29, 2005. http://www.newsday.com/news/health/wire/sns ap abortion records,0,2853022.story?coll=sns ap health headlines

31 Alan Guttmacher Institute, Fact Sheet, Teen Sex and Pregnancy, 1999. http://www. agi usa.org/sections/youth.html.

32 *Victims and Victors: Speaking Out About Their Pregnancies, Abortions and Children, Resulting from Sexual Assault*, edited by David C. Reardon, Julie Makimaa, and Amy Sobie, (Springfield, IL: Acorn Books, 2000).

7 The Law of the Gift

1 This is George Weigel's summary description of the personalist philosophy of Karol Wojtyla, later Pope John Paul II. *Witness to Hope: the Biography of Pope John Paul II*, (New York: Harper Collins, 1999), pp. 136-7.

2 My approach takes one of the features of *A Theory of Justice*, by John Rawls, (Cambridge MA: Harvard University Press, 1971), and stands it on its head. He proposes that people hypothetically place themselves behind a "veil of ignorance," and try to imagine the social arrangements that would benefit the least well-off. He argues that individuals would rationally choose social and constitutional institutions that would benefit the least well-off, if they did not know whether they might be among the least or most well-off in the society. This device is an attempt to create a world of disinterested individuals, who remain disinterested at least long enough to choose the institutional arrangements of the society. He treats the basic facts of our birth as issues of justice.

My approach keeps all the particularity of individuals in place, and offers a different approach to managing some of the problems that flow from it. Rather than seeing these particulars as an issue of justice that needs to be corrected, I see them as sources of individual strengths that people can potentially use for their own benefit, and the benefit of others. These individual attributes are more than endowments that people are entitled to cash in. They are gifts for which we owe gratitude. Rawls treats differences in economic productivity as suspect, and argues that disinterested people would rationally choose to assign the state the duty to redistribute income to the less productive. By contrast, I argue that people ought to rationally choose to be grateful for the gifts they have, not be covetous of others, and be willing to share with others in personal ways. This admonition to share requires gifted individuals to go far beyond the minimal requirements of acquiescence in the face of taxation by the state, and it defines "gifted" as meaning much more than economically productive.

3 Rhoads, *Taking Sex Differences Seriously*, pp. 159-187.

4 Chantal Delsol argues that moderns have assigned so much importance to equality that we have lost sight of the distinction between roles and functions. As persons

who perform functions, we consider ourselves interchangeable with each other. If we consider roles, however, no one can take the place of the particular person who plays the role of my mother, or my husband. The quest for utopian equality has blinded us to this important fact of social life. *Icarus Fallen*, pp. 139-148.

5 The crisis created by Harvard President Lawrence Summers is a case in point. For making the scientifically unexceptional statement that gender differences between men and women should be studied, he was given a vote of no-confidence by the Harvard faculty. But gender differences in development begin at birth. Some child development specialists go so far as to take it as a datum that "infant boys as a group are already developmentally delayed compared with girls." This is from a study that found infant boys to be more vulnerable than infant girls to the onset of depression in their mothers. Deborah Sharp, Dale F. Hay, et.al., "The Impact of Postnatal Depression on Boys' Intellectual Development," *Journal of Child Psychology and Psychiatry*, 36 No. 8 (1995), pp1315-1336, quotation on p. 1334.

6 Simon Baron-Cohen, *The Essential Difference: The Truth and the Male and Female Brain*, (New York: Basic Books, 2003), pp. 69-84.

7 The fact that large parts of our economic benefits are gifts from other people and from the system as a whole shows up most profoundly in two analytical places in economics. First, the theory of comparative advantage says that there are potentially gains from trade among those who are different from each other in some economically significant way. The other place the idea shows up is in the idea of consumer and producer surplus, the little triangles much loved in elementary economics classes. The surpluses arise because everyone trades at the same price. So, if I am an especially talented producer, who could make money selling at a price lower than the market price, I benefit from the fact that the marginal producer requires a higher price from consumers than I do in order to break even. If I am a consumer who would be willing to pay a huge amount for copies of Adam Smith's books, I benefit from the fact that the marginal consumer is only willing to pay $20. I get my books at a lower price than I would have without all those other consumers out there who don't share my enthusiasm. These surpluses are gifts to the vast majority of market participants.

8 Dinesh D'Souza, *What's so Great About America?* (Washington, D.C.: Regnery Publishing, 2002).

9 J. W. Harris argues that the self-ownership principle is not the most useful way to defend property rights as a "spectacular non-sequitur." "From the fact that nobody owns me if I am not a slave, it simply does not follow that I must own myself. Nobody at all owns me, not even me." J. W. Harris, *Property and Justice*, (Oxford: Oxford University Press, 1996), pp. 182-196.

10 Jennifer Roback Morse, "The Modern State as an Occasion of Sin," *Notre Dame Journal of Law, Ethics and Public Policy* 11, no.2 (1997): 531-48; "Making Room in the Inn: Why the Modern World Needs the Needy," in *Wealth, Poverty and Human Destiny*, Doug Bandow and David L. Schindler, eds. (Wilmington, DE: ISI Books, 2002), pp. 179-212; "The Limits of Equality: Why the Needy Need Us More than We Need Equality," *Thomas Jefferson Law Review*, 26, No. 1 (Fall 2003), 51-64.

11 For a spirited defense of the idea that all economic theories have implicit philo-

sophical, if not down right theological presuppositions embedded within them, see Robert Nelson, *Economics as Religion: from Samuelson to Chicago and Beyond*, (University Park, PA: Penn State University Press, 2001).

12 The late Sherwin Rosen initiated a substantial research program illustrating the importance of variation in human tastes and how these differences express themselves in implicit prices attached to the purchase of commodities. The analysis has roots all the way back in Adam Smith. Thus it is seriously misleading to claim that maximizing monetary income is somehow a central tenant of economic thinking. See Sherwin Rosen, "Hedonic Prices and Implicit Markets: Product Differentiation in Pure Competition," *Journal of Political Economy*, 82 No.1 (January/February 1974), 34-55. Adam Smith, *An Inquiry into the Nature and Causes of the Wealth of Nations*, Volume 1, Book 1, Chapter X. "On the Wages and Profits in the Different Employments of Labor and Stock," (Chicago: University of Chicago Press, 1976), Edwin Canaan, translator.

13 See Chapter 4, "Why Marriage isn't a Contract," of my *Love & Economics*.

14 Nelson, *Economics as Religion*, pg. 313.

8 *People with Problems and Problem People*

1 *The Gospel According to Tolkien: Visions of the Kingdom in Middle-earth*, Ralph C. Wood, (Louisville, KY: Westminster, John Knox Press, 2003), 136-48.

2 Hebrew Bible, Job, Chapters 3-5.

3 There is now fascinating evidence that human beings are "hard-wired" to ask questions of ultimate meaning. See for instance, *Why God Won't Go Away: Brain Science and the Biology of Belief*, Andrew Newberg, Eugene D'Auilli, and Vince Rause, (New York: Ballantine Books, 2001); and *Hardwired to Connect: The New Scientific Case for Authoritative Communities*, (New York: Institute for American Values, 2003).

4 *Biography of Pierre Simon de Laplace*, website of the School of Mathematics and Statistics, University of St. Andrews, Scotland. http://www groups.dcs.st and. ac.uk/~history/Mathematicians/Laplace.html. Quotation cited at http://www groups.dcs.st and.ac.uk/~history/Quotations/Laplace.html

5 "My Own Life," originally dated, April 18, 1776; *David Hume: Essays, Moral, Political and Literary*, edited by Eugene F. Miller, (Indianapolis: Liberty Classics, 1987) pg. xl.

6 This is reported by Hume's friend Adam Smith, in his letter to William Strahan, included in *David Hume: Essays*, p. xliv. (My colleague Thomas Sowell loves this anecdote, in equal parts because of his affection for David Hume and for Bid Whist.)

7 This discussion could be considered the personal equivalent of the discussion of whether societies or mass movements can ever develop a genuinely irrational or malevolent streak. Paul Berman makes the very interesting case that modern liberal democracies are blinded to the existence of genuinely evil movements celebrating death and slaughter, due to liberalism's article of faith in a rational universe. These evil movements must be explainable in some kind of logical way.

Under this view, the existence of death cults such as suicide bombers and terrorism, can only be logically explained, not by the evil of their perpetrators, but by the evil of the victims, who must have in some way, provoked the outburst of violence. The United States, under this view, is more to blame for terrorism than the terrorists themselves. The evil of the U.S., by contrast, is a stand-alone fact that requires no independent explanation. *Terror and Liberalism*, Paul Berman, (New York: Norton, 2003).

8   Hebrew Bible, Job Chapters 38-41.

9   Many other observers have noted the tenacity with which children will protect even gravely abusive parents. "In her book *Necessary Losses*, Judith Viorst tells this story: A young boy lies ina hospital bed. He is frightened and in pain. Burns cover 40% of his small body. Someone has doused him with alcohol and then, unimaginably has set him on fire. He cries for his mother. His mother has set him on fire. It doesn't seem to matter what kind of mother a child has lost or how periolous it is to dwell in her presence. It doesn't matter whether she hurts or hugs. Separation from the mother is worse than being in her arms when the bombs are exploding. Separation from mother is sometimes worse than being with her when she is the bomb." Quoted by Nancy Verrier, in her self-published book, *The Primal Wound: Legacy of Adoption*, 1993.

10   Nancy Thomas, *When Love is Not Enough: a Guide to Parenting Children with Reactive Attachment Disorder*, (Glenwood Springs, CO: Families by Design, 1997), pp. 82, 84.

9 The God of the Gift

1   Christian Bible, Matthew, 19:3-12. For insightful commentary on this passage, see *The Theology of the Body: Human Love in the Divine Plan*, John Paul II. (Boston: Pauline Books and Media, 1997), pp. 233-303.

2   Margaret F. Brinig and Douglas W. Allen, "These Boots are Made for Walking: Why Wives file for Divorce," *American Law and Economics Review*, Vol. 2, (2000) 126, examine the reasons offered for divorce in Virginia, one of the few states that allows people to offer cruelty as a grounds for fault divorce. Only 6% of those filing for divorce cited cruelty as a reason.

Another study asked couples to list problems in their marriage. Violence wasn't even a category. However, only 20% listed "gets angry easily" as a problem behavior for husbands, only 4% listed "has had sex with someone else," and only 6% of husbands were described as "drinks or uses drugs." Of the couples in this study, 12.5% ultimately divorced. This shows that the potential indicators of "high conflict" marriages were not a factor in the vast majority of marriages, and probably not even a factor in most of the marriages that ended in divorce. Paul R. Amato and Stacy J. Rogers, "A Longitudinal Study of Marital Problems and Subsequent Divorce," *Journal of Marriage and the Family*, 59 No. 3. (August 1997) 612-624.

3   Another survey of 256 people who had been divorced at one time or another asked "what was the principle reason you got a divorce?" Sixteen percent reported drug

or alcohol problems as the principle reason, while only 5% reported abuse as the principle reason. Fully 47% listed "basic personality differences or incompatibility" as the principle reason for their divorce, while 17% listed marital infidelity and 10% reported disputes about money or children. *Statistical Handbook on the American Family,* Bruce A. Chadwick and Tim B. Heaton, editors (Phoenix, AZ: Oryx Press, 1992), Table C3-6, pg. 98.

4   See for instance, Murray S. Straus, "Sexual Inequality, Cultural Norms and Wife-beating," *Victimology*, 1 (1976), 54-76; and R. Stark and J. McEvoy, "Middle Class Violence," *Psychology Today*, 4 (1970) 52-65; Kersti Yllo and Murray A. Strauss, "Interpersonal Violence Among Married and Cohabiting Couples," *Family Relations*, 30 (1981) 339-47. Jan Stets and Murray A. Strauss, "The Marriage License as a Hitting License: A Comparison of Assaults in Dating, Cohabiting and Married Couples," *Journal of Family Violence*, 4, No. 2 (1989) 161-180, show that cohabiting couples are higher rates of assault, and the violence is more severe, than among dating or married couples. Jan Stets, "Cohabiting and Marital Aggression: The role of Social Isolation," *Journal of Marriage and the Family*, 53 (August 1991) 669-680 attributes the increased domestic violence among cohabitors to social isolation.

5   Paul R. Amato and Alan Booth, *A Generation at Risk: Growing up in an Era of Family Upheaval*, (Cambridge, MA: Harvard University Press, 1997).
    Henri Nowen, *The Road to Daybreak: A Spiritual Journey*, (New York: Doubleday, Image Books, 1990), and Jean Vanier, "Handicapped Are Teachers of Civilization of Love," interview with Zenit news agency, February 7, 2002: http://www.zenit.org/.

6   Married men working full-time earned $47, 467 per year on average, while their never-married counterparts earned $29, 420, according to raw data from the U.S. Census in 2003, (quoted in *Why Men Earn More: The Startling Truth about the Pay Gap—and What Women Can Do About It* by Warren Farrell, (New York: American Management Association Books, 2005), pp. 237, footnote 2 to page xviii.

7   Rene Girard, *I See Satan Fall Like Lightening*, (Maryknoll, N.Y.: Orbis Books, 2001), and Gil Bailie, *Violence Unveiled: Humanity at the Crossroads* (New York: Crossroads Publishing, 1999) argues that Christianity reverses the social tendency to create social order around the sacrifice of scapegoats. On this account, Christianity's contribution is to instill in societies a concern and respect for the innocent victim. Rodney Stark, *The Rise of Christianity: How the Obscure, Marginal Jesus Movement Became the Dominant Religious Force in the Western World in a Few Centuries*, (San Francisco: Harper Collins, 1997) argues that Christianity competed successfully against Roman pagan religions by giving people a sense that their suffering has meaning, and is not as senseless as it sometimes appears.

8   Zenit News Agency, Vatican City, (Zenit.org) February 5, 2002.

A NOTE ON THE AUTHOR

JENNIFER ROBACK MORSE, PH.D., brings a unique perspective to the subjects of love, marriage, sexuality, and the family. A committed career woman before having children, she taught economics for fifteen years at Yale and George Mason University. She and her husband adopted a two-year-old Romanian boy in 1991, the same year she gave birth to a baby girl. Dr. Morse left full-time university teaching in 1996 to move with her family to California. She is now associated with the Hoover Institution at Stanford University as a research fellow. Her previous book is *Love & Economics: Why the Laissez-Faire Family Doesn't Work* (Spence, 2001).

In addition to caring for their own two children, Dr. Morse and her husband are foster parents for San Diego County.

This book was designed and set into type
by Mitchell S. Muncy,
and printed and bound
by Bang Printing,
Brainerd, Minnesota.

℮

The text face is Minion Multiple Master,
designed by Robert Slimbach
and issued in digital form by Adobe Systems,
Mountain View, California, in 1991.

℮

The paper is acid-free and is of archival quality.

40